OTHER WORKS BY PIERCE KELLEY

Elysium, (iUniverse, 2021)

The Jesus Trail, (Westbow Press, 2020)

Pilgrimage, (iUniverse, 2019)

Hiding in America, (AuthorHouse, 2018)

Hunted, (Xulon Press, 2017)

Massacre at Sirte (iUniverse, 2016)

To Valhalla (iUniverse, 2015)

A Deadly Legacy (iUniverse, 2013)

Roxy Blues (iUniverse, 2012)

Father, I Must Go, (iUniverse, 2011)

Thousand Yard Stare (iUniverse, 2010)

Kennedy Homes: An American Tragedy (iUniverse, 2009)

A Foreseeable Risk (iUniverse, 2009)

Asleep at the Wheel (iUniverse, 2009)

A Tinker's Damn! (iUniverse, 2008)

Bocas del Toro (iUniverse, 2007)

A Plenary Indulgence (iUniverse, 2007)

Pieces to the Puzzle (iUniverse, 2007)

Introducing Children to the Game of Tennis (iUniverse, 2007)

A Very Fine Line (iUniverse, 2006)

Fistfight at the L and M Saloon (iUniverse, 2006

Civil Litigation: A Case Study (Pearson Publications, 2001

The Parent's Guide to Coaching Tennis (F & W Publications, 1995)

A Parent's Guide to Coaching Tennis (Betterway Publications, 1991)

Anima

A Search for Inner Self

Pierce Kelley

ANIMA
A SEARCH FOR INNER SELF

iUniverse books may be ordered through booksellers or by contacting:

iUniverse
1663 Liberty Drive
Bloomington, IN 47403
www.iuniverse.com
844-349-9409

ISBN: 978-1-6632-4387-4 (sc)
ISBN: 978-1-6632-4392-8 (e)

Print information available on the last page.

iUniverse rev. date: 08/18/2022

Dedication

This book is dedicated to the memory of some of those who have gone before us and asked identical questions to the ones my generation now asks, and all future generations will continue to ask. The list is long and includes far too many to mention, but it certainly must begin with Sri Krishna, Ptahhatop, Abraham, Moses, Socrates, Plato, Aristotle, Siddhartha Gautama, Confucious, Jesus Christ, Mohammad, Sigmund Freud, Carl Jung, Jean Paul Sarte and one of my personal favorites, Herman Hesse.

DISCLAIMER

This is a not a work of fiction. It is based upon my life on this planet and it is a result of my memories and thoughts from all that I have experienced during this lifetime. The names of the people in this book are, at times, the real names of people I have met along my sojourn. At other times, I have created names to protect the privacy of friends and acquaintances, where necessary. No disrespect is intended towards anyone.

Again, everything in here is factually accurate to the best of my recollection, with a liberal dose of editorial license. I have left a few of the more painful experiences out. I hope you will find this book engaging and entertaining. Moreover, I hope that readers will find that there are many significant points of similarities and convergence, as well as a healthy dose of divergent views, too. Differences of opinions are absolutely inevitable, and welcomed.

It seems to me, from years of observing politics and people, that about half the people in the world will agree on any particular issue, while the other half will disagree, no matter what the issue. We are, however, when all is said and done, all part of the human race, and that is the nature of man. We continue to take bites from the apple, seeking knowledge and understanding, knowing that our efforts will be futile.

As Mark Twain once said, "When we remember that we are all mad, the mysteries disappear and life stands explained." If he is correct in that observation, what follows is the work of a fellow mad man.

Acknowledgments

I thank those who have supported and encouraged me on this and other projects, and there have been many, over the years, too many to mention by name, but they know who they are and so do I.

I wish to specifically thank my three younger brothers, Chris, Allan and Bruce, on this particular project, which is an autobiography. They have read drafts and offered their insights and recollections of events, correcting me, where necessary and, sometimes, where it was not.

Family and genetics play an enormous role in who and what we, as human beings, become, as we all know. Some are more fortunate than others in that regard. I was dealt a good hand. That and nurturing are said to be the two most important factors in determining who and what we become. Having been born in the United States of America was fortuitous, also, without any doubt whatsoever. I was fortunate in that regard, too.

Once, when applying for a job, I was asked to provide references. A friend of my father's wrote a very nice note on my behalf, saying many kind things, and then he added, "but that was no accident. His parents had much to do with that," and that was true. There can be no doubt of that with any of us. I am grateful to them for that and acknowledge their significant contribution in that regard.

Pierce Kelley

Inscriptions

"Your journey was never meant for you to reach your destination, but to find yourself along the way."

N. R. Hart

* * * * * * *

"Two roads diverged in a wood and I – I took the one less traveled by, And that has made all the difference."

Robert Frost (1874-1963)

* * * * * * *

"The unexamined life is not worth living."

Socrates, (circa 470 BCE – circa 399 BCE)

* * * * * * *

"If what I say resonates within you, it's merely because we are branches of the same tree.

William Butler Yeats (1865 - 1939)

* * * * * * *

"The two most important days in your life are the day you were born and the day you find out why."

Mark Twain (1835-1910)

****

Anima defined:

The soul, especially the irrational part, as distinguished from the rational mind.

Oxford languages

The soul or inner self of a person.

Wiktionary.com

The part of the psyche that is directed inward, in touch with the subconscious.

Wordgenius.com

The unconscious part of your mind that works automatically, without introspection or awareness.

Vocabulary.com

****

Introduction

Every sentient human being has learned, from a very early age, that there are questions regarding the origins of our world, the universe, creation, and a multitude of other issues that have been asked by all human beings since humans first appeared on earth. Most have learned that such questions have never been satisfactorily been answered by the scientific community or anyone else, and never will be. Still, mankind seeks answers to questions for which there are no totally satisfactory explanations.

Rather, religions have provided the answers to those most basic questions and most human beings align themselves with one of the five major religions in the world - Christianity, Buddhism, Hinduism, Islam and Judaism - and they accept the teachings of their churches, temples, mosques and synagogues as truth. Unfortunately, most people reject any explanations other than those provided by their spiritual leaders. They have "faith" in the validity of the explanations provided. Most never stray from what they have learned from their parents or pastors when they were children.

I, having been born into an Irish Catholic family, have heard the expression, "keep the faith," all of my life. The word "faith" is defined to mean that one has a "belief" in the truth of the religious dogma of the Roman Catholic Church, or any other religion, despite there being no objective proof. Devotees of three of the major religions, whose followers total nearly two-thirds of the people on earth, believe in what is found in the Bible. They are called "children of the book." Suffice it to say that there are passages in the Old Testament that defy belief, far too many to document, yet human beings fervently "believe" in what they have been taught by their parents and the leaders of their respective religions and all that is contained in "the book."

Most people on earth believe in "God" as the creator of all that is. The term "god" is synonymous with Yahweh, Jehovah, Great Spirit, Supreme Being, Creator, and other such terms but, in essence, it means that some "thing" or some "one" created all that is. Atheists and agnostics abound, but they are in a very small minority. If polls and statistics regarding such things are accurate, less than five percent of the people on earth fall into those categories.

Carl Jung is credited for originating the term "anima," though it derives from the Latin word "animus," which is defined to mean "rational soul, life or intelligence." Jung defines it to mean that part of your psyche – or spirit – that connects with the deepest, most subconscious aspects of the mind. Most people believe that human beings have a "soul," and they acknowledge that it is a non-physical entity of some kind which has a tangible effect on who and what a person is. Moreover, most people on earth believe that one's soul survives after the physical body is gone. Where that "soul" goes is another question regarding which there is much disagreement over the answer.

The question of what "soul" is and how the soul interacts with the brain is another issue entirely. Personally, I relate the concept of soul to my heart. We think with our brains but we "feel" with our heart. We can fool our brains through the use of rationalizations and much thought and debate, but our hearts don't lie. They tell us the truth, without any explanation whatsoever, but the heart makes mistakes, as we all know. I don't think that our souls do.

I think that most people leave such questions as the "meaning of life" deep within their psyche, knowing that it is useless to try to answer such questions. Actually, I think the answers to that question flows directly from the answer to the very first question all human beings now have or have ever had, and that is who and what created what is. Once that question is answered, even if it is an inadequate answer, the rest follows.

For me, my brain shuts down when I get to the question of how anything comes from nothing. I'm aware of the "Big Bang" theory and other explanations now being advanced, but who or what created the "thing" that exploded? Who created the atoms, molecules, gases and other "building blocks" of life? There are scientists who have written books trying to theorize how that could occur. How does something come from nothing? They don't know and, in my opinion, will never know. My brain hurts if I dwell on it too long.

I have chosen the word Anima to be the title to this book because I would like to arrive at some meaningful understanding, at least for me, of all that I have learned during my years on this planet. What have I learned? If I am to meet St. Peter at the pearly gates, what will I say?

I am mindful of what Plato has told us about Socrates, who wrote nothing, yet he is recognized as being the "father" of western philosophy. All that we know of Socrates comes from one of his most famous students, Plato. Aristotle was one of Plato's students. According to Plato, one of Socrates most-favored expressions was "I know nothing." He wrote no books and provided his students with questions, not answers. That style of teaching is now known as the "Socratic Method."

I ascribe to that theory and candidly acknowledge that I, like Socrates, know nothing. The things that I "think" I know are based upon assertions of facts that may or may not be true. Most of the things we humans thought to be true, going back millenia, have been dis-proven, like the sun revolves around the earth, or the earth is flat, to name just two of the more obvious dogmas of the past.

I have no better answers to any of those most basic questions than any who are reading this. I simply want to get a better understanding of my inner self, or my soul, if you will, by examining my life to see if I can make sense of it all. Consider what follows to be a case study of one human being - me.

I begin the journey with no expectations of what the end result will be. I am writing this book in hopes of getting a better understanding of my anima – what is in the deep recesses of my subconscious as my brain works tirelessly to sort out and think through all that has happened in my life. My conscious mind doesn't have the answers. Maybe my subconscious mind will come up with a few.

What follows is a narrative about my life. We all have different paths that we have followed in life, so we all have differing "facts" upon which to base our own analysis. I think I am much like everyone else in that regard. Most people would agree that we are all basically alike, deep down. Yet all would also agree that we are all completely different, too.

There is no one else like me on earth, and there is no one else on earth exactly like you! There must be some universal commonalities, right? There can be no doubt about that, right? Hopefully, readers will have some interest in seeing what conclusions I have drawn from my years on this planet. Otherwise, they would put the book down and not read another page. We'll see. Again, this is a "case study," and the one case being studied is mine.

This is not intended to be my "Memoirs." I'm not writing this to tell people about all that I have done or failed to do in my life, like a Winston Churchill, Mahatma Gandhi or Nelson Mandela might write. That's not me.

I'm not so accomplished to warrant that kind of analysis. I have made mistakes, and I doubt that there is anyone on earth who would not say the same thing. We have all made mistakes in our lives, it's just a matter of how many and how bad those mistakes have been. As my father once told me, I have a checkered past, some good things and some bad, much like most everyone else, I'm sure.

Given all of the foregoing, what follows is a summary of my life. I do so to provide the factual basis for the conclusions I will ultimately draw in the last chapter of this book. Also, I do so to help me make sense of it all, and to put it down on a piece of paper. It's one thing to think about these topics, but it's another step to say them out loud, and then quite another to put them in print for all to read, especially when you know that others will be reading some of the most intimate details of your life.

With that as an "Introduction," or a brief explanation of what is to follow, here goes...

Chapter One

Birth to School Days

I was born on July 14, 1947 in Boston, Massachusetts to Robert Pierce Kelley and Marjorie Sullivan Kelley. "Bob" was still an officer in the Navy, since the military did not immediately discharge all soldiers and sailors from service following the end of WW II. Marjorie was a housewife, raising my sister, Carol, who was three-plus years older than me. I was named Robert Pierce Kelley, Jr., and I was called Pierce.

As many of you know, July 14 is Bastille Day in France – the day the peasants stormed the Bastille, a medieval fortress and armory that was considered the most significant symbol of "royal" authority in the land. It was also a prison for political prisoners. It was the beginning of the French Revolution, which ended the reign of Louis XVI, the last monarch of France.

As an aside, because of the dates being identical, I have always felt a kinship to the French and that holiday since I was old enough to know of it. One of the leaders of the "Revolution" was a man named Maximilien Robespierre. Because of the similarity between his name and mine, I identified with him for the same totally irrational reason. For decades, I had no full understanding of who he was or what he did in 1789 to contribute to the uprising, yet the fascination remained.

At the time of the uprising, he was a thirty-one year old man who had become a lawyer and a statesman of great stature. He espoused many noble and laudable positions to benefit the "common man." He was considered to be, by many, the principal ideologist of the revolution. His fame was relatively short-lived as he was executed by way of the guillotine six years later. Though there are a few other similarities, I am no "Robespierre." Despite that, I continue to mention it, as I have just done.

Regardless, I was given a "good" name and I was born into a "good" family. Three years later, my family moved to Miami and, in September of 1950, a month or so after we arrived in south Florida, another child joined the family – Christopher Paul Kelley. Once he was out of his crib, we would share a room until I went off to college fifteen years later, but I digress.

At first, my father worked at a Sinclair gas station at 63rd street and Collins Avenue on Miami Beach owned by my grandfather, Frank Sullivan, while going to law school at the University of Miami. He was good with numbers and organizing things, having been an officer in the supply corps while in the Navy. He was no mechanic, however, and his children learned precious little from him about mechanics. His favorite tool was the hammer. I inherited those deficiencies, as did all of my siblings.

My father was a very intelligent man, though, having graduated from Harvard in 1938. He graduated from law school in 1953. He was also a handsome and athletic man. He would remain in the Naval Reserve until he retired, as a Captain, forty years later.

My mother graduated from Regis College, a private Roman Catholic college located in Westin, Massachusetts, run by the Sisters of St. Joseph. Though she never worked outside of the home, she was active in political and social circles in Miami and Dade County. She, too, was an intelligent person, and she was a beautiful woman. I was given good genes.

I have absolutely no recollection whatsoever of my days in the Boston area before my parents moved us to Miami. I did, however, manage to contract the much-dreaded disease known as "Red Sox Fever," although it wasn't diagnosed until a few years later. Still, I continue to proudly identify myself as being "from" Boston, though I truly have no vestiges of anything to do with that great city, except for being a Red Sox fan, a Celtic fan and, to a lesser extent, a Bruins fan. I also learned to love swordfish and New England Clam "Chowda," as my father would say.

Other than pronouncing the word "tomato" incorrectly, my mother lost the accent quite quickly. My father, on the other hand, "pahked cahs in the Hahvad yahd" until the day he died. I think he was quite proud of the accent.

Both were of Irish heritage. I didn't know anything about what discrimination they experienced in their younger years until much later in life, but both experienced some degree of social prejudice because of that heritage. There were NINA laws in effect, or so I was told, due to a deep-seated hatred for the Irish by the blue-bloods of New England. The term meant "No Irish Need Apply," and it was, for many, a harsh reality in Boston until the Kennedys, and others changed that. I doubt that there were any "laws" on the books to that effect, though I have definitely heard the expression.

Things began to change in 1885 when an Irish-American immigrant, Hugh O'Brien, became the mayor of Boston. After that, the Irish began, slowly but surely, to gain political power and, later on, a higher degree of social acceptance. By the time my parents entered adulthood, their heritage identified who and what they were to some appreciable degree. I think my mother, much more so than my father, felt this and she is the one who not only welcomed the move to Miami, she may have been the one who decided upon it.

My parents bought a house in North Bay Village, on North Bay Island, which is located on the 79th Street Causeway joining Miami Beach to Miami. The "Village" included Treasure Island and Harbor Island and, though primarily a residential area, featured the Harbor Island Spa and many fine restaurants like The Place for Steak, which many mafia mobsters reputedly called home.

We lived at 7530 Coquina Drive in a four bedroom, two bath house for the next fifty years, or thereabouts. It was a quiet community where we had vacant lots to play baseball and football and occasionally throw rocks at all of the other neighborhood children like the Militanas or the Rizzos. I was fortunate to have a good "environment" in which to live as a youngster. There was little diversity in that community, although most were probably Jewish.

Being good Irish-Catholics, my parents shunned the public elementary school located on Treasure Island, less than a mile away, and sent us half an hour away to St. Patrick's Elementary School on 41st street in Miami Beach. That's where we went to church every Sunday, too.

On school days, a bus would pick us up at the end of the block, nearly a quarter of a mile from our home. We walked, by ourselves, to the "bus stop." There was no danger in doing so. It was a good, safe place to live.

Dominican Nuns taught all classes at St. Patrick's. Monsignor Barry was the head priest. We all wore uniforms and the nuns wore white habits and black hats with long black tails. As my brother, Christopher, aptly pointed out, they all looked like penguins.

At first, he had a hard time figuring out which one was his teacher. I had to identify his teacher for him. We were provided with a welcoming and caring education at the elementary school level, though the nuns did use rulers across knuckles and they weren't, apparently, aware of any prohibitions against corporal punishment.

Also, my mother, intent on being socially-upward, convinced my father to join the McFadden-Deauville Club, which had the largest fresh-water pool in the United States at the time. It was an Olympic sized pool and many Olympians trained there. It also had a diving area where there were Olympic sized platforms, including the 10-meter one. We all learned how to swim at an early age.

By the time I was entering the first grade at St. Patrick's, after attending kindergarten there, another child joined the family – Allan Richard Kelley. We were carrying on an Irish tradition – having large families. Catholics were going to rule the world by outnumbering the others.

We children had no idea of the privileges which we were given. We weren't rich, and not even remotely wealthy, but our parents wanted the best for us. We went to church as a family on every Sunday, without exception. We said our prayers before every dinner meal, which was always eaten as a family, together. We ate fish on Fridays, and we were encouraged, if not required, to do well in school. We were "nurtured."

I can't say that my upbringing was much different from any of the other children I met in school during those early years. I thought, and still think, that we were much like every other family I knew. Looking back, I don't know what I could ask for that could have made my life any better. I, like all of my siblings, were off to a promising start. I had done nothing to deserve that, other than just stay out of trouble, I guess. I was a normal kid.

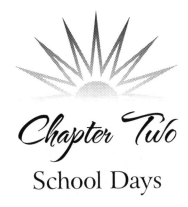

Chapter Two

School Days

The years between kindergarten and middle school are entirely different from the middle school years, and then there are the years spent in high school, which are completely different, too, but I will lump those three together in this chapter. During all of those years I lived in a house owned by my parents, together with my siblings. I recognize that not everyone had such a traditional path to follow, but that was my path and I can only speak authoritatively about myself and my journey. Again, the hope is that there are some universal truths in here.

First graders are, as a general rule, about six or seven years old, depending upon what month they were born in. Children are about thirteen when they enter the seventh grade, and they are usually about sixteen when they enter high school. I, like most others, was eighteen when I graduated. Huge changes take place during those years, and some people handle things better than others.

Here is when the issue of nurturing comes in. Some people are better parents than others – that's a fact, plain and simple. It's also true that some people get parents who are much smarter than the parents of other children – that's the genetics part of the equation. I was fortunate to have parents who gave me good genes and they also nurtured me and provided opportunities for me and their children to be successful.

I was a baby-boomer, having been born in 1947, and the men and women during those years, having just withstood a world war on the heels of the Great Depression, welcomed some degree of normalcy – marriage, a nice home, in a good neighborhood, with children, peace and tranquility, as well as upward mobility – the American dream. My parents were no different in that respect. Although we weren't wealthy, we certainly didn't lack for anything. They joined a country club and had a healthy social life. We benefited from that.

Not to get too far ahead of the story, but back in those days divorces were rare. I didn't know any children who came from what was called a "broken home." As we all know, nowadays, over half the marriages end in divorce, and a simple one-on-one husband-wife relationship is no longer the norm – there is no "normal." A marriage is no longer only between a man and a woman.

As I learned when I first began working in a legal-aid office in Washington, D.C., while in law school, for many low-income people, especially the African-American families in the District of Columbia, they had no access to the judicial system and families were virtually inter-changeable. That must have been incredibly difficult for children of those relationships. There were many such dis-advantages for people of color back then.

I was fortunate to have been born into a "stable" family unit. I am fully aware of the fact that I am disregarding issues of race, national origin, sexual preference and a whole host of other issues from my profile. That is who I was and who I am – pretty much middle-America, although that, too, has changed dramatically in the intervening years.

I have read where 90 percent of Americans were caucasians in 1950 and 95 percent of Americans identified as Christians at that time. That is no longer the case today, but I was a part of that startling statistic. My history is, therefore, much like most Americans my age. I am a septuagenarian, caucasian Christian.

The way Catholic schools operated back then, you had the same nun for every class. You went to the classroom for whatever grade you were in and you stayed there all day. The quality of the education depended upon the quality of the nun as a teacher. Some were better than others. St. Patrick's was a big school, and it housed all grades from kindergarten to high school in the same building, but there weren't that many students, so that system worked just fine. Class sizes were never over thirty.

I was a good student. I didn't do anything to make myself a good student, but I had no problems academically and was usually near the top of the class. Again, there might have been thirty children in my class, but I scored in the one-hundredth percentile in math for the entire country on one of the standardized tests given to us in the third grade, so I showed some promise. I was also gifted athletically.

I was also an altar boy. It was an honor to be one. Since the masses were in Latin back then, we had to be able to say all the correct responses in Latin. That was long before homosexuality became an accepted choice, and the idea of priests being pedophiles couldn't have been imagined, at least not for me or anyone I knew. Sadly, those days are gone, too.

Those days were simple and uncomplicated. We had a routine which was followed almost unfailingly – we got up, ate breakfast, walked to the bus stop, went to school, rode the bus home, played outside until it was dinner time, ate dinner with the family, watched a little television, and then went to bed. On weekends, we went to the beach as a family, went to church as a family and, with few exceptions, such as friends here and there, that was life, and it was a good life.

Parenthetically, it is interesting to note that for me and all children of that era, the television was a "new" invention, having come into existence in the early '50s. We had one television, which was in the "television room," and we all watched the same things, as a family.

Also, air-conditioning was a "new" invention, for both the home and the car. For years, we only had one air-conditioner in the house and it was in our parents' room. Everyone spent a lot of time just sitting in that room, getting cooled-off.

We had two cars, one for my father and one for my mother. They weren't expensive ones. My mother drove a Chevrolet station-wagon and the "new" air-conditioner was installed to sit on the floor between the driver's seat and the passenger's seat. The boys always sat in the back. Our mother and our older sister always sat in the front. I don't remember what my father drove, but it wasn't a Cadillac, that was for sure.

The boys, and there would be four of us by the time our parents were finished making babies, always played sports at the local community center, which was, for us, Normandy Isle park. We played football, softball and basketball there. It also had a pool and a tennis court. We went to North Shore Park, on 73rd street, for baseball, starting with Little League, when we were about seven or eight.

Our sister, Carol, never played any sports at Normandy Isle. She swam, some, at the country club, but she was never encouraged to be athletic. My parents bought a piano, which sat in the living room, and she learned to play the piano. Her interests were clearly shown to be in all things academic.

That was a sign of the times, though. Girls weren't encouraged to be athletes. Their trajectory in life was aimed towards Home Economics classes in school, with an eye towards becoming a teacher, a nurse, or a secretary.

That was not the case for Carol, however. She was gifted academically, though, and her brilliance in that regard was obvious from a very early age. She was reciting nursery rhymes and reading books at age three, or so I was told. She was born in December of 1943 and I wasn't around to see any of that.

Her success in school, and her interest in classical music, reading books, dwarfed her fellow students at the small, Catholic school we all attended. That forced a major change in the lives of us boys by the time she was about fourteen years old, but I'll get to that later. She played the piano, she read books – a lot of books – and she swam, if she wanted to. She was being groomed to be a star. She sat on a pedestal.

Summers in Miami were always hot – extremely hot. We played sports in the morning and then swam in the ocean or pool in the afternoons, most days. One day, when I was ten years old, my mother said to me, "Pierce, let's go play tennis."

Being the athlete that I was, I said, "Sure, Mom. Let's go!" and off we went. The club where we were members had three tennis courts. She introduced me to the game of tennis. Not all parents would do that. She did.

I enjoyed just hitting the ball back over the net, much like hitting a baseball, with eye-hand coordination being the primary requisite for success. I took an immediate liking to it, because I hit more tennis balls in one point, sometimes, than I did in a whole day of baseball, and I was good. Plus, I was extremely competitive. I wanted to win.

Not too long after I started to play, I remember playing with a kid my age named Michael Lerner at Normandy Isle. He was one of my teammates who lived within a block of the park. The court, and there was only

8

one, had metal nets and cracks running throughout. We didn't know how to keep score, so we just played to a hundred and counted each point as ten.

Also, we didn't know that you had to let the ball bounce on a serve. We wanted to intercept it at the net. We didn't know anything, but we had fun, and then we went swimming in the pool at the other end of the park. I took to tennis like a dog takes to water.

My mother and I played at the Bath Club, an exclusive country club on Collins Avenue which didn't allow Jewish people or negroes, as they were called back then, into the club as members. As most everyone knows, I think, Miami Beach was built by Jews and it was, and still is, heavily populated by Jewish people. I was blissfully unaware of any of that. The Bath Club is now owned by a black, Jewish man.

Years later, I invited my Jewish friends over there frequently, although it cost money to bring a guest into the club and my father had to pay for it. He never complained about doing so. I don't think we, as a family, had racial biases or any anti-semitic attitudes, but there were few black families living in Miami Beach back then and there were no black or Jewish students at St. Patrick's. For that matter, there were few Hispanics, too. That didn't happen until 1959, when Castro came into power in Cuba. I was raised in a sheltered community, in that respect, much different from a large, urban area, and certainly nothing like a rural community.

After a few months, I began to improve at tennis. I learned how to keep score and I could keep balls in the court, especially on the forehand side. One day that Fall, which would have been in 1957, the resident tennis professional, Mike Dolan, who spent his summers in Charlottesville, Virginia at a club up there, called my mother and asked if I would play in a little tournament they were having for the junior players. He needed one more player to get to an even number. I readily agreed. I didn't care. I just liked to play.

One of my favorite pictures from my tennis-playing days is of me in that tournament, with seven other kids who were dressed in tennis "whites," and all but one were much older than I was. I had on long pants and a t-shirt. It makes me laugh to look at it, but I can see a twinkle in my eye like that was a big deal for me. I lost, badly, I'm sure, but I enjoyed it. That was the beginning of what would become a life-long love affair with the game of tennis.

That December, over the Christmas vacation, I met someone who would become one of my best friends and my fiercest opponent – a kid named Tug Miller, who was one year older than me. My parents and his parents introduced us to each other and we began to play. Both sets of parents were encouraging their sons to learn how to play tennis.

We played each other for the next seventeen days until we had to go back to school. We were as evenly matched as two people could possibly be. We kept a running score of sets won and he would beat me one day and I would beat him the next. It was neck and neck for the next fifty years. In the process, we both became excellent players.

We continued to play on weekends at the Bath Club and we improved to the point where we could play with our mothers, and then, after a while, with our fathers, and then, about three years later, I was the Club Champion, beating Tug in the finals. I think he destroyed a couple of rackets when I did, but I'm not sure of that. He destroyed quite a few over the years. My mother broke me of that habit by saying that she would take my rackets away and never buy me another one unless I stopped throwing rackets. That worked.

I played my first tournament in August of 1959, when I was eleven. I played Billy Harris, who was the number one player in the state and the country at the time. He beat me 6-0, 6-1, but I unfazed. I would have played him again the next day. I was an athlete and I enjoyed playing tennis. I had a passion for it.

As I look back, one of the things I am most proud of is that when I started to play tennis, within six months, my father joined my mother and me on the courts, saying "Well, I guess you two must be good enough now for me to play you." He continued to play for the rest of his life. He and I won the State Father-Son Championships when I was eighteen. He wasn't a good player, by any stretch of the imagination, but he loved it, and he went from weighing 230 pounds to about 175 within a few years.

The major benefit of my father starting to play tennis with us was that we, as a family, began to spend all of our weekends on the tennis courts. My brother, Chris, started to play at about that same time and he became one of the better players in the state by the time he was twelve, and our brother, Allan, played number 1 for his high school team and traveled with me to tournaments as an adult. He was a great runner and wanted to be an Olympian, but injuries ended that dream.

Another benefit of the family becoming a "tennis family" was the people who we met. My father became best friends with Edward Annis, president of the American Medical Society. He debated John F. Kennedy on national television over the wisdom of "socialized medicine," which Kennedy advocated.

He also became best friends with Don Shoemaker, editor of the Miami Herald, who gave me my first racket. Some of the original owners of the Miami Dolphins were members of the Bath Club and, though they weren't tennis players, they had a cabana not far from ours. Everyone who was a member of that Club was someone with money and a high social standing.

Also, when I won the Club Championships, I beat Norman Woolworth, heir to the Woolworth fortune, in the quarter-finals. Tennis became the single most important activity in my life during those years, and my parents supported and encouraged me. I was talented, but I had the support and encouragement of my parents and my family.

My maternal grandfather, Frank Sullivan, spent much of the last five years of his life, driving me to and from practices and tournaments, watching me play, after his wife died. My paternal grandmother, Helen Pierce Kelley, came to watch me play every chance she got, too. I had the full support of my entire family.

A major event occurred when my sister, Carol, entered the ninth grade, which would have been in 1962. Because she was so gifted academically, my parents decided to send her to the best private school in Dade County – the Everglades School for Girls. It was an extremely small group of extremely bright, and wealthy, girls. Carol not only fit right in, she excelled. She was a National Merit Scholar by the time she graduated.

She went on to Wellesley College, in Massachusetts, and graduated cum laude, and then to the George Washington University law school, where she was an editor of the law review. She graduated third in her class. I never had thoughts that women were intellectually inferior because of my sister and my mother.

That wasn't the case when it came to athletics. My sister was no athlete, but she was a knowledgeable and enthusiastic sports fan. In fact, she would be the score keeper for volleyball or softball games and she knew all about college and professional sports. When she was older, she had season tickets to all of the professional teams in the Washington, D. C. area.

However, since we weren't wealthy, our father decided that the boys weren't going to a Catholic school anymore, where he had to pay tuition, plus a whole lot of other expenses to support the school. We were summarily sent to a public school. For Chris and Allan, it was the Treasure Island Elementary School, which was five minutes away. For me, it was Nautilus Junior High School, half an hour away.

Nautilus probably had about a thousand kids in it for the seventh, eighth and ninth grades, ninety-eight percent of whom were Jewish, if not more. I knew many of the boys, and all of the athletes, because I had played with them in all the sports for years at the local parks. Because I was a good athlete, I was accepted.

I played on the volleyball, basketball and softball teams for all three years and, at virtually every practice, as I recall, Coach Greenhut would call roll and say, "Goldfarb! (here); Steinfeldt! (here); Rappaport! (here); Hornreich! (here); Kelley!...Kelley?...how did he get here?" and everyone would laugh, every time.

My nickname was "shagitz," which means non-Jewish boy. I don't think I was ever called Pierce. I was called Kelley occasionally. Most of the time I was called "shagitz," and that continues to this day whenever I speak to any of those guys. The Jewish girls didn't have too much to do with me as all they wanted was a Jewish boy, but that was okay. I was a late bloomer in that regard.

Incidentally, it was an extremely talented group of athletes. Several played in college and one, Neil Walk, played at the University of Florida and then was the second player drafted in the 1969 NBA draft, behind Kareem Abdul Jabbar. I started in front of him in all sports, except basketball, since we both were lefties and played the same positions. He grew to be 6'11" and had a lengthy pro career, primarily with the Phoenix Suns.

By the time I was thirteen, I had become a real "tennis player." I obtained a ranking of number 14 in the state of Florida in the 14 & under division and I was on my way up the ladder. I was good at every sport, and I was voted "Most Athletic" at Nautilus but, as my grandfather told me, I was good in football, baseball, basketball, volleyball and everything else in my school and around Miami, but I was really good in tennis, not only in the state of Florida, but also for the whole country. Fortunately, I stuck with tennis. That was good advice.

In fact, though I am jumping ahead a bit, when I went away to college, my roommate was Rick Ascott, and he was named Mr. Basketball in high school for all of Dade County. He only had a few scholarship offers. I must have had fifty or more full scholarship offers. I chose Tulane, but that's a story for a little later on.

I won't go into much detail regarding my progression in tennis, though it was, and remains to this day, an extremely significant part of my life and who I am. Suffice it to say, most every day after school, and after practices at Nautilus, I would be on a tennis court until dark. I'd take a bus, or hitch-hike, to North Shore Park, where my grandfather would be waiting for me. He'd bring me home. I had a passion for the game.

Again, I jump ahead, but twenty-five years later I wrote a book entitled "Introducing Children to the Game of Tennis," which was called THE perfect introduction and primer for parents of beginning players by the United States Tennis Association and Tennis magazine. Jimmy Evert, father of Drew, Chrissie, Jean, John and Clare, all star players, wrote the Foreword for me. In it, he says that he taught all five of his children to play tennis so that they could learn social skills and meet a diverse group of people.

Tennis is a great game and I played because I loved to play, not because of any pressure put upon me by my parents. They supported and encouraged me. I also wrote an article, at about the same time my book came out, in Florida Tennis magazine, about the true champions I had met along the way. In it, I said that desire was the most important component. All had talent, but many, many players with talent never rose to the level of champion. The ones who had talent AND desire were the ones who were true champions, and there weren't that many of them. I was not quite of that ilk, but I was very good, and I competed with all of them, winning every so often.

I wasn't a particularly good student, but I was in all of the Honors courses and did well on all of the standardized tests, like the SAT exams. Harvard turned me down, at the very last minute, as I was on its "wait list," and so did Princeton, but I would have been accepted into most every other college, I'm sure. I'm also sure that my father was very happy that I didn't get into Harvard. Instead, I received a full scholarship to what was then called the "Harvard of the South," which saved him a lot of money - a whole lot of money.

I'll share that Tulane story with you now regarding how I chose it. So, as I said, I was receiving full scholarship offers from a large number of schools – University of Miami, Florida, Florida State, Oklahoma, Texas, Georgia … virtually anyplace outside of California. At the time, USC and UCLA had teams with the best players in the country on it, like Arthur Ashe, Stan Smith, Bob Lutz and Charlie Pasarell, as well as some of the best players in the world, like Ian Crookenden from New Zealand, and Mexico's Davis Cup team members. Those schools, which included Stanford, were not interested in me. They had a lock on all of the players from California, Arizona, Oregon and Washington. Tulane had offered me a full ride.

So, as I was mulling over the offers, in no hurry to make a decision, my parents said to me one night over dinner, "Pierce, there's a tournament in New Orleans over the Christmas holidays and we were thinking it might be a good opportunity for you to go look at Tulane. What do you think?"

It was the Sugar Bowl tournament and it was one of the biggest national events for junior players. I was well aware of it, but didn't expect to have my parents ask me if I wanted to go. At that point in my life, I was in my senior year and I had never had anything alcoholic to drink. I was a good Catholic boy, but I was ready to spread my wings. I immediately agreed, thanking them, and saying only that it sounded like a good idea.

Now, although I was a virgin, in every sense of the word, I was no saint, and I knew enough to know about New Orleans and Bourbon Street. This was a golden opportunity young boys like me only dream about. The Orange Bowl had a junior tournament involving many international stars a week or so before Christmas, and I would play in it and be ready to play in New Orleans.

So the day after Christmas, I boarded a plane at the Miami International Airport and flew to New Orleans, something else I wasn't accustomed to doing at that point in my life, by myself. I then took a taxi to City Park, located about ten miles outside of the city. They had a large complex there with thirty courts or so, as I recall, and a big building where many of the players were housed, dormitory style.

As I remember, there were rows of beds for maybe fifty boys on one side and someplace else on the other side of the building was a place for the girls. Having played the junior circuit for a few years, and being nationally-ranked, I knew many of the players there. I think I was ranked about number thirty in the country at the time, but top ten coming back for my last year in the eighteens. I had some friends there with me in that dormitory who were a bad influence upon me. They will be nameless.

I arrived late on a Sunday afternoon, with play beginning on Monday morning and ending the following Sunday. It was a big tournament with a full draw of a hundred and twenty-eight boys in the 18 and unders. I'm sure that I was a seeded player, but I don't remember what number. I played doubles with a friend from Miami who made the trip, Mike Keighley, another good player.

On Monday night, a gang of about five of us were in a taxi on our way downtown once play ended for the day, after we ate and showered. We were dropped off right where Bourbon Street intersects with Canal Street and we started walking, right down the middle of the street, with hundreds of other people, most of whom were either inebriated or on their way.

Everyone was smiling and greeting one another. It was a carnival atmosphere. I had never seen anything like it. I don't know that I've seen anything like it since, either. I hadn't seen Mardi Gras yet. That's a totally different animal.

So we would play matches during the day, all day long, and then, at night, we would go down to Bourbon Street. Now those of you who have been to New Orleans know what Bourbon Street was like back then. It hasn't changed all that much in the last fifty-five years, actually. I have still not found anyplace on earth like Bourbon Street, to this day.

I think the drinking age was twenty-one at the time, but it might have been twelve. It didn't matter, none of us were legal. That was of no concern to the "barkers" who invited us in to all of the strip joints on the path, and there were many. They would open the doors wide, showing naked ladies on stage and say, "Come on in, boys! Your first drinks are on the house! Free!"

I could not believe that any of that was legal! I had never seen anything like that in my life. Granted, I was sheltered, as you know from what I have written so far, but this was like another planet.

What was a poor boy like me to do, other than go in? It would have been un-manly to do otherwise. My friends would have ridiculed me and left me standing in the street. I had no choice. We went to several that night, and on every night thereafter.

And those weren't the only attractions, though they were the main ones. Pete Fountain was a world-famous clarinet player and he had a place on the street where we went in to listen to his music a couple of times – no cover charge and first drinks were free. Al Hirt, a world-famous trumpet player, also had a place – same thing. And there was Preservation Hall, which was a small, little dive near the end of the street where black musicians played and people, including us, would walk in, listen, put money in a basket, stay as long as we wanted, and then leave.

There was also a place called Pat O'Brien's, which is still there, and they served a drink called a "Hurricane." It was a fruit drink with a large amount of alcohol, but you couldn't taste it. We drank it like it was water, and we were thirsty, with the predictable outcome.

We did this every night. I did well in the tournament, and Mike and I got to the finals of the doubles. We lost to a guy named Frankie Connor, who was an excellent player, who went to Trinity College in Texas, which was a great tennis school, and his partner, who was a good player, too. He beat me in singles, too, in the quarter-finals.

He then went on to become a professional golfer. He was a funny guy and a great athlete. That was the last match of the tournament and I went straight to the airport and caught a flight home. I never made it to Tulane's campus.

When asked how my trip was, I responded, "Mom, Dad, I'm going to Tulane!" and I accepted the offer.

I will share one more tennis story with you from that period of time in my life – more will come, I'm sure, but this will make you laugh, and we'll get to the more serious stuff soon enough. So I was a senior in high school and I played in a men's event and did well. I beat some good players and was in the finals against a guy named Frankie Tutvin, who was on the University of Miami's team and an excellent player. He went on to play Davis Cup for Canada for about fifteen years after graduating from UM.

The match was scheduled for 11:00 on a Sunday morning, and my father, brother Chris, and I drove up to Ft. Lauderdale and arrived fifteen to twenty minutes beforehand. The tournament director, Bob Perrin, had everything set up and had placed the trophy on a table in front of the court. It was at least three feet tall, if not bigger.

There were linesmen, a chair umpire, fans in the stands and it was a beautiful day. So, Frankie was late, and he called to let everyone know that he was on his way. Bob gives us the news. It doesn't bother me and I'm just sitting around, awaiting his arrival.

Twenty minutes later, Frankie pulls into the parking lot, gets out of his car and starts to walk over to the stadium court. Now Frankie is a very funny guy, and a friend, but he was always the one pulling stunts on everyone else, making everyone laugh. He was, and still is, a character.

So unbeknownst to me, my father walks over, picks up the trophy, and starts walking to our car, saying "Too bad, Frankie! You've been defaulted! You're too late!"

Everyone laughs and we walk onto the court, and get ready to play. My father comes running up to me and says, "Pierce, you've got to win this match!"

I say, "I'll do my best, Pop," and he repeats himself, saying that I've got to win. I ask, "Why, Pop? And he says "I broke the trophy!"

I think I laughed, but I said, again, "I'll do the best I can, Pop."

So I win the first set and lose the next two. We shake hands. I wasn't terribly disappointed. I played well, but Frankie was just a better player at the time. I beat him the next time we played.

But Pop, undeterred, picks up the broken trophy off of the table where it still stood, walks over to Frankie and says, "Here you go, Frankie! Good match!" and starts laughing. Frankie didn't know what to say or do. He just stood there with a "shit-eating" grin on his face. We got in the car and drove home.

Forty years later, my brother, Chris, sees Frankie at the Jockey Club in Miami, where he was the pro, and reminds him of that event. Frankie remembers and says, "It was the biggest trophy I ever won in my life, too."

That was Pop. He was a bull in a china shop. It makes me laugh just thinking about it.

I was a star athlete, going to one of the best colleges in the country on a full scholarship, and life was good. My biggest concerns were the tennis matches and whether I won or lost. That was 1965. Most people reading this book will know what life was like in the United States at that time.

Three very significant events occurred during my high school years of 1962 to 1965 that affected my life and the life of all Americans in a profound way. The first was when I was in the tenth grade in Mr. Shumard's Civics class when news came over the loudspeaker that president Kennedy had been shot. We all sat quietly for a little while, thinking he would surely recover, and then we were sent home.

Being an Irish Catholic from Boston, it was especially hard on me. I think it affected my entire generation in the same way. It was an unimaginable thing to happen. How could they kill our president? Even today, it's hard not to think about how things would have been different if JFK had lived. Even today, we really don't know who did it. I think the government knows but, for whatever reason, refuses to tell us the truth.

The second most significant event occurred in 1964, when John, Paul, George and Ringo burst onto the world stage. The most memorable part of all of that, for me, was how young girls and grown women reacted to them. It was truly revolutionary, in more ways than one.

The third most significant event was taking place in Southeast Asia, where American soldiers had been acting as "advisors" to the South Vietnamese army. We were told that they weren't allowed to carry guns, but they accompanied the South Vietnamese soldiers into battle. In 1965, President Lyndon Johnson made the fateful decision to put guns in the hands of our troops and allow them to fight. Everyone in the country thought we'd kick ass and take names, but that didn't happen.

On a personal level, I went through a crisis of my own. Sometime in my junior year, acne attacked me, and I had a bad case of it. It put scars on my face and I was extremely self-conscious and hid during those days. The scars were removed through surgery, but my life was dramatically affected. I still have remnants of the scars to prove it.

The only good thing to come of it was that it made me dedicate my life to tennis. That was my salvation, a silver lining, if you will. It made me a better player. I didn't have the same distractions other boys my age had, and ones that I would have had but for the acne.

I really don't know how or why, but my girl friend at the time was the best looking girl in the school. She went on to become a model with the Ford Agency in New York, after spending one year at the University of Florida, where she was selected as the Homecoming Queen. I don't know what she saw in me. We're still friends, and I had other beautiful young women interested in me, but I was very self-conscious about my complexion.

The Beatles made their appearance on the Ed Sullivan show on February 9, 1964. In February of 1965, President Lyndon Johnson sent combat troops to Vietnam and launched a campaign to bomb North Vietnam and the Ho Chi Minh Trail the following month. We had been in Vietnam under President Kennedy as "advisors," but that is when the Vietnam war is said to have officially started, as far as the United States of America is concerned.

I graduated from high school in June of 1965. To summarize, the "school days" portion of my life were idyllic, and I expect that my experience was much like everyone else's my age at the time. We all had dreams and aspirations. We expected to live the "American Dream."

We were naive, watching silly television shows like Father Knows Best, Happy Days, I love Lucy, Car 54 Where are you, the Mickey Mouse Club, and so many more, but we were about to get caught up in some powerful forces that changed our country, and the world, forever.

The era of "sex, drugs and rock 'n roll" was just about to begin. The war in Vietnam was on the other side of the globe and had yet to hit home. For those of us living in Miami, all of that was a million miles away.

As I said before, I was a star athlete, going to one of the best colleges in the country on a full scholarship, and life was good. My biggest concerns were the tennis matches I won or lost. The "School Days" portion of my life was over. I was on my way to the "College Years."

Chapter Three

College Days

Tulane University is situated in what is called the "Garden District" of New Orleans, in between streets called Broadway, Freret and Claiborne. The historic and picturesque trolley cars stopped right in front of the school and took students along the six mile route to and from the downtown area and the French Quarter. Loyola of New Orleans was on the other side of Freret Street, with the Holy Name of Jesus Catholic Church in between.

Audubon Park, a 350 acre park owned by the city, and named in honor of John James Audubon, who lived in New Orleans in the early 1800s, is adjacent to both schools. At the time, it had a zoo, with a pool for sea otters, a golf course, and a circular route for cars to drive around and through. Beautiful trees lined all of the streets in the neighborhood.

The stadium where the Sugar Bowl football game was played, called Tulane stadium, sat in the middle of Tulane's campus and I walked through and under it every day on my way to practice. The three clay courts where the tennis team played our matches was in the shadows of the stadium, next to the track. The field where the varsity baseball team played its games was right behind both.

Tulane University first came into existence in the mid 1800s, and was given its name later in the nineteenth century when a man named Paul Tulane made an extremely generous donation to the school. A woman named Josephine Newcomb made a similar donation at approximately the same time. Newcomb College was for women students only, but men and women took classes together. Women had their own dormitories, though, on the opposite side of the campus.

The enrollment at Tulane, including the women students from Sophie Newcomb, as it was called, was less than five thousand, including the graduate programs. It was, and still is, a small, private school, with an excellent reputation. There were few classes where the ratio of students to teachers was more than thirty to one, which is, more so now than then, unheard of.

It was an idyllic place to go to school. It also had a reputation as a "party" school, which was well-deserved. It still does. The fact that Bourbon Street is so close and so easily accessible gives it an unfair advantage over every other school in the country.

I now have four grown children. When my oldest was eighteen and thinking of places to go to school, one of his friends recommended Tulane and told him that it was the number one "party" school in the country, which it was and still is, according to whoever ranks schools in that category. My son responded, after telling his friend that I had gone to school at Tulane, by saying "it must have changed since he went there." Such are kids.

I enrolled in the school of Arts and Sciences. I had no interest in things like engineering, architecture or pre-med, so it wasn't much of a decision. In retrospect, I realize what that meant back then and continues to mean is that students receive an education regarding topics such as English, foreign languages, political science, philosophy, psychiatry, sociology, music and art, with a dabble into the sciences, like geology, astronomy, or mathematics, depending upon your major.

Back then, freshman students had few choices. We were required to take some basic classes, and then, at the beginning of our sophomore year, we had to choose a major. We also had to choose a minor. Students had to complete 128 hours of classwork to graduate and 36 of those had to be in one particular department in order for it to be a major. 18 hours of study in another department was required for it to be a minor.

Being an athlete on a full scholarship meant that I would receive room and board, in addition to tuition, books, fees, and the rest, including a voucher for $15.00 for meals on Sunday when the athletes' training table was closed. That $15.00 was never used for food. "Room" meant living in an athletic dormitory with other athletes.

Also, as a scholarship athlete, the athletic department helped to create your schedule. I never had afternoon classes as that was when our team practiced. That was the same for all athletes in all sports. That made things extremely difficult for engineering and architectural students, because they had so much "lab" work, which was always in the afternoons. I never had a problem with any of that.

When I arrived on campus, my schedule had been pre-arranged for me. I was assigned to a room reserved for athletes. There was a room within the cafeteria that was reserved for athletes. I just had to show up and do what had been arranged for me. It provided a "structure" for me, which most students don't have. I was fortunate in that regard. However, that didn't mean that campus life would be "structured."

Since my roommate, Rick Ascott, "Mr. Basketball" in Miami, was going to Tulane on a full scholarship, we decided to room together. We were "allowed" to do so. The basketball coaches were the ones who allowed this to happen, as did the tennis coach, and both probably regretted the decision as the year went on. I was not to blame. I was guilty by association, and so was he.

We lived in an eight man suite with four rooms, each with two beds in each room, with a bathroom consisting of four toilets and four showers in between. We didn't know who our six roommates were to be, but I wasn't expecting upper classmen. I was expecting other freshman, like we were. I was wrong.

We were put with six other basketball players, two seniors, two juniors, one sophomore, and one other freshman. The senior was Craig Spitzer, a 7'1" center who would go on to play in the NBA for the Chicago Bulls; Michael Muldoon, a 6'9" junior from Racine, Wisconsin who was a forward; Bob Benjamin, a 6'8" junior from Niles, Michigan, who was also a forward; O.J. Lacour, a 6'0" senior guard from New Orleans; Alan Goodman, a 5'9" junior guard from New Orleans; and Joel Miller, a freshman, who was a 6'4" guard. Since O.J. and Alan were from New Orleans, they were rarely there, and spent most days at their homes. Since Ascott, my roommate, was 6'4", I was the shortest person in the suite at 6'3".

I have said on many occasions, and I continue to believe, that college is, for the most part, a socialization process. It is where young people meet other young people and they socialize with one another. It is the time of life for those fortunate enough to attend college to find out who they are. They are called the "formative" years, and they definitely were for me.

It was a time when I, like most everyone else, was away from the structured life in the home of my parents. There were some rules which could not be broken, like those that would get you arrested or kicked out of school, but, for the most part, you could do whatever you wanted to do. You didn't have to answer to anyone, at least not on a regular basis. The most important thing was, however, that you carry a 2.0 average, which meant "C" work. An "A" was worth 4 points; a "B" 3 points; a "D" was good for 1 point and an "F" meant 0 points.

One of the reasons Tulane didn't do well in the other sports was that most football players flunked out after their first year. Some basketball players did, too, but not many. I don't think any tennis players ever flunked out, but I could be wrong about that. I know that no one flunked out while I was there.

That meant, among other things, what time you went to bed; what time you woke up; when you ate; how much you had to drink; what you did and who you did it with; among many, many other things, such as whether or not to go to class, were entirely up to you. It was a time when one was as "free" as he or she would probably ever be in life.

Back in those days, for many, that meant attending as many parties at fraternities, sporting events and gatherings of all kinds as one could. Or, simply going to a bar, and there were many on campus and in the surrounding area, whenever you wanted to. The fact that you might have been under-age was not an obstacle. Again, Tulane was the number one party school in the country.

My suite-mates were a bunch of characters who really weren't as concerned with excellence on the court as they should have been. I think they were 2 and 22 that first year. Now, the freshman basketball team was 19-0 and changed the dynamic for the next three years. That was back during the time when freshmen weren't allowed to compete against the upper classmen.

Being a scholarship athlete had its requirements, though, and that was a good thing. Every afternoon, weather permitting, we would have practice, beginning at around 1:00 and continuing until dark. That provided a structure to my collegiate life, a much-welcomed one at that.

Tulane was still in the Southeastern Conference in 1965-1966, but it left the conference after that. Our teams just couldn't compete against all of those state schools, like Alabama, Florida, Georgia, Tennessee and the rest in football and most other sports. They had so much more money and, quite significantly, a much lower academic threshold, although Georgia Tech and Vanderbilt were still in the conference at that time, and they are excellent academically, too. That wasn't true for our tennis teams.

We had one of the best tennis teams in the country for decades and won the Conference 17 out of 24 times from 1939 to 1965. That was one of the reasons I chose to go there. I think we lost two dual matches in the three years that I played there and we finished in the top ten at the NCAA tournament twice. We didn't play one year due to ROTC commitments from a couple of our players, not me.

At the time, freshmen weren't eligible to play any sports other than against anyone else other freshmen. It was a silly rule, intended to protect the young football players from injury, primarily. It was abandoned a few years later, but I couldn't play on the varsity team that first year.

I did, however, go with two juniors and a senior to Europe over the summer of 1966 and we played for ten weeks in England, Switzerland, Sweden, Austria and some other places, which was an adventure. Two of the guys met and married women from Sweden.

I had offers from the Naval Academy, West Point, and the Air Force Academy, but I wanted to be a tennis player and didn't want the four year commitment to military service after completing college. That was before the Vietnam War became an issue. That had nothing to do with my decision in that regard.

Tennis was, and still is, a major part of my life, but I was active in all aspects of college life there. I was a member of the Sigma Chi fraternity; I was elected the Vice-President of our senior class; I was elected to the Student Senate and was in "Who's Who" for college students, and I played all of the intramural sports and was a star, friends with most of my fellow students.

I was a fair student, but I wasn't a good student. I was, however, good enough to do well on the law school application test, the LSAT, and get accepted to some of the best law schools in the country. I almost got into Harvard law, but I received my rejection letter in late August just before school was to start. I was on the "wait-list" for months. I decided to go to George Washington, in Washington, D.C., which is the next chapter of my life.

That's not the "take-away" from my collegiate days, however. Not by a long shot. Being an athlete, I knew all of the other athletes, and they were my best friends. Some still are. They are the ones who influenced me the most in my growth as a human being – and there were some real characters in there.

However, I would have to say that whoever I am and whatever I am is, in large part, a result of my days at Tulane. It was a time of transition from being a somewhat sheltered, naive, adolescent and becoming a dramatically different sheltered, naive young adult. Those were good days and the friends I made there influenced me in a positive direction. I left New Orleans a more confidant young person, ready to move to the next stage of life, which became, in a roundabout way, law school.

I didn't have all that many serious relationships with girl friends at Tulane, but I always had dates for the parties. It wasn't a time to be married or in a serious relationship. It was a time for meeting lots of people just like me, looking to have a good time and not be too serious about much of anything. That was true for me, except for my tennis. I was serious about that.

I wrote a short story about those days and some of those characters. It fairly accurately summarizes the general tenor of that time of life – still very innocent and un-jaded, full of optimism and hope for what lay ahead. It is entitled Senor Muldoon. It is in a book of short stories I wrote thirty years later.

The summer between my collegiate days and law school continued to involve more tennis. I was still a "tennis player." I played the NCAA tournament in Princeton, New Jersey, where we finished in the top ten, and some other tournaments in Florida and on the Southern "tour," until the middle of July when my brother, Christopher, and I drove from Miami to Tacoma, Washington, to play the Pacific Northwest tour.

It took us three days to complete what was just shy of a three thousand mile trek. Our father let us use a 1967 Ford Mustang and we drove that thing at top speeds most of the way. Our favorite part was through Montana where there was no speed limit.

We arrived in Tacoma on July 20, 1069, the day the Apollo 11 crew stepped foot on the moon. Neil Armstrong, Buzz Aldrin and Michael Collins were the three astronauts on board. We listened to it for hours and we set foot on the Tacoma Park courts at exactly the same time as when they touched down, which was pretty remarkable, and memorable.

Chris is three years younger than I am and was a good player in his own right. He had completed his first year at Georgia Tech, where he was on scholarship. He had been ranked in the top twenty in Florida for years.

It was a full 128 man draw and I figured to do well, but I was upset in the quarters by a guy from Stanford who wasn't as good as I was, but he beat me that day. I was still somewhat disoriented from the trip, or at least that was my excuse. It took some time to get used to the slick hard courts, too. In Florida and the south, most tournaments were on slow clay courts.

So you'll get an idea of what those days were like, we played tennis all day long, every day, unless it rained or we were out of the tournament, but at night, we'd go out to dinner and then to the bars. We didn't get drunk every night, but we did have more than one or two every night.

Although the game of tennis had opened up the year before when, in Bournemooth, England, the first "open" tennis tournament was held and amateur players were allowed to play for prize money. The best amateurs in the world were allowed to play against the best professionals in the world, which was a colossal shift in the game. An Englishman named Mark Cox beat Pancho Gonzalez in the first round, which shook up the tennis world, as it wasn't expected.

It took a few years for money to really get into the game and even more years for the money to filter down below the winners and runners-up. At first, most of the money went to the top players and there wasn't much for guys like me at the bottom of that exclusive ladder. There was no money on the Pacific Northwest Tour, but they did provide housing and meals.

The best part of being in Tacoma was that we met Paul Larson, who was also on the Stanford team. He put us up at his parents' house and became a life-long friend. He is now a successful lawyer in Yakima, Washington, and still a good player.

From there we went to Seattle to play the next tournament on the schedule. I lost to Ross Case, who was a top-flight Australian who got to the quarters of Wimbledon the next year. He was a world-class player and better than I was that day.

The most memorable part of our time there were the boat races on Lake Washington. The tennis club sits up high above the lake and we could watch boats like the Miss Budweiser fly across the water. We had never seen anything like it.

Paul took us on hikes in the Cascade Mountains and up to the top of Mount Ranier, as well as showing us other sights to see in his neck of the woods. He's a first-class fisherman and took us out on his boat, too. We went to a Diana Ross concert and had a great time there, due in a large part to Paul and his family.

I should add at this point that Chris and I didn't really have all that much money, but Pop had given us a gas credit card, so we didn't have to pay for gas. All of the tournaments usually provided food for lunch and dinner and, since we were staying at Paul's, the only money we spent was for beer at bars.

From there, we took a ferry across to Vancouver Island, Canada, where the next two tournaments were to be played. We landed in Victoria, a beautiful city called the "City of Gardens." They have, literally, billions of flowers blooming at that time of year – yes, billions. It was beautiful.

I can't remember where we stayed, but the tournament provided housing to out of country players like my brother and me. Again, every day was spent playing tennis and every night was at a bar. I had some money saved up, but it was a finite amount. This was before credit cards were available, or before I was eligible for one, since I had no income, so everything was on a cash basis. I probably had several hundred dollars in cash, and maybe more, but not all that much, and it went down considerably on a daily basis.

Our parents had given Chris some money, too, but they told him not to tell me how much they had given him and not to loan me any money. At one point, near the end of our journey a month later, I remember saying to him, "So how much money do you have, Chris?" and he reluctantly responded "Two hundred dollars." My response was, "Good! We have two hundred and twenty dollars." I had nothing left, as you will learn as the story progresses, but I digress, again.

My brother and I, who I love very much and shared a bedroom with since shortly after he was born until I left for law school, were not a good doubles team. We lost in the quarter-finals of both of the first two tournaments. We just didn't play well together, so I told him that we were going to have to find different partners, and we did.

Victoria was an absolutely magnificent place to play. The club sat high up upon a cliff, commanding an amazing view of the Strait of San Juan de Luca, which separates it from Vancouver and the mainland. It also gave us a spectacular view of all the flower beds below. It is said to be one of the most beautiful cities in the world, especially at that time of year when the flowers are in bloom.

I won the tournament in both singles and doubles, despite being down match points in two matches in singles. I also won the doubles, with a man named Jim Wilson, who was from Colorado. He wasn't as good a player as my brother, but we played well together. He was a great guy and fun to be around. We had another adventure with him at a tournament in Denver, a month later.

The most memorable match for me from that tournament was against a guy named Gus Pelizzi, who was a 6'7" lefty from Rice University, and he was a good player. He had a huge lefty serve and the courts were the slickest and fastest courts I had ever played on. Of course, that made my serve that much better, too.

So we were having a battle of the serves. I was holding my serve and he was holding his. The problem was that I wasn't coming close to breaking his serve. I think I won three points in seven games. That was back before tie-breakers.

I really didn't know what to do. He was that good, plus he had a huge forehand, and I couldn't hit a ball to him on that side. I was having some trouble holding my serve, and was down a few break points in a couple of games, but we were even at 7 games apiece and it was his turn to serve.

It was at that point that one of the most remarkable things in my tennis career occurred – he double-faulted four times! I did nothing to win that game. He gave it to me. I have no idea what happened to him, maybe it was the sun. I don't know.

I won my serve and the first set, and then, somehow, won one more game on his serve in the next set to win the match 9-7; 6-3. He was a nice guy and a good player. He just had an inexplicable lapse for one game. I remember it well, and I remain grateful for his generosity.

I also remember being stopped by a police officer, after having bought a case of beer, and having a car full of revelers, including a few girls, and after consuming more beers than were, probably, legally permissible.

Fortunately, I was able to dissuade the officer from arresting me, telling him about why we, visitors from Florida, were in Victoria, and why it appeared that I was driving around like I was lost. I assured him that we didn't have any beer in the car. He was a nice man and he, apparently, believed me. That could have been a disaster.

From there, we drove north a few hours to Cowichan Bay, a small fishing village on the San Juans' side of the island to play the Pacific Northwest Grass-courts Championships. The tournament put us up in a motel that wasn't quite finished yet. Our room was fine, but the place wasn't open for business. We arrived late the night before and ended up sleeping in our car in the parking lot next to the courts that first night.

The first thing we did was go rent a small boat and ride around the harbor. We'd been told that pilot whales were in the harbor and we were hoping to see some. We'd never seen a whale before. We didn't see any, but we had fun trying.

Ask any tennis player if they've ever played on grass and I'll bet over ninety-nine percent will say no. It's a treat. The only place in the country where you'll find grass courts, with rare exceptions, at least back then, was in the northeast, at the exclusive country clubs in Philadelphia (Merion), Boston (Longwood), New York (Forest Hills), Long Island (Meadow Club), Orange, New Jersey and Newport, R.I., home of the Newport Casino and the Hall of Fame.

Chris had never played on grass before, so he was really looking forward to it. I had played that grass-court circuit several times, which began after Wimbledon and ended with the U.S. Open at Forest Hills, so I was looking forward to it, also. They had a restaurant/bar at the courts and we basically lived there for a week.

There were many good memories from that tournament, but the best is winning the tournament. Again, Jim Wilson and I won the doubles, too, but the singles finals of the tournament was epoch. It was, by far, the longest match I ever played. My brother said he would never watch me play again.

I beat a guy named Craig Hardie who played number one for the University of Arizona and was an excellent serve and volleyer. He was a tall guy and he could bang both serves and follow them to the net. He was good on those slick grass courts where the ball stays low, skimming off of the grass, getting heavier and heavier as the matches wore on, but I was good on that surface, too, and this was before the tie-breakers.

He won the first set 24-22 – yes, that's right 24 games for him, 22 for me, in about two and a half hours. Then I won the second set 19-17 and then the third 6-3 in another two hours, making it a 4 and a half hour match. It was painful to play but I just don't understand how all of those spectators, and there were over a hundred of them, sat through what must have been torture for them. It was for my brother, and for me.

The most amazing part was that Craig broke my serve at 16 games apiece and was serving for the match and led 30 – love in the game. Somehow, and I don't remember how, I evened it up at thirty – all, but then Craig missed two absolutely simple drop shots. All he had to do was get the ball over the net and he would have won the point, but the ball hit the top of the net, twice, and stayed on his side. I couldn't believe it, he couldn't believe it, but I broke serve for the first time all day.

I then won my serve and broke him again. I'm sure that he had an enormous let-down, knowing that he had just blown it. Even now, over fifty years later, I remember matches that I lost where I should have won, and I always tell myself to get over it, but the memories remain. That's a memory of a match I absolutely should have lost, but won.

From there, we drove back to Victoria, took the ferry back to Port Angeles, Washington, a two hour trip, and then we headed south to Los Angeles, where Jim Wilson had a house and he invited us to visit. I know, that was a really long drive, but we'd never been to Los Angeles before, and we had a gas credit card. It seemed to be a good idea at the time. On reflection, I don't think I'd do it again. That was a long drive and, eventually, we had to get back to Florida, and we were to play a tournament in Denver along the way home.

We stopped in Tacoma to see Paul and spent a night there, and then drove to San Francisco, where another guy on the tour lived, and he invited us to stay with him. We took the Pacific Coast Highway, otherwise known as Route 1, and that took a long, long time, as we had to stop about every hundred yards to admire the views.

We spent several days in Huntington Beach, just south of Los Angeles, on the coast, not far from the beach. We lived in Miami Beach, which is south Florida, and we expected the waters of the Pacific to be much like the waters of the Atlantic, and L.A. is southern California, so we thought we'd be swimming – surfing, no less. We were wrong! It was as cold as ice, and that was in August! We went in the water, but we didn't stay in all that long.

From there we drove to Las Vegas. We were on fumes as far as cash was concerned, which was probably a good thing. We walked around, played the one-arm bandits a little, didn't see any shows we were interested in, and didn't stay long. We were headed to Denver for our next tournament – we were on U.S. 15 to U.S. 70 for a long time.

I was the top-seed in the tournament and there was money in it, though not a whole lot by today's standards. We needed the money as we had little left. Unfortunately, it was raining the first day of the tournament so they put the matches inside on a basketball court – a fast, slick, wooden surface, one that I'd never played on.

I got out of the car, went out on the court, and proceeded to lose to a big, tall guy, who lost the next round. He was a serve and volleyer and I couldn't get the ball by him. I had excuses, but the result was the same. I lost in what was a big upset. My brother won a match or two, but he didn't win any money, either.

Other than that, there were three noteworthy take-aways from the tournament: number one, we spent all of our available cash on buying Coors beer when we left Denver; number two, I learned about tarot cards; and number three, I lost a match in the semi-finals of the doubles that I still can't believe. Each deserves an explanation.

As far as the Coors beer was concerned, that was the rave of the country, but it was before refrigerated trucks, apparently, because you couldn't buy it east of the Mississippi. We had only heard all about it, but we had never been able to find any before. We bought what we could and finished it before we made it back to Florida. That was disappointing, though the beer was good.

As far as the tarot cards were concerned, my brother and I were staying at someone's house, and I have little recollection of who they were. It was arranged for us by the tournament. That Sunday morning, I was to play the semi-finals of the doubles at 1:00 in the afternoon. Jim Wilson met us there and he and I were playing together again, and we were the top seeds.

Before the three of us went out to practice, the woman of the house, who wasn't too much older than we were, got out these cards and asked if we knew anything about tarot cards. Neither of us did, so she shuffled the cards and proceeded to show us how it worked.

I don't remember what she told my brother, but she told me that something unexpected was going to happen and that it wasn't going to be good. It wasn't going to be anything terrible, but it definitely wasn't going to be good. I didn't think too much about it and found it to be interesting, but not anything I put much stock in. It was like a palm-reader or fortune-teller kind of thing.

We packed up our things and headed out to practice around 11:00. We would be heading back to Florida after the matches. We practiced for an hour or so, getting warmed up for my match. Jim met us there. Then we went to get something to eat at an International House of Pancakes, not far from the courts.

We had a light breakfast and sat there talking, just killing time until the match was to start. We stayed for about an hour. When it was time to leave, Jim, who was the only one to drink coffee, said, "Well, one thing is for sure. I won't fall asleep out there. I had about ten cups of coffee."

We all laughed, and I didn't think too much about it. I wasn't a coffee drinker and didn't know much about caffeine at the time. I soon found out.

We were playing two guys from the University of Texas who weren't all that good. They were on the team, but down the ladder. There was no way we could lose that match, and my brother and I needed the money, badly. I was overly confident, and rightfully so.

However, when it was Jim's turn to serve, he hit me in the back as I was standing at the net with his first serve. He proceeded to double-fault three times, hitting me once more, and losing his serve. It got worse from there.

I was going crazy, yelling and screaming, trying to encourage him to rally. We were and we still are friends, but I wasn't angry at him for having too much coffee, and I did not want to lose that match. Needless to say, we did, in two straight sets that weren't all that close. Jim lost his serve every time. I won my serve every time, but we were only able to break the Texans' serve a couple of times. I was distraught.

I think they gave us a hundred dollars for our efforts, so that meant my brother and I had fifty dollars to get us home. That was back when you could only get gas with a gas credit card. It was a long drive from Denver back to Miami, and we drove straight through.

It was late August and Chris had to be back in school in a week or two. I wanted to continue to play tennis and had no desire to go to law school. I had been accepted at the University of Florida, the University of Miami and George Washington, which was the last one to start classes. I chose the latest entry date, hoping that something good would happen, but I was draft eligible and I no longer had a deferment if I didn't go to law school.

Before leaving for our trip out west, I had applied for the National Guard, which was a deferment, although it did involve some military service, like boot camp and training, as well as one weekend a month at the Armory and two weeks in the summer. I applied for the officer's program and was told that I scored the highest ever for that base on the mental exam and I was in the top tier of the physical testing.

However, when I met with the Commandant, and he asked me why I wanted the National Guard and not the regular army. I told him that I didn't want to go to Vietnam. I explained that I wanted to be a professional tennis player. He wasn't impressed.

Shortly after arriving back home, I received notification that I wasn't accepted into the Officer's program, but that I could become a radio technician and go to San Diego for training, if I wanted to do so. I didn't want to do that, but if I didn't accept it, I would lose my "ace in the hole." I was still 1-A and still draft eligible.

The night before I was to begin classes at George Washington, I was still uncertain what to do. I was out drinking with my good friend, Gregg Golding, and I told him, in no uncertain terms, that I wasn't going to law school. I was going to go in the National Guard. I'd go to basic training and then go on tour. Ten hours later, I was on a plane to Washington, D.C.

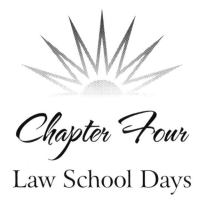

Chapter Four

Law School Days

My mother awakened me at 9:00 that morning to tell me that I had a phone call. I was still pretty hung-over. The call was from the George Washington Athletic Department offering me a scholarship to law school to coach the men's varsity tennis team. The timing was uncanny. What was I to do? I had no choice. That was a "no-brainer."

My sister, Carol, lived in the outskirts of Washington and I could stay with her until I found a place to live. She would pick me up at the airport later that afternoon. My plane was to leave in two hours. BAM! Just like that, my life took a predictable, yet still unexpected turn. My mother drove me to the airport, and that was that.

That was early September of 1969. Woodstock was from the 15th to the 18th of August, two weeks before. The country was changing and the changes were coming fast and furious. New Orleans had been seemingly unaffected by the Vietnam War, whereas Washington, D.C. was totally consumed by it.

The war was definitely the single-most significant issue of the day, but there were others – many others. Books like <u>Sisterhood is Powerful</u> and <u>Soul on Ice</u> were out there, as was the Black Panther movement, and people declaring themselves to be gay, not to mention the civil rights movement … and then there was the music, the sex and the drugs.

At Tulane, being an athlete in an athletic dorm, I didn't hang around anyone who even so much as smoked marijuana. There were plenty of people getting drunk and having sex, but it was an entirely different atmosphere. I didn't know anyone in law school who didn't smoke marijuana, or do something much stronger. Drugs were everywhere.

Music concerts were plentiful, too. I saw the Grateful Dead, the Doors, the Allman brothers, the Stones, and a whole lot more in and around the area. Emmy Lou Harris was just starting to get a name for herself and I would sit at the bar and talk to her for hours at a place called the Child Herald on 16th street. I actually thought I had a chance with her. I was wrong, but she was very nice and she humored me.

I still say that women were the single most significant catalyst for change, though, during those days. They were burning bras and wearing short skirts that barely covered what was underneath those skirts, and they were extremely sexually active. Guys were always that way, or wanted to be. It was a vibrant, if not explosive, time to be alive. I was caught up in a torrent of energy that was, truly, unimaginable, at least for me, prior to that time.

However, not everyone agreed with those changes. In fact, an overwhelming number of people opposed those sentiments. Richard Nixon easily won the election, with George Wallace, governor of Alabama for years, winning almost 14 percent of the vote nationwide, finishing a not too distant third. Nearly two out of every three voters were staunchly conservative and opposed to everything the students and other liberal-minded people, like me and other students, supported.

Walking the streets of Washington, D.C., though, you would never have guessed that. Hubert Humphrey, the democratic candidate, won 80 percent of the vote in the District. The country was deeply divided, to the point where physical violence was always threatened, but not on the streets of our nation's capitol or on college campuses.

Of course, the most popular democratic candidate, Robert F. Kennedy, was assassinated on the very night he won a huge victory in the California primary. If he had lived, the outcome might have been entirely different, one never knows. He was a very popular and charismatic figure. This took place a year after Martin Luther King had been assassinated and less than five years after his brother, John, was killed.

The only stabilizing part of my life was tennis. I was the coach of the men's varsity team, which practiced at the public courts at 16th and Kennedy. The team had finished 7th out of 8 schools the year before in the Southern Conference and the top players had graduated. The Southern Conference included Furman, Richmond, the Citadel, VMI, Davidson, William and Mary and Washington and Lee.

The caliber of play was nowhere near the teams in the SEC, ACC, SWC or the team I had played on, but the competition wasn't nearly as good, either, and there was potential there. Everyone on the team really wanted to improve. They were open to all of my suggestions and I truly enjoyed being a coach. Also, making them do things as I did made me do those things, too, so it was good for my game as well.

I also taught them how to jump rope, made them run and made them practice drills involving hitting balls at cones down the lines and cross-court, using those cones as targets. There were some extremely interesting and talented players on the team, one of whom was the most intelligent man I ever met. We became the best of friends and he became a research scientist at the National Institute of Health.

Every afternoon from about 2:00 until dark we practiced. I'd drive a station wagon full of players and equipment out to the courts and we'd play. We practiced up until the first of December when it got too cold to play outside, and then we went inside.

The anti-war marches had begun and in November the largest march to date took place, involving hundreds of thousands of people. I participated in those marches. At Tulane, I wasn't allowed to wear my hair long. In fact, at the spring Athletic Banquet the Athletic Director, Rix Yard, said that the Tulane tennis team would be competing at the NCAA tournament so long as I got my hair cut. Everybody laughed, but I got my hair cut, and it wasn't long at all, especially not compared to what was stylish in Washington, D.C.

By Fall, my hair had grown some, but it grew out, not down, kind of like Bozo the clown, not down my back, like Jackson Browne. I had an Afro, but Afro's were cool back then, so that was okay. I started to wear what was, essentially, a uniform – blue jeans and a flannel shirt. Nobody wore long-sleeved shirts and ties to class, and definitely not coats, except for winter coats. It was a lot colder in Washington, D.C., too, and I'd never lived in a cold climate.

Again, much like at Tulane, the courses were pre-determined. I had no choices to make – Contracts, Criminal Law, Torts, Evidence and a Legal Research and Writing class. My Torts professor, Robert Park, was a tennis player, and we became the best of friends. There was a tennis tournament for law students and professors and he and I played together in it and won it easily. I think we lost a few games along the way, but not many. He was very happy about that.

But I didn't want to be there. I wanted to be in Australia, playing the Australian Open, drinking Foster's beer, eating shrimp off the barbie and chasing Australian girls. Instead, I was freezing my ass off going to and from classes and being the tennis coach. I wasn't happy.

Sometime during that Fall semester I had to board a bus and go to Baltimore to take a physical. I was still 1-A and draft eligible. Although law school was an exemption, I was required to submit to the physical, which I did, and passed.

On December 1, 1969, the United States of America held a lottery to give each and every American male a random number relating to their birthday, which determined the order in which men would be drafted. July 14 was the 331st number drawn. I would be spared. My brother, however, born September 20, was the 60th number drawn. He was in danger, but he was in school, so he still had a deferment.

I guess I could have dropped out of school right then and there, but I had agreed to coach the tennis team and I didn't want to quit or, worse yet, fail, so I stayed in school. In the back of my mind, I always knew that I was expected to become a lawyer. There was never a doubt about that, really, although I wasn't ready to give up my tennis and do all of what was required to become a lawyer. The Fall semester was almost over, so I stayed in school.

I remember going home for Christmas that year, needing to read a thousand page book on Contracts. Final exams were to start the week after the New Year. I also remember getting on a plane the day after Christmas, going back to Washington, still needing to read those one thousand pages. I couldn't study on the beach in Miami Beach. Somehow, I managed to pass with an 80, as I recall, which was a "C". I passed all of my other classes, too, but I was nowhere near the top of the class.

The second semester was more of the same, except a class on Constitutional Law was added to replace the Criminal Law class. I think there was a course on Property Law added, too. I can't remember. Reading legal opinions and legal theories was a laborious and time-consuming process. You couldn't "speed-read" and it took a long time to read each and every page, as in hours and hours of time with your head stuck in a book, usually in the dark and dreary law library adjacent to the law school.

I was miserable. I didn't want to be there and tennis was my only salvation. When I was on a court, doing what I did best, it relieved me of all of the stress I was experiencing in every other part of my life. I really didn't have much of a social life.

The anti-war movement was growing stronger by the day and things were becoming more violent. I remember soldiers standing on street corners as I walked to school. I also remember tear gas episodes and running away from it. I also remember just barely making it into my apartment building as crowds of people were being chased down the street by police officers with batons.

There were a whole lot of slogans and "war cries" during that time, on both sides. "Love it or leave it," was one. "Next time you're in trouble, don't call a cop, call a hippy," was another. And there plenty on the other side of the spectrum, like "Ho – Ho – Ho Chi Minh is gonna win!" Or "A police officer's baton can turn a liberal into a radical." People would yell at each other. It was a very tense situation every day, all day, except on a tennis court.

Also, I started to get more involved with things going on outside of the classroom. George Washington University was among the very first schools in the country to encourage students to do things in the community and get credit for doing so. Although I didn't have the time for it, I signed up at a local Neighborhood Legal Services Program at 1411 N.W. Ninth Street as a volunteer.

I also became the coordinator for a Police Observer program whereby students rode with police officers in their squad cars on routine shifts. I would attend class, usually, but I wasn't doing too much reading at night. I was getting by, but I certainly wasn't getting ahead.

During the months of January and February, it was too cold to play outside, so our midnight trips to the indoor courts was all the play I was getting. I had been able to make arrangements with Pauline Betz Addie, who was one of the great women players of her day and was the owner of an indoor facility, and a friend, to allow us to play for free after 11:00 at night, when there was little or no play. So we'd drive out to Fairfax and play several times a week. All of the kids were agreeable and I had no trouble convincing them to join me.

Looking back, I really was not the best influence on those kids. For example, I told them that the way you were supposed to play the game was work hard, play hard, try hard, and then go drink some beer. That was the way I played the game. So, after practice, we'd drink a beer or two. I had no trouble convincing them to join me with that, either.

Probably the worst thing I ever did with them, though, was after our last team match of the year. We had traveled to Philadelphia to play against Swarthmore, who was coached by a good friend of mine, Mike Mullan. We lost 5-4 and I was so pissed that I made them run laps after the match, which they begrudgingly did.

We had the conference tournament to play the next week, so nobody argued with me about that, but I'm sure that they weren't happy about it. We'd had a pretty good season and won 15 out of 20, as I recall, losing to Columbia, Notre Dame, Maryland and a few others. Nobody wanted to lose that match, but we did.

However, unbeknownst to them, on the way home, I stopped in Baltimore for us to attend a Grateful Dead concert. They were absolutely blown away. I was driving the school car and it wasn't, obviously, a pre-approved activity. We, or I, could have gotten in a whole lot of trouble for doing that, and I almost did.

The concert was in a huge auditorium and it was standing room only. There were about ten of us and there was no way we could all stay together, though we tried. Over time, as the music started, we got separated.

There were police officers and men in uniforms walking through the crowd, and there was a strong aroma of marijuana permeating the arena. I noticed one man in uniform approach one of my players, but I couldn't see what was going on. Suddenly, a crowd gathered around the officer and I couldn't see anything.

Then, the crowd erupted into a large cheer and dispersed, including the officer, leaving my number 4 player standing there with a joint in his hand. I went over and asked him what happened and he said someone passed him the joint just before the officer got there, and he was caught red-handed, so to speak.

Then, instead of arresting my player, the officer took the joint from him, took a puff on it, and handed it back, evoking cheers from the crowd. He got rid of it and I gathered up the rest of the team around me so that I could keep an eye on them. That was a close call.

We finished 2nd in the Southern Conference tournament, which was a huge upset, not expected by anyone. The tournament was held in

Greenville, South Carolina on the campus of Furman University, which won the event. We came close to winning it but lost a few close head-to-head matches to them in the final rounds.

Our season ended sometime in early May, and I still had about a month of classes ahead of me. The anti-war marches continued throughout the early spring and there was a demand made by the "leaders" of the movement for what was called a "student strike" for the week of May 1-8.

Lots of things were going on all over the country on various campuses, especially out in Berkeley, but also at Columbia, where students took over a building. The largest march to date took place on May 1, called "May Day," involving hundreds of thousands of people in Washington, D.C., and I participated. Things were truly getting out of hand, but it was still kids like me, voicing their protests over the war in Vietnam.

Then, on On May 4, 1970, four students were shot by National Guard members at Kent State. That made things much, much worse. Just a few days before that, I had decided to drop out and go play tennis, and I did, on the very last day I could do so without getting a failing grade. My record would just reflect a "W" for "Withdrawn," with no "F's" on my report card.

Unfortunately, for me, a few days after doing so, schools all over the country canceled all classes and gave everyone a "passing" grade, as in "pass" or "fail." If I would have waited a just a few more days, I would have received credit for the entire semester, but I didn't, and I didn't.

Instead, I was off to play tennis full-time. For the next six months, I played with and against the best players in the country and the world. I played against Roy Emerson and Manuel Santana, who were numbers 1 and 2 in the world at the Canadian Open Championships in Montreal and beat players who were in the top ten in the world over the ensuing six months. I could tell countless stories of those days, but I won't.

At the end of that year I was ranked number 46 in the country, which correlated to about the top 100 or 150 in the world at the time. The United States and Australia were the two top tennis powers in the world back then. That was before eastern European countries began to play in earnest, as they now do, once big money got in the game. Spain was very good, too. I was at the top of my game and moving up.

Unfortunately, my timing was off by a few years. Although money was now in the game, there wasn't much of it to go around and most of it went to the very top players, not to guys like me. Plus, society was changing. Being a great athlete was no longer an "end-all, be-all" thing. In fact, it was, to a large extent, looked down upon. "You're a tennis player? So what?"

I can't say that I ever felt that way. I always loved playing the game with and against the friends I made along the way, many of whom remain friends to this day, but I lost the focus of working hard to be the best player I could be. I was changing, too.

Years later, I wrote a short story about what it takes to be a champion, and my friend, Jim Martz, published it in his Florida Tennis magazine, saying it was one of the best articles he ever published. I had lost what it took to be a champion. I had known many "champions," and I knew what it took to be a champion.

A friend of mine, who I practiced with many times, played exhibitions with and against, and went to a few concerts with, Brian Gottfried, rose to be the number 3 player in the world about that time. While I was in school, he was out playing all over the world. I saw him one day at a tournament and asked if he had been to any concerts recently. He looked at me as if I had two heads and said, "Concerts! I don't have time to listen to the radio!" To be a champion, at anything, you have to live, eat, sleep and breathe it, and he was doing just that.

To be honest, I didn't have the talent that Brian had, but I had a great serve and volley game and I could compete with anyone on a fast court. I knew I could be better, and I was continuing to improve, but I had lost the "desire" to be the best and, as I wrote in that article, I think desire is more important than talent. You've got to have talent, but if you don't have desire, you're not going to get there.

On top of that, I could return to George Washington in January and resume law school. However, if I didn't, I would have to re-apply, with no guarantee of being re-admitted. I decided to go back to law school, but this time I had a purpose. I was going to be a part of what was a movement called "Equal Justice for All."

When I went back, in early January, I didn't even bring my rackets, as I recall. I had decided to focus on school and other projects and programs offered, for credit, by George Washington University. I wasn't a hippy, but I believed in the things my generation was doing in the areas of civil rights, women's rights, and all of the other "causes" of the day, and my hair was long.

I immediately proceeded to sign up for the following: Work on an ACLU project investigating police brutality in Prince Georges County, Maryland; volunteer for a Law Students in Court program whereby students could actually appear in court and argue cases involving landlord-tenant issues; volunteering at the same Neighborhood Legal Services Program in the inner city; volunteering at St. Elizabeth's Psychiatric Hospital, assisting patients thought to be mentally ill and in need of involuntary hospitalization; and volunteering at the Public Defender's Office as an investigator, among other things. I was absolutely crazy. I wasn't playing much tennis, though, so I had lots of time that I had never had before.

I moved into a house on "S" street, much further from school than before, with three other law students and two other people – 4 guys and 2 girls, which was unusual for me, but not for the times. I started to smoke marijuana, which I hadn't really ever done too much of before. I started to drink more often, and I went to class and the law library a whole lot more. I was changing.

I did much better in school that semester, and went home for the summer, that being the summer of 1972, intending to teach tennis someplace, volunteer at the Legal Services office in Coconut Grove, learn to play a guitar, and just rest – do nothing else. The Harbor Island Spa, a world-famous place, was less than half a mile away, and there were three courts there that were rarely used. The manager agreed to allow me to use those courts as long as I agreed to teach the people who came to the spa from all over the country and the world, and charge them a reasonable fee for doing so, and I agreed to do so.

I met with the managing attorney at the Coconut Grove Legal Services office, and she gladly allowed me to volunteer there, as much or as little as I wanted, and I had a $10 guitar, ready to be played, though I didn't know how. I was dead-tired after the semester of law school and ready for a break. I really missed not having the physical outlet that tennis provided me. I was, and I am, at heart, an athlete. I was all set, looking forward to a calm, peaceful, enjoyable summer.

That was when one of the first of what would become an increasingly large number of "wild hairs" would emerge in my life, totally unsuspected and definitely unplanned. My life was altered and I was very fortunate to escape unharmed, though not unaffected.

Chapter Five

Red

This period of my life, which consists of only a few months, those being the summer months of 1971, deserve an entire chapter. It's not that I'm proud of this period of time. In fact, there is much shame to it, but it represents such an incredible departure from who and what I was, and who and what I was to be, that it merits that attention. I'm lucky to have survived it.

So I would ride my bicycle less than a mile to the Harbor Island Spa from my house on North Bay Island, right across the 79th street causeway, which connected Miami from Miami Beach. North Bay Village consisted of three islands: North Bay Island, Harbor Island, and Treasure Island. All told, maybe two thousand people lived on the three islands. My father was the Municipal Judge at the time.

The courts were located in the back, behind the six-story building which housed hundreds of people, mostly women, who were there to get massages, their hair done, take whirlpools, swim and, basically, to lose weight. It was, and still is, a world-famous place.

The three hard courts, which had lights, were in the back, with a separate entrance, so I didn't have to walk through the enormous building to get to them. I was completely isolated and had the place to myself. I had a little club house, with a bathroom next to it, and the first court, or the "pro court," was right on the water. It was very nice, but nobody was there to play tennis.

I think I was charging $25 per half hour for lessons back then, and I wasn't getting too much business, which was okay with me. My brother, Chris, would come over and we'd play and he'd help me with lessons if I needed him to. My brother Allan, who is seven and a half years younger than I am, would have been about 15 then, and he was playing number one on his high school team, so he would join us, too. We had the place to ourselves! It was great.

Then, one fateful day, as I sat there doing I don't know what, three middle-aged guys walked in and asked if they could play there. They weren't members of the Spa. They were just the "general public." Since I was in charge, I said, "Sure. Go back there (where the third court was) and play as long as you'd like." I think I said it would be $5.00 per hour to play. I can't remember.

So the three of them went back to play. I watched them and saw that they weren't players, but they were having fun and they weren't bothering anyone. No one else was playing. They played, they paid, and they left. No problem.

They came back the next day, and this time they had a little music box. They asked if they could play some music. It was the middle of the afternoon, and no one was there except for my brothers and me, so I said, "Sure, go ahead, as long as you're not bothering anyone, you're fine." Again, they played, they paid, and they left. No problem.

So the next day they come back and they have two women with them, who were younger and fairly attractive. They were several years older than I was and I wasn't interested in them, though they were pretty to look at. They sat on plastic chairs at courtside and watched. They didn't play the radio too loud and they weren't bothering anyone. Again, they played, they paid and they left.

By this time, I knew their names, they knew our names, and we were "friends." One was named Don, a short, muscular man, who looked a little like Don Johnson, the famous actor. Another was named Kenny, and he was the larger of the three, almost as tall as I was, but more muscular and much heavier. He, too, was a handsome man, and then there was a man with red, curly hair, freckles all over his body and gold teeth, with gold chains hanging around his neck. Needless to say, that was "Red."

All three were dressed appropriately for tennis, with collared shirts, tennis shorts and tennis sneakers, not basketball shoes. They were well-mannered, and they were funny! They laughed a lot and said funny things to make us laugh, too.

So now they were "regulars." They came just about every day, unless it was raining, and they started bringing coolers, and they offered us beers. You get the picture. Every day was a party.

More people started to come by, some of whom were actually tennis players, and more women, and they started smoking dope, too, which I didn't object to, and I might have partaken in, though I can't recall exactly when I began participating in what was going on.

One day, when things were in full stride, a North Bay Village police officer came walking in. I immediately rushed out to the back courts to alert them to the fact, thinking that them smoking marijuana might be something the police officer would find offensive. They weren't concerned.

"Oh! Don't worry! That's Johnny! No problem. Hey, Johnny! How you doin'?" they asked. Johnny came, said hello, watched for a little while and then left. I didn't know what to make of that, but I did find it to be a little unusual, to say the least. Still, I didn't protest, complain or do anything to stop what was going on. To be honest, I was enjoying it.

So weeks go by with the situation progressing and more and more people are participating. I even arranged a tournament for all of the players who were now there several days a week, at least, and on both Saturdays and Sundays. People were having fun, and so was I.

Of course, I wasn't playing my guitar much at all. I wasn't playing much tennis, though I did begin filling in on doubles matches when they needed a fourth, and I had my brothers to play with every so often, although they weren't there all the time, as I was.

I had no plans to play tournaments or go back on circuit at that point. I was finished with those serious tennis-playing days, or so I thought. I even stopped volunteering at the Legal Services office. I had become a part of what was debauchery, basically.

However, my friend, Frank Froehling, who I had practiced with quite a bit in 1970, after dropping out of law school as I did, came back from Paris, after losing in the semi-finals of the French Open, called me and asked me to play him in an exhibition match in Hollywood against him, which I readily agreed to do, so I had to prepare for that, and I did. He beat me 6-4, 6-3, but I played reasonably well, and certainly wasn't disappointed. After all, he'd been playing with the best players in the world and I'd been playing with Red, Don and Kenny.

Over the course of several weeks, maybe as long as two months, those being all of June and July, while all of that was going on, I learned who these three characters were. Don was a bookie, and he, from what I could gather, handled some big bets, really big bets. Kenny was an accountant, and he handled the books for someone, and I never knew who that was, but I was pretty sure that it wasn't entirely a legal operation, and then there was Red.

He was a drug-smuggler. He drove a bright, red Cadillac convertible, with the top down. He wasn't trying to hide from anyone, but he was as Irish as he could be, and he was funny. I truly enjoyed knowing him, despite his obvious flaws. In fact, twenty-some years later, I wrote a novel about him, based on things he told me about his life story. It is entitled A Tinker's Damn and a lot of it was true.

One day, I was riding with him in his car to pick up something to eat from the local Burger King, and he says to me, "See this car behind us? Don't look, but the license plate will begin with the letters ABC," or whatever letters he said. I can't remember.

He pulls off to the side of the road, the vehicle passes by, and sure enough, the letters were exactly what he said they would be. He explained that it was either DEA, Florida Law Enforcement, some task force or some other law enforcement agency, and that they follow him around all the time.

Although I should have been aware of the fact that I would, without any doubt whatsoever, be on somebody's list as a suspect for something bad, I hadn't given it as much thought as I should have. I am pretty sure that I didn't get a job with a couple of governmental agencies because of that, a few years later. It was a wake-up call for me. I had gotten myself in a situation that I needed to get out of.

The only thing I could think to do was get out of town, and the only way I could think to do that was to go back on the circuit. So I started to run and jump rope, things I hadn't done in a while, and I started to play some friends who were good players, like Rick Fagel, Frankie Tutvin, Eddie Dibbs and others.

After a couple of weeks, I felt like I was good enough to go back and play, though I hadn't played a tournament in nearly eight months. Technically, I was still ranked number 46 in the country, so I could get into most any tournament I wanted to. Nowadays the rankings are updated monthly, if not weekly. Back then, it was only once a year. That was before ATP points came into being.

The first tournament I could find to play in was the Georgia State Open in Athens, run by a friend of mine named Dan Magill, who was the coach of the Georgia team. I had played against his son, Hamilton, and beaten him. That would have been during the first part of August. I said my good-byes and headed north. My brother, Chris, came with me.

Chris and I had a friend who was on the Georgia tennis team and had a house close to the courts where we could stay. That was a good thing. He was a popular guy and had many friends come to visit him, especially after he lost in singles. That was a bad thing.

Since I was still, officially, the 46th ranked men's player in the country, and ranked in the top five or so in the Southern Tennis Association, as well as the Florida Tennis Association, I was a "seeded" player. That meant that I would be "placed" in the draw so that I wouldn't meet one of the other top seeds until the quarter-finals.

It was a full 64 draw, meaning that there were 64 players in the tournament and the winner would have to win 6 matches to win the tournament. I don't remember who I played in the early rounds, but my most vivid memory of the tournament was when I was to play the finals on a Sunday morning at 11:00 against Juan Diaz, the number one player from the University of Florida. He might have been the SEC champion that year. I can't remember. He was from Cuba and a very nice man, in addition to being a very good player.

Unfortunately, for me, the night before, being a Saturday night, our host had a party at his house. Since I was sleeping on the couch, the party was all over and around me. I have no idea what time I got to sleep, but I woke up at 11:00 – yes, 11:00, when the match was to begin. Everyone else in the house was still asleep.

I panicked, threw on some clothes, grabbed my rackets and ran to the court. When I arrived, it was after 11:15. There is a somewhat universal fifteen minute default rule and I knew it. Dan Magill looked at me and said, "You're late." Then he looked at Juan and said, "If you want a default, you have it."

Juan looked at me and said, "No, I want to play." I saw Juan a few years ago at a party in Gainesville hosted by Steve Beeland, another great player from the University of Florida, and thanked him, again, for that. He didn't have to do it, but he did. Not everyone would have done it, probably most.

So I was still waking up. You're supposed to be up for at least two hours before a match, and players always want to warm up for a while before playing. I liked to be up early, hit for about an hour, shower up, rest, and then go on the court, ready to play, but that didn't happen that day.

Juan won the first set 6-3. I lost my serve once and never broke his serve. I didn't behave well that day. I was groggy, not fully awake, and angry at myself for what had happened, and I was yelling at myself, trying to get me going. I'm not proud of that.

However, after pouring water on my head on change-overs and constantly yelling at myself, I was able to hang in and keep it close. By that time, everyone was using tie-breakers. There would be no 24-22 sets, like there were in Cowichan Bay, Vancouver Island, Canada, when I won the Pacific Northwest Grasscourt Championships a mere two years earlier.

At six games apiece, we played a NINE point tie-breaker. A year or two later, the twelve point tie-breakers were adopted and that's what's used uniformly across the globe nowadays. Player A would serve twice, then player B served twice, then player A served two more points, and Player B would get the last three serves, if necessary. The first player to five points won the set.

So Juan served first and we went back and forth until I had the last three serves. I don't remember exactly how it went, but I won the tie-breaker and, thereby, second set. Player B then started serving the next set, so that way one player wouldn't get the last three serves two sets in a row. Again, I don't remember the points, but I ended up winning the third set, and the match. I had done well. I could still play.

From there, we planned to head north. The U.S. Open was to be played at the end of August and I planned to be there for it. I wasn't going to get straight in the draw, so I would have to qualify, which wasn't going to be easy, and there would be 127 other really good players trying to get in the main draw, just as I would. That was a few weeks away.

I was really beat up after that tournament. My body was not ready for all of that exercise. I was stiff and sore for the next few days. After the tournament ended, we went back to Atlanta, where my brother was going to school, at Georgia Tech, and we stayed with friends of his. We went out to the Bitsy Grant Tennis Center the next day to practice, waiting for the next tournament to begin.

The "big boys" were playing the grass court circuit, but there was a Southern Circuit going on, too. Plus, all throughout the south, and really all over the country, there were weekend tournaments, and I knew where most of them were and played in many of them.

Since I had decided to get back on the circuit so late, there was no way I could get in any of those big tournaments, and I didn't even try. Besides, I needed to get better. I was out of shape. So I looked for the smaller ones.

I found us a tournament in Newport News, Virginia, and it was the typical three-day event with 32 players in the draw. The usual way the tournaments were run was to play two singles matches the first day, a Friday, and then two more on Saturday, with the finals set for Sunday morning and the doubles finals for Sunday afternoon.

The tournaments uniformly provided housing, food, parties on both nights, and an open bar. There were times when I was limited to a certain number of drinks. Those were normally the tournaments I had played before and they knew me. Again, they were all over the South, the Middle Atlantic, the Middle States, New York, the New England states and elsewhere. They also gave us money for travel expenses. Most of those tournaments weren't awarding prize money back then, but some were. This one was.

What I remember most about that tournament was how hot it was. It was 100 degrees temperature and 100 degree humidity. I also remember playing one of my players from my George Washington team, Burt Abrams, who lived there. It was hot as hell.

I ended up in the finals against Bobby Heald, who ended up being ranked number 1 in the Middle Atlantic region that year. I lost a very close match, 7-5 in the third, after leading 4-1. It was the first and only time I ever cramped in my life. He was another great guy and great player. It was a good match that I should have won, but you've got to play tournaments under pressure to play well under pressure, and I hadn't been playing enough tournaments.

I remember winning $100 for my efforts. As is evident, the money really hadn't arrived in the game by that time. I ended up being number 3 in the Middle Atlantic division because of that loss, instead of number 1 that year.

My brother and I went out to dinner on our way out of town on our way north to the next tournament, and I immediately spent over half of my earnings. Greg Hilley had joined us and I bought dinner for all of us. I was a sport.

Next up was a tournament just outside of New Haven, Connecticut at a place called Wentworth-by-the-Sea. After sweltering in the heat of Athens, Georgia and Newport News, Virginia, we were so looking forward to that. None of us had been there before, but we had visions of loveliness, cool breezes, adjacent to the Atlantic Ocean. It didn't turn out quite like that, but we sure did have fun dreaming about what it was going to be like.

It turned out to be a very good draw as a number of the best players in New England and the surrounding area showed up. I ended up losing in the quarter-finals to Norman Holmes, who was a very good player from Florida, a couple of years younger than me. I think he might have might have reached the round of 16 at the U.S. Open that year. He was probably favored to win. He out-played me on the slow clay and beat me, fair and square, in a close three set match.

Next up was the U.S. Open, and it was still being played at Forest Hills. It moved to its current location of Flushing Meadows a few years after that. My brother couldn't get in the draw, which was extremely difficult to do, because aspiring players from all over the world wanted in, too, so he went home. I stayed at the house of another one of my George Washington players, Sanford Schwartz, whose parents had a beautiful house, on the water, in Brooklyn.

I did well and won five matches, needing to win only one more match to get into the main draw. If I did, since the draw had already been made for the main event, I was to play Ken Rosewall on center court. My opponent was a man from Ecuador named Eduardo Zuleta, and he was on their Davis Cup team.

I had beaten him a year earlier on hard courts and he wasn't happy about it. After the match he swore that I would never beat him again. I didn't care much for him and he, obviously, didn't care much for me.

So we had a long, hard match on a slow clay court, but I got to 4-1 in the tie-breaker in the third set, with me to serve the last three points, if necessary, after he served once more. I don't know how I did it, but I lost the last four points and the match.

Looking back, as I have about a thousand times over the years, I think I tried to end it with a great shot, instead of being patient and playing the way I had the entire match. I really don't know, but I was absolutely devastated.

I hadn't trained properly, and I still wasn't in the best of shape, but I should have won that match. To play Rosewall on Center Court would have been a career highlight, but it just wasn't meant to be. Instead, I took the next plane back to Miami, not even staying around to play in the doubles or mixed doubles events, which I regret not doing.

Once home, I played a tournament on Miami Beach and lost to Eddie Dibbs, in two close sets, in the final, 8-6; 9-7. For some reason, we didn't play tie-breakers. He was ranked in the top ten in the world not long thereafter. I had beaten him two years earlier.

Also, I found out that Don had been shot in the head and killed, execution style, by a mafia hit-man, because he had been "meddling" in their business; Kenny was still doing books, but now for a small construction company, and Red had been arrested, after leading police on a wild, high-speed chase through the streets of Miami, after picking up four IRA members who had robbed a bank in Canada of a million dollars. I never saw or heard from him again.

That was "closure" for that part of my life. As I said before, I was lucky to survive and I don't really know what all those governmental agencies put in their reports about me, but I'm sure it wasn't good. It got me back to playing tennis again, and I was on my way back to law school. I wouldn't be be coaching the men's team this time, but I brought my rackets. I was playing again.

Chapter Six

Back to Law school

I now had a small, one bedroom apartment right near Dupont Circle, where I lived alone. I was back to playing tennis again, but not at the same level of commitment. I was a much better student this time around, and law school takes a whole lot of time.

However, I continued to be active with all of the many extra-curricular activities I had been the previous years, including working at Neighborhood Legal Services as a volunteer. I did pretty well with my grades that year and I accepted a full-time position as a Law Student Assistant with the Neighborhood Legal Services office for that summer. Bill Botts was the other summer intern. Fifty some years later, he is still dedicated to the "cause" of social justice. I admire him enormously for that.

Most of the work I did while there was either with family law matters, such as divorce, or landlord-tenant matters, where people were faced with evictions due to their inability to pay the rent. There were always major issues involving repairs that needed to be done to the apartments, which were never done, of course. I was able to try some of those cases in front of a judge, not a jury, and actually won a few, but not many.

Susan Schapiro was the managing attorney; Jerome Morris was one of the attorneys; and there was a full compliment of support staff and some other lawyers, Reggie, Ruby and others, whose names I can't remember. All of those people, including the support staff, truly believed that what we were doing was meaningful.

I, and we, were part of a movement called the "War on Poverty" which was part of the Civil Rights movement of the '60s, started by JFK and enacted into law by LBJ. It was an exciting thing to be a part of and I enjoyed being a part of it all. Those were exciting times. We really thought that we were making a difference.

Washington was a really hot place to be in the summer time. I was riding a bicycle at the time through the streets of D. C. and I remember just being unbearably hot, except when in the air-conditioned office. The office was an old, three-story wooden building, adjoining other old, three story buildings, among blocks of old, three story buildings, that were not well insulated. I worked long, hard hours back then, because there were so many people in need of our services.

I was still playing tennis, though, and I would get up in the morning at sunrise to play with friends at the Georgetown University Courts. One such person was Bobby Johnson, who was the son of Dr. Robert Johnson, of Lynchburg, Virginia, the man largely responsible for helping Arthur Ashe realize the success he did as a tennis player. He would pick me up in his car at sunrise and we would play for an hour or more, as time permitted. I was almost always late.

He was always very patient with me as I wasn't used to getting up that early. We would play almost every weekday morning, hitting drills, before going to work, on the hard courts. I won local tournaments and that was how I was able to achieve a ranking of number three in the Middle Atlantic States that year. My left-handed serve was the weapon that allowed me to continue to play at a high level, even though I wasn't playing as much as I had during most of my life prior to that.

George Washington re-hired me to be the coach of the varsity men's tennis team for the school year 1972-1973, and that helped me out financially. I had become less interested in tennis in the intervening years, but I still had some of the same players on the team. I know that I wasn't as good a coach the second time around, but I enjoyed them and I enjoyed my time on the court, as I always have.

I was now a third-year student and I would be graduating in May. I became more interested in trying to figure out just what I was going to do with my law degree, which I would soon be receiving. I had become caught up in all that was going on in the country regarding calls for social change, and the spirit of the sixties, which had carried over into the early seventies.

The war in Vietnam was still raging on. However, the huge anti-war demonstrations had fizzled out by then, due to the fact that so many men were no longer faced with being drafted. I was somewhat saddened by that. Once men were no longer worried about being drafted, their opposition to the war faded. I guess that was to be expected, but it was, nonetheless, disappointing.

My time with Neighborhood Legal Services, helping poor people with legal problems, as well as all the time I spent with the Public Defender's office there, St. Elizabeth's Mental Hospital, the ACLU project, the Law Students in Court program and all the rest, made me want to use my legal education to help other people, instead of chasing tennis balls as I had for most of my life. It changed me. By the time I graduated, I was definitely a different person from the one who had reluctantly entered law school in September of 1969.

Also, somewhere along the line I lost the desire to be the best tennis player in the world, or the best tennis player I could be. I didn't lose my desire to play, I just lost my "desire" to be a champion. I still loved to play, and compete, but I was no longer the "tiger" I had once been on a tennis court.

The best part of that summer before my last year in law school, and the most memorable, was the very last part of it. After I ended my summer internship with Neighborhood Legal Services, two weeks prior to the time school would begin, I took a three thousand mile trip on my motorcycle up through New England.

I had purchased a Honda 175 motorcycle from a fellow student at some point, and I don't remember when that was, but it was a whole lot easier to park a bike in D.C. than find a parking space for a car. Before that, I'd ridden a bicycle through town, and that was a challenge for different reasons, like not getting killed by passing cars. I'd never ridden a motorcycle before, but I bought it despite that. How I learned to ride it is a story in itself.

One of the lawyers at NLSP, Jerome Morris, lived in Fairfax, Va, in a complex that had a huge grassy area between buildings that was the size of a football field. I took it over to his house and we, after drinking some tequila, started to try to ride it. He had never ridden before, either. His wife, Jane, tried her best to convince us that it was a bad idea, but we were determined to give it a try. How hard could it be?

You engage the clutch by using your left foot; You shift gears with your right foot; you give it gas with your right hand; and the left hand operates the brake. Simple enough, right? No, it wasn't.

Jay and I fell down many, many times. The grass and the tequila softened the landings. We laughed constantly. Jane laughed as much, if not more. She was laughing at us, not with us, of course. He was sure that he could do it better than I could, and I was sure he couldn't. Neither one of us was right.

About two hours later, a police officer arrived and put an end to our shenanigans. Since we were on private property, and not on a roadway, he couldn't give us a ticket for DWI, but he could have given us one for disorderly conduct, I guess. Except, we weren't disorderly, we just couldn't ride that damn motorcycle, and we were drunk. We put it away, at his strongly-worded suggestion, and continued with the Saturday night festivities.

However, the next morning, when I got on that motorcycle, I could ride. Damned if I know how that happened, but it did. I didn't drive too fast, and it took a while before I was comfortable on it, but that's how I learned how to ride that bike.

I drove north on I-95, through New York City and over those bridges, up into Connecticut, Rhode Island, Massachusetts, out to Cape Cod, then up through New Hampshire, on up to Maine, and then down through Vermont, into western New York and then down into Pennsylvania, before riding through Maryland to get back to D.C. I camped out the whole way. How I survived is a miracle.

The Honda 175 is not a big bike, and it's not that heavy. That's one of the things I liked about it. If I fell, it was easy to pick back up. Not so with the bigger bikes. However, the light weight had some unforeseen consequences.

I was riding up the side of a mountain one windy afternoon in Vermont when a gust of wind blew me from one side of the road to the other. I had absolutely no control over the bike - none whatsoever. I ended up off the road in the grass. Fortunately, there was no car coming in the opposite direction when that happened, and there was a grassy area for me to land, when I did. It was sheer luck ... a miracle, if you believe in such things.

Another memorable event from that trip on a motorcycle was while I was camping, in a tent, on top of the dunes at the National Seashore out on Cape Cod. I went to bed the night before, after watching a full moon rise from start to finish, and was awakened by heavy rainfall – a tropical storm had hit! I walked back to my bike, completely soaked, and went to a laundromat to dry my clothes and wait for the storm to pass. That was interesting.

That year, 1972-1973, we had a good team coming back, with several guys who had been on my team during the 1969-1970 season, including Mark Geier, Sandy Schwarts, Edward Kahn, Jan Sickler and Bert Abrams, but it wasn't the same for me. I was a tennis player going to law school in 1969, but in 1972 I had become a law student who was a tennis player, and the transition wasn't a smooth one. That was going to take some time.

My grades had improved and I had become a better student, but I was, by no means, anywhere near the top of the class, as my sister had been. She had been an editor of the law review and graduated third in her class. That was not me. If there were grades given for "clinical law," or learning law on the street, I would have been at or near the top of the class.

My 1969-1970 over-achieved, but my 1972-73 team did not. We had a decent record, but finished in the middle of the pack at the Southern Conference Championships. I blame myself for that. I wasn't the inspirational leader I had been.

Once my law school education concluded, and I couldn't wait to get out. Almost all graduating law students were going to have to take a bar exam before actually becoming a lawyer, and that included me. Many would take jobs right out of law school and study for the bar at night. Others would just study for the bar and plan to begin work after successfully "passing the bar" exam. I chose a different path. I wasn't quite ready for that.

I didn't know what I wanted to do, but I'd been either in school or on a tennis court for my entire life, it seemed, and I wanted to do something else before beginning my career as a lawyer. I knew that once I did I would be working long, hard hours and I'd be wearing a coat and tie all day every day. I wasn't ready for that.

Pierce Kelley

This next stage of my life was the most significant departure from a "normal" progression into the responsibilities of adulthood, and there is a story behind it, albeit not a totally rational explanation, at least not in the eyes of my parents or the world at large, but it made sense to me. How that came to be is a story in itself.

Chapter Seven

The Shenandoah River

While the rest of my classmates were attending graduation ceremonies at George Washington University, I was on my way to Luray, Virginia, with my brother, Allan, to go canoeing on the Shenandoah River. I don't remember if that was the first time I'd been canoeing in my life, but it might have been. Allan had gone to Camp Carolina a couple of times before, and he had been in a canoe a few times.

That was in June of 1973. Allan, who is seven and a half years younger than I am, had just graduated from Archbishop Curley High School in Miami, and he had been accepted to Duke for the Fall. He was riding on the back of my Honda 175. That was quite a load to put on that little engine.

Our plan was to spend a weekend on the river. We had sleeping bags with us and we bought some supplies for three days and two nights out. We rented canoes from the Shenandoah River Outfitters, located about ten miles outside of the thriving metropolis of Luray, which is famous for its caverns, and is located just west of the Blue Ridge Parkway and, at that time, had a solitary stop light.

Joe Sottosanti was the owner of the business and he put us on the river in a seventeen foot, aluminum, Grumman canoe, right under the only bridge crossing over the river for another fifty miles or so. He gave us a map and explained where to camp, where the various rapids on the river were, and where he would pick us up on Sunday. He also gave us two paddles and two life-preservers and wished us luck.

That was right around the time when the movie "Deliverance" came out and, instead of having the expected effect of scaring people from daring to go on wild rivers, people began to go canoeing in earnest. Everyone my age remembers the movie, which starred Burt Reynolds, Jon Voight, Ned Beatty and Ronnie Cox, among others, and everyone remembers the "squeal like a pig" line from the movie.

It also had a fabulous guitar and banjo duet with an albino backwoods teenager and Ronnie Cox which has become an "anthem" for bluegrass musicians. The river scenes were absolutely compelling and my brother and I were excited about doing it together. Since he was ten years old when I went off to college, he and I hadn't had the same amount of "bonding" time that Christopher and I did.

Allan played on the high school team and he, too, played tournament tennis. He was a good player, but not as good as his two older brothers. He was an excellent runner, though, and set school records in distance events which still stand. He wanted to be an Olympic runner, but injuries prevented that from happening.

We were both looking forward to the trip and excited when we shoved off and headed downriver. Back then, not many people knew too much about what became known as "whitewater." When a river gets big enough, it forms rapids, which bubble out and appear to be white, hence the term.

There are various categories of whitewater rivers, and they vary from the east coast of the United States to the west coast. East of the Mississippi, the range is 1 through 7, with 7 being totally impassable, and 6 being almost impossible. The biggest rapid on the Shenandoah River was at Compton Rapids, which was a class 3, so not too bad, and it was the only class 3 rapid on the river, at least for the stretch we were doing.

Still, us being novices, we really didn't know what to expect. Since we left on a Friday, we were the only ones on the river. I'm 6'3" and I weighed 175 pounds back then. Allan is 6'1" and he weighed about 150 pounds. So I was in the rear of the canoe, or the stern, and Allan was in the front, or the bow.

For those of you who aren't canoeists, that's a significant difference. Both paddle the same way, with one hand gripping the top of the paddle and the other hand holding the paddle in the middle. Both changed hands when paddling on the opposite side of the canoe.

The "bow" person's job was to keep an eye out for obstacles in the river, like rocks, tree limbs or whatever, and the primary stroke he would execute was the "J" stroke, which is a straight front to back motion, leaning forward and putting the paddle in the water and then "drawing" the paddle back as far as he could, and then lifting it out of the water, and doing it again. The purpose of that stroke is to propel the canoe downriver in a straight path, but the bow man has little to do with controlling the general direction of the canoe.

The other stroke for the person in the bow is called the "draw" stroke. That's when he, or she, puts the paddle straight out from the canoe at a 90 degree angle and then pulls the paddle straight towards the canoe, usually bumping right up against it. The purpose of that stroke is to dramatically alter the direction of the boat over a very narrow area, like maybe a foot, to avoid some major problem. He sees the obstacles that can't be seen from a distance. That usually occurs somewhat suddenly.

The person in the stern performs the "draw" stroke, just like the bow man does, as far as technique is concerned, but the other major stroke for him is called the "C" stroke, and that's when he puts the paddle as far forward as he can in the water and then makes the shape of a "C" in bringing it back. That's to cause a dramatic shift in the stern of the boat and change the direction of the canoe significantly. The paddler in the rear, or stern, truly controls the direction of the canoe going downriver. If a canoe goes from side to side, or off into the banks of the river, it's the fault of the person in the rear.

So Allan and I were doing just fine, learning how to canoe and enjoying the scenery. There were no homes along the river, no bridges over the river, and virtually nothing else on the river except for trees, open meadows, and maybe an occasional deer or two. We were fully engaged and enjoying every minute. We were both "city boys," having been raised in Miami. We'd been athletes our whole lives. This was an entirely new activity for us.

Then, a couple of hours later, after having a pre-packaged lunch on a particularly beautiful spot, we heard what sounded like a train off in the distance. We didn't know what it was, but we heard the noise. There was little noise prior to that, except for birds singing. Planes were flying overhead to Dulles Airport, or maybe National, in D.C., but they weren't making any noise. We could see the white trail they left in the sky, but we couldn't even see them. We were way out in the country, having a blast, but the sound of the "train" kept getting louder, and we didn't know what it was.

So we come around a bend in the river and see two enormous rocks in the river, and I mean enormous! They must have been at least thirty feet out of the river. We could see down below the rocks where there was about three hundred yards or more of white water boiling out of and above the river. The two rocks were standing side-by-side and there was no way to get in between them. We had arrived at Compton Rapids.

We both analyzed the situation and began talking much more rapidly to each other. I told Allan that we needed to go left. He was quite insistent that we should go around them to the right. I repeated myself and explained my position. He repeated himself and explained his thoughts on the matter, all the while the noise became louder as we got closer and closer to the rocks.

"Left!"

"Right!"

"Go left!"

"No, go right!"

And, before we knew it, we crashed into one of the rocks sideways, causing almost everything in the canoe to go in the water and, most alarmingly, causing the canoe to be pinned up against the rock.

We grabbed what we could, like our paddles and preservers, holding onto the canoe, trying to free it. After a while, with no success, we found a way to get up on top of one of the rocks to survey our predicament. There was no one around and there was no chance anyone would be coming along behind us to be of assistance.

We sat for a while, not saying a word to the other, though both of us were silently blaming the other for what had occurred, and then it started to rain. At that point, we were glum. We were wet; we had lost all of our belongings, which had floated downriver; we were cold; and we were in trouble!

At that point, I had the bright idea to get a limb of a tree, or something, to try to pry the canoe off of the rock. To this very day, my brother says it was his idea. I then swam to the side of the river, walked upstream about a hundred yards or more, and found a twenty foot long limb of a tree that had fallen to the ground. I then swam back to the rocks, with limb in hand. It floated, so that wasn't a problem. To this day, he says he did that, which is ridiculous – he was eighteen and I was twenty-five … who do you think did that?

Together, we were able to position the tree limb underneath the canoe, finding some way to leverage it up, and when we did, it popped up, away from the rocks and started to float downriver, with us in tow. We managed to direct it to the side of the river, avoiding the rapids, and then we emptied the canoe of all the water inside. Fortunately, there was no structural damage to the canoe, not even a dent.

Once we were back in the canoe, going downriver, we found almost everything we had lost along the way. It stopped raining, and the sun came out. We found a nice place to camp and did our best to make the best of our situation.

Of course, the food was totally destroyed, the sleeping bags were soaked and useless, except to give us a little something between the hard ground and our bodies. The matches were useless, too, and we were not happy campers.

I love my brothers, but I don't remember too much conversation with Allan that night. I'm sure that he was as mad at me as I was at him, but we didn't yell at each other, or fight with each other. We just didn't talk much with each other, and that was our first night on the river. We had one more to go.

The rest of the trip was somewhat uneventful, but still really enjoybable. Of course, after that first mishap, it would have taken a fatality to match it. It really was and is a beautiful trip and I would encourage anyone to take it, just remember to go left at the two big rocks in the river.

Joe Sottosanti, or his teenage son, Michael, picked us up at the designated landing spot on Sunday at the designated time. We made no mention of any problems along the way. "No, we had a great time. No problems at all," we lied.

However, that's not the end of the story. It is just the beginning. We rode in the van back to the headquarters, where we were able to shower, and just as we were ready to leave, while making idle conversation with Joe, I told him that I had just graduated from school, not saying it was law school. He asked if I had a job and I answered in the negative. He then asked if I wanted to go to work for him there. He needed some help with his canoeing operation and he had a partner who could use some help, too.

I had nothing else to do at that point in my life, except study for the bar exam. When I asked what, specifically, I'd be doing, he said that he could use help with taking people down the river on rafting trips and, during the week, I could help his buddy build houses. I couldn't think of a good reason to say no, so I didn't. I told him that I had to take my brother back to our sister's house in Maryland and that I'd be back in the morning.

Allan and I rode back to Potomac, Maryland, where Carol lived, on what was a long, difficult ride, especially for Allan. We were both exhausted, not having slept much for two nights, and still somewhat in shock over what had happened to what was to have been a great weekend of whitewater canoeing. We made the best of it, we really did, and we both enjoyed the weekend, despite the mishap.

Parenthetically, I would tell you that it led to a lifetime of canoeing, rafting, kayaking and comraderie. We, including our brother, Christopher, have been on over a hundred rivers all over the country since that time. Last Fall, the entire Kelley clan of males went down the Chattooga River in rubber duckies on section III, and then down the Ocoee River in Tennessee.

All four Kelley brothers were there, plus my two sons, Allan's two sons, Bruce's son, and Christopher's son-in-law, plus a few close family friends, as we have done for over twenty years now. That fateful trip spawned a lifetime of adventure on rivers.

For me, however, it was, as I said before, the beginning of a dramatic departure from the path my parents had planned for me. I'm sure that they were totally baffled by my hasty decision and I'm sure that they weren't too keen on the idea. Neither they, nor I, had any idea how long that would last. It was a completely new venture – it was to be an adventure, and I was excited about the prospects.

Chapter Eight

Shenandoah River Outfitters

Please keep in mind that I was raised in Miami Beach, Florida and had spent my entire life either in school, on a tennis court or some kind of ball field. Living in the country was something I'd never done. I'd never even gone to summer camp, as my brothers had. What I was about to do was going to be a whole new experience.

My first night, after arriving back at the Shenandoah River Outfitters campground, was spent in a tent. I was awakened to the sounds of horses parading around me. Apparently, I slept too late and Joe let the horses in to wake me up. I was okay with that. It was a new experience.

My first task that particular day was to help bale hay, which was, to state the obvious, another novel experience. My particular assignment was to walk the fields with another man, and each of us was to grab a two foot by three foot bale of hay and toss it up to two other men, who were on a long, wooden wagon, being pulled behind a tractor, who were stacking the bales up about seven or eight high. The bales probably weighed about twenty or thirty pounds or so. Before long, we were throwing them up two at a time, using both hands.

It was a gorgeous day in the late spring in the Massanutten Mountains of Virginia. The Shenandoah Valley is bordered on the east by the Blue Ridge Mountains and on the west by the Appalachian Mountains. The Massanutten Mountain is fifty some miles long and in the middle of those two.

The Potomac River runs to the north; the James River runs to the south, and the Shenandoah River runs from south to north and is on both sides of the Massanutten mountain. There is a "north" fork of the Shenandoah and a "south" fork. We were working within a few hundred yards of the "south" fork of the river and could jump in the river to cool off every so often, which we did, occasionally, throughout the day.

It was an absolutely gorgeous day and I was having an absolutely wonderful time. For me, this wasn't work. It was fun. I think I was being paid $2.00 per hour. My parents were so proud!

So there are some hazards to baling hay, as I was doing, as I soon learned. First, is the obvious – the bales of hay scratched your arms and made them itch; second, it was hot and I was soon sweating profusely; and third, there were, occasionally, snakes in the bales.

I discovered the snake problem when I picked up a bale and a black snake leapt out and ran, yes, ran, slithering along the ground, as fast as it could. One of the men told me to be sure to kick the bales before picking them up, because snakes get caught up in the bales sometimes. That would have been a good pointer to have been told beforehand, but it wasn't. I'd never seen a snake before in the wild.

I made sure to kick bales before picking them up, and a few more came out over the next few hours, but they were black snakes and the men I was with said not to worry about them, that they were "good" snakes. "They bite, and it hurts, but they're not poisonous and it's nothing to worry about." Easy them for them to say.

Later on, though, a different kind of snake came out and a totally different response took place. "It's a rattler!" said one. "Kill that hellion!" said another, but two others wanted to catch him, and they did.

I stood back, watching what was going on, impressed by the speed of the response, as well as the skill demonstrated in actually capturing what was, as far as I knew, the most dangerous snake in the world. It is not, but it is definitely one of the most dangerous in the United States, together with the cottonmouth, the coral and the copperhead. Plus, there are several different types of rattle snakes, as I later learned, all of which are extremely poisonous and can kill humans with their venom. They put the snake in a bag in the back of their truck.

We quit work for the day soon thereafter and it was with much dismay that I was handed the bag, with snake inside, from our leader, Don. It was the kind of bag which holds corn or grain, which had been able to contain the snake inside, thus far. He told me to stand in the back of his pick-up truck and hold it while he drove home, which I did, with much trepidation.

The trip of several miles back to headquarters was on a bumpy, dirt road and I was afraid of falling. I held the bag off to the side of the truck as far as I could reach. I was going to drop it in the road if I fell or if the snake got out. I survived and the snake was put in an empty aquarium. That was my first day.

Needless to say, it was a much different day than any other I had ever experienced in my life, but I enjoyed it. That is true. I did, even the business about the snake. I was experiencing a side of life I'd never seen before.

I was still sleeping in a tent off to the side of the main office of the Shenandoah River Outfitters, where I could shower, and get something to eat. The fare consisted of cold sandwiches, chips, crackers and the like, the kind of things you take on a trip down a river, but I didn't mind. I would have to ride my motorcycle ten miles to town to get a meal at a restaurant, which probably would have cost me more than I earned that day, and I didn't want to do that.

I had no idea how long I'd stay there, or what else was in store for me, but I was game. We baled hay for the next day or two and then began to build a house, which was very exciting for me. Don was a carpenter, and a good one, and so was his side-kick, Cliff.

There was another man working with us, named Mark, who had been a football player at James Madison University, located in Harrisonburg, Virginia, an hour or so away. This was a summer job for him and we got along just fine. He was a big, strong man and we were the "labor" part of the job.

First, the site was cleared by Joe Sottosanti, who operated a back hoe, digging out the roots of the trees and leveling the ground, after we cleared the area with chain saws, cutting down the trees. Don and Cliff operated the chain saws and Mark and I carried away the tree trunks and debris.

Then Joe dug the holes for the footers, after they measured out exactly where the house was to go. This was all new to me, so I was absorbed by the process, taking in all of this new information, including the terms and tools. I'd never been around chain saws and back-hoes.

Every so often during a day, we'd have to drive down to the headquarters, or store, and put canoeists on, or take them off of the river. My job was either to drive the van which took the paying customers to the river, with the canoes on a trailer behind, or pick them up from the river, after the trips were over. Learning the put-in spots and the take-out spots was a bit of a challenge, too, but Michael, Joe's teenage son, was usually with me, and he knew everything about what to do and where to go, so I was learning from him.

On weekends, since it was the summer time, the canoe business totally dominated our activities. They were putting large groups of people on rafting trips but, as much as I would have liked to have been a part of that, I wasn't. I was hauling passengers and toting canoes. I wasn't good enough to be a guide yet, especially after I told them about my exploits at Compton Rapids with my brother.

Those canoes weighed about 70 pounds, each, so it was difficult, but not impossible to carry them by myself. At first, two of us would carry them one at a time, but after a while, it was easier just to do it by myself. It really was.

So this went on for a few weeks, and I was all-in with everything. I wasn't playing any tennis, obviously, and I wasn't reading any books, newspapers or watching any news reports, and studying for the bar exam might have been the last thing on my mind.

Nixon had been re-elected in 1972 and the Vietnam war was raging on. The Watergate break-in had taken place in August of 1972, but he wouldn't be removed from office until 1974. I really don't remember exactly what was going on in 1973 in the rest of the world. Where I was, it was all about living out in the country, building a house and putting canoes on the Shenandoah River, or taking them off.

I was following the news of the day as best I could, but none of the people I was working with were too concerned about it. I remember when Spiro Agnew resigned later that year. We heard that on the radio. Nixon resigned in August of 1974, but that was after a long and drawn out process which began on June 17, 1972 and it made the news almost daily in the two years following the break-in.

Not too long after that, Don took us down to a barn where horses were kept. We were to build a corral for his sister to give riding lessons. That's when I met his sister, Christie, and we hit it off quite famously. Not long after that, I was living in her house and we were sharing a bed.

Christie added another new dimension to life. I'd never had a live-in relationship with a woman before. Women would come and go for varying stretches of time during my law school days, but never like this. It, too, was a new experience, and a very enjoyable one at that.

Also, Christie added something else besides a romantic partner, because she was a horse-woman. She would take people out on trail rides into the mountains for day trips or overnights. Soon thereafter, I was riding a horse and acting as the rear trail guide.

My job, as the rear trail guide, was to call Christie if someone fell off their horse. At first, I was happy to be able to stay in the saddle, so I was hardly a qualified "guide." I'd help set up tents and do things to help with the camp fires, the meals, and the clean-up, but basically I was just there to be with Christie and not get in the way.

Over the next few months, after clearing the land, pouring concrete for the footers and the foundation, we laid out the walls, using pine 2 x 4s, put on a roof, using hot tar and shingles, dug the lines for the septic system, put in a septic tank, framed out the inside walls, did the electric and plumbing and everything else necessary to make that building into a house.

I was learning things every day that I knew nothing about, and after work, I was having fun doing things I had never done before, like what it means to roll in the hay, literally.

In addition to that, I was learning how to ride a horse and do all the things that horse people do. Also, Christie's horse, Cricket, had foaled the year before and I got to spend time with the young colt, named Torque. That was another new experience for me and, little did I know, but Torque would become a big part of my life in the years to come.

I wasn't playing any tennis, although there was one public tennis court in Luray, and I did give a few lessons on it. Months had gone by now, and I wasn't studying for the bar exam. I was basically living in an alternate universe, and enjoying it.

Christie, who was all-country, taught me how to gig for frogs, which I knew absolutely nothing about. We would go out late at night, with pitchforks and a flashlight, to some local ponds and shine the light on water's edge. The best time to go was on a full moon, because you have to see what you're doing. Fortunately, I never successfully gigged a frog, so I never had to clean it and actually eat it. We had fun, despite the lack of success.

The months passed by and life was good! I bought a 1953 Ford pick-up truck, some "Farmer John" blue jeans, and a cowboy hat for when I went on trail rides. I had to look the part, right? While all of my fellow classmates were in three piece suits, with starched white shirts and ties, wearing shiny, black shoes, earning tens of thousands of dollars, I was earning $4.50 at hard labor, and enjoying it.

Also, since Christie had a nice young doberman pup, I decided to get one, too – a young, female Irish setter, who I named Daffy. She was a great dog and the two of them got along quite well. They'd follow along behind the horses on trail rides, and basically had the run of the land.

The 1953 truck started about half the time, but that was okay, because I learned how to jump start it by popping the clutch, something else I knew nothing about. I didn't even know how to drive a stick shift vehicle before buying that thing. I just had to make sure to park it in a spot with a good incline so I could release the emergency brake, put the vehicle in neutral, let it run down hill a ways with my foot on the clutch, engaging it, and then release the clutch when it was going fast enough to start the engine, and then it started every time.

The Florida Bar Exam was given at the beginning of October, as it always is. My father had done whatever was needed to be done for me to be eligible to take the exam, including paying whatever fees were required. I took some time off, maybe two weeks, giving myself a week and a half to study, since I hadn't done anything to prepare for the exam before then. Applicants don't get the results for a month or two later.

When Fall came around, all of the men I was working with - Don, Cliff, Mark, Joe, his son, Michael, and others - took time off to hunt. Of course, I had never hunted before and had never even held a gun, or a rifle, let alone fired one. I was about to learn.

My grandfather Kelley, who died in 1951 and I have little recollection of, had left a nice shotgun and my grandmother Kelley, who I loved very much, gave it to me. My father had no use for it. There was never a gun in our house. I brought it back north with me after taking the exam.

Looking back, I can only imagine what my parents were thinking at the time. I have to say that they really gave me a lot of slack and allowed me to "sow some wild oats." I'm sure that they were, quite understandably, concerned about what the heck I was doing.

My mother told people that I was taking my retirement first. I'm surprised they didn't have me seen by a psychiatrist, but even if I was mentally unbalanced, I posed no danger to myself or others, so they couldn't have had me committed to a hospital. They were stuck with me.

So this shotgun, which was somewhat of an antique, but a very high quality gun in its day, had two barrels, one for a slug and the other for a bird-shot shell, which was somewhat unique, apparently. That's what I was told. I had no idea, but that was my weapon for hunting squirrel, rabbit, ducks, quail, pheasant and anything else that came along, including, of course, deer, which were plentiful in the area.

There were no deer in Miami, New Orleans, Washington, D.C. or anyplace else I'd ever been, except in a zoo. Seeing deer in the wild was thrilling. They're such beautiful creatures, and so harmless. When did you ever hear of a deer posing a threat to a human? Never, but men hunt them with a passion.

However, before deer season opened, which came in mid to late November, when the cold weather arrives, there is squirrel season, and that, too, is an extremely important time of year. I wasn't all that bad at killing a few squirrels, and I even skinned them and gave a couple of the carcass to Christie to cook for us.

I don't know how many readers have eaten squirrel, but everyone knows that they're not that big. They don't have much meat on their skinny, little bones. No matter how much you season them, it really wasn't all that good, either, but I did it.

As for rabbits, that was even worse. Rabbits are completely harmless. Squirrels can be a nuisance, especially if they want to get in your house and nest, to get out of the cold and have their babies, but rabbits don't do anything to harm anything or anyone, so killing them was more difficult.

It was especially hard when, after you killed one, you had to skin it, and clean it, put it on ice, so the meat didn't go bad. Most of the time, I didn't hit them. Those little guys are so unpredictable! They zig and zag this way and that way, so they're hard to kill. I remember killing one, skinning it, on an absolutely beautiful Fall day, and then vowing never to kill another one, and I didn't.

As for deer, that was another matter. That was a matter of man-hood! There was definitely something wrong with you, in that environment, if you told people you weren't a hunter. Besides, venison, which I'd never eaten before, really tastes good. It does. There, too, my ineptitude was my saving grace.

I remember my first experience with going deer hunting with "the boys." First, you wake up way before the crack of dawn, meet up with everyone else, have coffee and a good breakfast, and then drive down to a special spot where deer are known to frequent, and get up into tree stands before the deer know you're there. Once firmly embedded on your perch, you sit silently for hours, not moving a muscle, except the muscles in your eyes, so as not to attract any attention.

I never did like getting up early in the morning, especially when it was really cold outside, so I never liked that part of it. I was from Miami Beach, remember? But I did it. I was just following along with the program. I was in the back seat, along for the ride, with my trusty shotgun in hand.

Now those of you who are hunters, or have been in the military, or lived in the country, know that a shotgun is really only accurate from a very close range, as in not that many yards. The buck shot wouldn't kill a deer anyway, so you could only fire the one shell, the slug, at a time. A slug is a cylindrical shaped bullet that is solid metal. It would definitely leave a mark on anything or anyone it hits but, again, it's not accurate, except at close range.

Have any of you readers ever been to a turkey shoot, where they have prizes for people? The organizers put up some paper targets about ten yards from the line where people shoot behind. Few people hit the target, let alone the bulls-eye. For me to be successful, an unsuspecting deer would have to wander directly in front of where I was sitting, ten feet or higher up in a tree, stop, pose and not move.

However, before getting up in that tree, I needed to rid myself of the coffee I had consumed, knowing that I'd be stuck up in the tree for who knows how long. Little did I know that doing that was like sending a message to any deer within miles of where I stood that I was there. They don't see that well, but their sense of smell is phenomenal.

Needless to say, I didn't see any deer that day, but I did hear these strange sounds that sounded like a baby crying. When I asked what made that sound, Joe told me "deer." I am very happy to be able to say that I didn't kill a deer that day or ever, though I did go into the woods with bad intent on many other occasions.

I didn't fare too well with the ducks, either. The men had a foolproof method of killing ducks, which were abundant on the river. They set up a "blind" down river a ways and then had me and another guy come down river and drive the ducks towards the spot where the men lay in wait. We arranged for a take-out place and eagerly baited the trap and began the "hunt."

A couple of hours later, we exited the river, not seeing the men in the blinds, or any of the ducks we scared up and caused them to move down river. When we asked, Joe, Don, Cliff and Mark told us, "Yeah, we fooled you, but not the f---ing ducks!" They hadn't seen or killed any.

Birds were a different story. Since there were many corn fields in the area, as well as hay fields that had been cut, it was a target-rich environment for bird hunters. Quail and grouse were the prime targets, though pheasant and turkey were also potential victims, although they weren't nearly as plentiful.

Men would line up, maybe twenty yards apart, and march, in unison, from a designated spot across these fields, waiting for the birds to fly up to be shot at. It was important that we kept in a straight line as best we could so as not to get ahead of a fellow shooter and then, quite accidentally, be shot. Everyone was more afraid of me than anyone else. I was the rookie.

I was happy just to be out there. It was exciting. I really didn't care about shooting the birds as I knew the amount of meat on the bird would be negligible, and probably not all that tasty, but I was bound and determined to be part of the expedition, and I was a willing participant. I was not, however, a hunter.

There were many other similar adventures living out in the woods in the Shenandoah Valley, site of many of Robert E. Lee's victories, far too many to share anymore than I already have. That is the part of the country where he earned a reputation for being a brilliant tactician. He had help from Stonewall Jackson, Jeb Stuart and his other almost as famous generals.

It was a beautiful place, especially in the spring, summer and fall, but not so much during the winter months, and that is when I decided it was time to leave – when the winter of 1974 approached, much to Christie's disappointment. I'd been there for over a year, and it was a good year.

I left over a month early this time, in early September, to give me plenty of time to study for the Bar exam, and that was my explanation as to why I was leaving. Christie would follow me down to Miami Beach, hoping to keep the relationship alive, but it was not to be.

We remained in contact for years and years, but that chapter of my life had come to an end and she just never could have fit in to the life I would eventually turn to, which was that of being a lawyer in a big city. She was "the girl from the mountains of Virginia."

However, as a parting present, she gave me Torque, who was now a two year old colt, and I had trained him to the point that I could ride him bareback, after putting a hackemore over his nose, and do just fine. He stood nearly 14 hands tall and I could jump on his back with no trouble whatsoever. I put stanchions on the back of my Ford 150 and we headed south, back to Miami.

My days with the Shenandoah River Outfitters were over, but I still wasn't ready to start looking for jobs as a lawyer. I guess I'd had my fill of Virginia and the Shenandoah River Outfitters. I still had no idea what I wanted to do with my law degree or where I wanted to go from there.

Chapter Nine

Texas and Colorado

The trip south was eventful. Imagine seeing a beaten-up, red, 1953 Ford pick-up truck, with a horse in the back, driving down the Interstate at about the minimum speed. How would you react? That's how every single driver who passed us reacted, which meant every other driver on the road. Everyone slowed down to take a look at us, including cars going in the opposite direction.

Did I mention that I had acquired a second Irish setter? I did, to keep Daffy company. His name was Poe, and the two of them sat in the front passenger seat as there was no back seat in those old trucks. I had a gun rack on the rear window, with my shotgun in it. I don't think people can do that anymore, can they? I don't know. That was a long time ago and things have changed quite a bit since then.

I took side roads whenever I could as I really disliked the interstate. Cars were going way too fast for me. Torque didn't like it either, especially when the big rigs went zooming by. The whole truck shook.

Somewhere in the mountains of North Carolina, I was driving down a four lane country road when two semis passed me, one on each side, doing about thirty miles per hour faster than I was. I was doing the speed limit, barely. It startled all of us - Torque, the dogs and me.

Fortunately, there was a state trooper sitting someplace off to the side of the road who saw that happen and he pulled them both over. He was standing in the road when I arrived to where he had stopped them to check my rear lights. Once he saw that they were operating properly, he let me pass. I told him that I was doing the speed limit and he just said, "I know. I saw what happened," and that was it.

Further south, in Tennessee, I was driving down the Interstate, listening to a radio station somewhere outside of Knoxville, going as fast as I could. Cars were slowing down to pass me, as usual. However, I listened with interest when the disc jockey on the radio told drivers to "be careful on I-75 because there's a slow moving vehicle in the south-bound lane of traffic and cars in both directions are slowing down to take a look at it!" That was me.

The menagerie arrived in Macon, Georgia, where my brother, Christopher was living, without further incident – the operative word there is that we "arrived." My plan was to leave my truck and my horse with him and then hitch-hike to Miami with the two dogs, which I was, somehow, able to do. Back then, people were much more trusting than they are now. That could never happen now. I wouldn't even think of it. Not many people hitch-hike anymore.

My parents weren't all that happy about having the two dogs in the house and, in fact, forbade it, so I kept them tied up outside in the yard. They were happy that I was going to actually study for the exam. I took a month-long course, in fact, which involved daily activity, including some class work with others taking the test.

I would get up every morning and go to a library for several hours, then take a break and play tennis for a couple of hours, and then back to the library for more hours of study. I would then play tennis, again, and then study more at night. I was determined to pass the test. Surprisingly, I was still able to play pretty well, even though I hadn't been playing very much at all in the past couple of years, as you know.

A couple of weeks after arriving back in Miami, I called my brother to see how things were going, with my father listening in on the conversation on the other line. When I asked about my truck, my brother responded by telling me that it had been towed away and he didn't know where it was. When I asked about my horse, he said that he went out to check on him, but he wasn't where he was supposed to be and couldn't find him.

My father thought that was hilarious. I didn't share his enthusiasm. He said it was like Mrs. Murphy's cow, or something like that. I wasn't happy and told Christopher so. He called back the next day to say that Torque was fine but the truck was a goner. I never did see that truck again and I never received much of an explanation as to what happened to it.

Christie had followed me to Miami, and she had rented an apartment on the beach, but there wasn't much time for her during that period of time, because I was really busy, and she went back home after a couple of weeks. I felt badly about that, and though it didn't end well, we still loved each other, but that was never going to work. I knew it, but she didn't want to accept it. That was on me. That was my decision.

However, some time after I took the exam, while still in Miami, I reconnected to my old high-school girl friend. She had returned to Miami for a visit to see her parents and we got together while she was there. She had divorced her first husband and was now living in Denton, Texas, which was located about half-way between Dallas and Fort Worth. She was a stunningly attractive blue-eyed blonde and, as the song goes, "the first cut is the deepest." I decided to chase after her.

After taking the bar, I began working for her sister's husband's construction company and I had made some money, not much. With a verifiable income, I was able to buy a new Dodge pick-up truck. I put some stanchions on the new truck and headed up to Macon to get Torque and go to Denton, Texas.

My parents weren't too keen on that move, but I think that they were glad to see me get out of their house. I am absolutely certain that they thought that I was either completely out of my mind or very close to it. Looking back, I must say that they were probably right.

So on my way out to Texas, I stopped by New Orleans to spend a night with my friends, Donnie Simpson and Johnny Arthurs, after stopping in Gainesville, Florida, to hit some tennis balls with Juan Diaz at the University of Florida. I spent the night with my friend, Steve Beeland. His wife was delighted to see me and my menagerie and still bristles when the topic comes up.

Both Donnie and Johnny remember the visit quite well, too, and their wives were delighted to see me leave. Torque left them all some gifts that kept on giving. That's what horses do. I don't think I've been forgiven yet by the wives. They still mention it every so often.

Somehow, and I have no recollection as to how I did it, but I found a trailer in Argyle, Texas, with a fenced yard for Torque and the dogs. I also found a job with Fox and Jacobs, one of the biggest home builders in the country, with no trouble at all. I was to be paid $7.50 an hour, which was a huge pay raise for me.

Unfortunately, I didn't do nearly as well with the girl friend as I had hoped. Some very wealthy Texan had swooped in. Imagine that.

We got together a few times but, as Jackson Browne sang, "She must be somebody's baby, because she's so fine," and she was. We're still in touch, but she's been married for decades and still is.

Fox and Jacobs was building a huge complex in the area and I was hired as a "carpenter's assistant." I was to work with a guy who was the carpenter, and our job was to put roofs on houses. He'd do the skill stuff and I would do the manual labor, basically, but I was learning things and working on roofs, which was a whole lot different from being in a classroom or on a tennis court, and I was still enjoying the experience.

At this point, some readers may be questioning my sanity, just as my parents and most of my friends were back then, but to me it made sense. I was just trying to become a better person. I really didn't have much knowledge or experience out of school or off of a tennis court and I knew that once I started practicing law, I would never have the time to gain any of that experience.

To me, I was growing horizontally, whereas I'd been growing vertically my whole life. I had graduated from one of the best universities in the country, as well as one of the best law schools in the country, plus I'd been one of the best tennis players in the world, so I wasn't doing too badly, but I recognized my limitations. One of my limitations was and continues to be that I will never be a carpenter if I live to be a hundred years old. It took me a while to realize that.

My partner, an African-American man about my age, whose name I can't remember, and I were tasked to do FOUR roofs in a day – that's right, FOUR! Now, there was a decking crew, that had already laid the plywood over the rafters, so we were doing the trim work and whatever else needed to be done before the "tile" crew went to work.

Still, doing four houses per day was a lot of houses. We went up one street and down the other for days and days. There was a crew for just about every aspect of the job. I worked on the decking crew for a while, too, at one point, and the framing crew, too, learning more and more things along the way.

However, when I decided that it was never going to work out for me with my old girl friend and it was time to go, I gave the boss a week's notice that I'd be leaving. He was surprised when I did, because most construction workers don't do that. They just don't show up the next day, after getting paid.

When I did, I was assigned to the clean-up crew, and that was the worst job I ever had in my life. I operated a broom, basically, sweeping up the carports, the driveways, the walkways and back decks -whatever could be swept up. It was the most boring job I ever had or ever hope to have.

We started at 7:30 every morning and took a half hour lunch break at 12:30, and we'd quit, or "roll them up" at 3:30. By 9:00 I'd be asking, "Is it lunch time yet? By 3:00 I'd be ready to shoot myself. I was so glad to leave that job.

Plus, we worked seven days a week. There was no weekend for me. I don't have too many good memories from my days in Texas, other than work, work and work some more, but I don't regret those days. I learned a lot and it was another life experience, and I would chase after that girl again, if the opportunity presented itself to me.

However, on December 31, 1974, while still there in Argyle, Texas, I received a phone call from my father telling me that my mother had died from complications relating to her breast surgery ten years earlier. Apparently, her spleen was severely compromised from the ordeal, but I never did fully understand why she died. I don't think that her doctors handled the situation very well.

I'd spoken to her a day or two earlier, while she was in the hospital, undergoing tests. We'd talked for a little while and then her lunch meal was delivered. She said, "I have to go now. You want me to get all better don't you? I have to eat." I said good-bye, told her that I loved her, and that was last time we spoke. The news came as a shock to everyone, even her. I am as sure as I can be that she had no idea that her days were numbered. I would have gone back immediately if I had any idea that might happen.

I went back for the funeral, and it was good to see the whole family, but it was really tough on my father, but probably just as tough on my youngest brother, Bruce, who was thirteen years old at the time. He really didn't fully understand all that he had lost. The rest of us did, and we all knew the significance of losing her.

She was a beautiful, loving, intelligent woman and the family was devastated by what happened. She was the heart and soul of the family. If she had lived longer, Bruce would have been a different person. She had a way of making you do what she wanted you to do, but making you think that it was your idea. He probably would have ended up being a lawyer, like the other four of us were.

By that time, our sister, Carol, had become extremely successful in her practice as a tax lawyer. She had clients ranging from the DuPonts of Delaware, to the Vice-President of the United States, as well as many leaders in the business world, and presidents of Universities, such as Duke. Her office overlooked the White House.

Our father needed her, as did our entire family, and she instantly became our matriarch. She handled all of the expenses and affairs regarding the funeral and burial. Our father wasn't really able to do any of that at that time, although he was only fifty-seven years old. His wife, my mother, was only fifty-three. She died one day shy of her fifty-fourth birthday.

Shortly after I returned to Texas, I left Texas with Torque still in the back of a pick-up truck and the two Irish setters in the front seat with me. I now had a back seat, but the dogs didn't like it back there. I didn't have a whole lot of money, though, and I was headed north to Aspen, Colorado, where my good friend, Gregg Golding, was living. We had been the best of friends since our high school days.

I had no job prospects, but Gregg was pretty sure that he could get me a job washing dishes at the Aspen Steak House, where he worked as a waiter. He was living with a girl at the time and he assured me that my arrival wouldn't be a problem. I told him to be sure to find housing for Torque.

I arrived late at night in the middle of a cold and dreary February night and unloaded Torque at a local stable, owned by a very nice couple, Frank and Carol. They operated a business of taking people on sleigh rides or rides in wagons through the streets of Aspen or up the mountain into Maroon Bells, a particularly beautiful part of a spectacularly beautiful area. Neither Frank nor Carol were there at that time of night, but Gregg assured me that it wouldn't be a problem.

However, a problem immediately arose the next morning, when Gregg's girl friend announced that my two dogs and I were going to have to leave. Gregg could stay if he wanted, but he decided to get out of Dodge with me. I apologized profusely, but he told me that it was no big deal. He'd been trying to find a way to easily and gracefully get out of that relationship and he wasn't the least bit upset. He'd already found us another place to live, unbeknownst to her. Still, I felt badly about that. He didn't. To this very day, we still laugh about that turn of events.

True to his word, I had a job waiting for me at the Aspen Steak House the next night. It was only open in the evenings and it only served steak. Before beginning work, every employee was fed a meal of steak, potatoes and a fresh vegetable. I hadn't eaten steak, potatoes and fresh vegetables in months. I hadn't ever washed dishes before, either, except at our house as a child, but I eagerly embraced the opportunity and I thoroughly enjoyed the steak dinners.

Gregg was and still is a skiing aficionado and he had an extra pair of skis for me. However, there is a rather steep fee to ski at any of the three big ski areas in and around Aspen, those being Aspen Mountain, Buttermilk and Aspen Highlands, but there are ways to get on the slopes for free, which Gregg knew well. We gate-kept, which means that, when there was a race, we would stand off to the side of one of the "gates" skiers had to successfully negotiate and make sure that they did so.

Also, we could shovel snow and get free ski passes. We would show up about an hour before the lifts began operating and clear off the pathways for the lift lines. Others, including Gregg, could also ski down runs to clear any obstructions and to make sure that the runs were safe and free of debris. I wasn't a good enough skier to be able to do that.

Regardless, we were always able to ski whenever we wanted to, which was usually on weekdays, before the crowds descended upon the community, as they always did. Oftentimes, we would just get the pass and use it during the week, rather than fight the crowds on weekends. I had skied a few times with my father and his brother, Fred, in Vermont, so I knew how to ski, but I wasn't too good at first. It was fun, though.

Since work at the Steak House didn't begin until after 5:00, I decided to find another job, because the pay wasn't all that good and Aspen is an expensive place to live. Gregg helped me get a job at the Holiday Inn just outside of town on Highway 82. He worked there during the day, sometimes, as a waiter. I was hired on as a busboy.

One advantage of working at the Holiday Inn was that there was an employee area where employees could change, use restrooms and shower. Also, I got to meet more people, including the female staff members and the bartenders. The shower area would prove to be of enormous benefit to me in the days which followed.

As fate would have it, directly across Highway 82 from the Holiday Inn was the Aspen Tennis Club. I walked into the pro shop one afternoon and introduced myself to the pro, Tom Peck, who would become a great friend. I was dressed in a flannel shirt and blue jeans which had patches on them to cover holes. I certainly didn't look like a tennis player, but Tom needed a 4th for doubles that day and he invited me to play. I had my racket in the truck and gladly accepted the invitation.

Tom and his partner won the match that day, but Tom saw enough to see that I was a player and told me to come back anytime I wanted. I became a regular. He never beat me again, but he was a great guy and a whole lot of fun to play with. He even let me give some lessons there. I made a lot of friends through Tom and his club.

Also, Tom needed some help in the pro shop and I was able to get Gregg a job. His responsibilities were to answer the phone and make reservations. When people came in to play, usually every hour, he would check them in and take their money, if they weren't members. He was able to lie down on a couch most of the time. Also, he was able to play whenever he wanted if there was a court available. He liked that job. It was the best one he ever had, I believe, until he became a salesman for World Book encyclopedias many years later, where he has been very successful.

I was able to adequately perform my duties as a dishwasher, and I really enjoyed the steak dinners employees were given – for a while. It was funny, and I still tell this story every so often, but after a couple of weeks, I was like "Can I have a hamburger? Or chicken? Or anything else besides steak?" The answer was no and I soon tired of steak! I hear that people who work at fast-food places can't eat the food they serve and sell. I understood why. However, I really didn't like that job too much and, after a few weeks, I found another one.

A high school was being built in Carbondale, a small town about thirty miles away, "down valley." I was hired on as a laborer. My pay was around $5.00 an hour, as I recall.

Work started at 7:30 in the morning, weather permitting. The rule was that if the temperature was above zero, we were going to work. One thing about construction workers is that they are never late for work - never.

It was really hard for me to get up in the dark and the drive down was, at times, dangerous. I wasn't used to driving on a road with snow and ice on it. At that time of the morning, and at that time of year, the roads were always icy. I couldn't be late, so I had to drive faster than I wanted to, most of the time, but I never had an accident, fortunately, and I was always on time.

Gregg had found himself another girl friend by that time and I found myself a trailer that had nothing but a bed in it. There was a communal toilet and shower, but it was a nasty place and I never showered or used the facilities there. I had the Holiday Inn, and that's where I began to take my showers.

It stays extremely cold in the mountains of Colorado until about the end of May, usually. In fact, it snowed June 1 that year. Everyone has heard of the band "Three Dog Night," but I didn't know what the expression meant. I found out very quickly, except I was having "two" dog nights. It meant having the dogs sleep on top of you to keep you warm. There was no heat in that thing, or if there was, it didn't work too well.

When the weather warmed up enough, I put up a tent right next to the job site, which would become the parking lot for the school, probably. I tied Torque to a stake in the ground and he roamed around as far as the line would allow him to. The two dogs slept outside of my tent, on either side. I would wake up, throw some water on my face, brush my teeth and walk a hundred yards to work.

That may have been a low point in my life, but I didn't feel that way about it. As hard as it might be to believe, I was enjoying it. I enjoyed the hard work and I enjoyed the variety of life I was experiencing. I was a good worker and I got along well with everyone I was working with out there.

Construction workers are a tough group of men. Building a high school is a large project, especially the gym, which had an extremely high ceiling. It was not an easy job, but I was good at what I was required to do, which was mostly physical labor kind of things.

Getting joists and rafters up on the roof of those buildings was not like building the sky-scrapers in Manhattan, but it was hard work, and I was part of the crew doing the hardest parts of the job, as far as physical strength is concerned. As the carpenters used to say, we were doing "man's work." Still, it required some knowledge of the carpentry trade and you had to know your way around the job site so as not to be dangerous to yourself or the others you were working with.

We worked from 7:30 in the morning, when we "rolled out" the electrical cords, until 3:30 in the afternoon, when we "rolled them up." When the work day was over, the men, and all of them, went to a bar in Carbondale and proceeded to get drunk, or close to it, every day. Next morning, they would all show up, each and every one of them, and go to work, without fail. It was something to behold.

I don't think any of them could say a simple sentence without having at least two curse words in it, or if they could, I don't believe that I ever heard them do it. They were a hardened group but, for the most part, a pretty happy group of guys. They loved what they did and they loved their beer. I can't say that there was a single man that I didn't enjoy meeting on that job.

One guy, whose name I can't recall, was a real cowboy, and I mean a really good cowboy. He worked alongside of me and we became friends. He was, apparently, a championship caliber rider and roper and when the school project was near completion, months later, he wanted me to go out to California with him to work at the ranch owned by the Hearst family. He had a standing job offer there.

The owner of the company was a man named Red, and he usually went to the bar with us, or he'd go to some other bar where none of the workers were. He had been a football player at the University of Southern California and was, I was told, a first-class opera singer, which was hard to believe. He had red hair and was a jovial guy.

However, he had a bad habit of having too much to drink, at times, and would offer women he had met at a bar the night before a job. That happened on more than a few occasions. On each such occasion, he was heard to say, "I did it again?" And indeed he had.

Most of the women didn't last too long, because they just couldn't do the work, but there were a couple who tried really hard to fit in. It just wasn't possible. The work wasn't always the problem, though it was difficult, but the language of the men drove them off after a while. The men weren't going to change. The laws regarding a "hostile work environment" hadn't come into existence yet.

Most afternoons, however, I would drive "up valley" to the Aspen Tennis Club and play tennis, after showering up at the Holiday Inn. There was a guy there named Jimmy Garcia, who owned and operated a Chinese restaurant, and we'd play for dinner. I never lost, but he was always glad to play. He was a pretty good player, and a chinese dinner, consisting of mostly rice, wasn't too costly for him. I enjoyed those days.

I also remember taking Torque, in a one-horse trailer that I had purchased, which was a major achievement, so he no longer had to ride in the back of my pick-up truck, out to Maroon Bells, jumping on his back and riding up the mountainside. That was pretty special. It's an absolutely gorgeous place. Colorado has 58 mountain peaks over 14,000 feet high. We were up in the clouds.

I also enjoyed going to the Hotel Jerome, located right in the middle of Aspen, which is on the National Register of Historic Places. It was built in the late 1800's by one of the co-founders of Macy's Department Stores, and it was said to be as fine a hotel as could be found anywhere in the world back in the day, and one of the first to have electricity throughout the building.

On the second floor, was a magnificent ballroom, and the Jerome was a place for "high society" to gather back in its prime. Rooms rented for $4.00 per night, said to be the equivalent of $1,000.00 per night nowadays. On the first floor was a spectacular bar, called the "J Bar," after it's owner, which is still in pristine condition.

Hunter Thompson, of Rolling Stone fame, and author of Fear and Loathing in Las Vegas, was a regular there. He ran for sheriff at one time on a platform of making marijuana legal, and almost won. I never met the man, but Gregg's younger sister, Gayle, worked with him for years until his death in 2005.

So that was my life for the next several months – working construction in Carbondale, building the new high school; living in a tent beside the job site with my horse tethered fifty yards away and my two dogs sleeping alongside the tent; playing tennis at the Aspen Tennis Club; and working at the Holiday Inn every now and then to keep my "guest" privileges alive and well, and I enjoyed every minute.

Aspen is known for being a "party" town and I found that it was a well-deserved reputation. There was no college or university nearby but there were hundreds of young people, most of whom were just out of college, all looking to have a good time. I met many such people and enjoyed that aspect of my days there, as well.

However, all good things must pass, and so it was to be for me and Aspen. My brother, Christopher, was getting married in Macon, Georgia in early September, and I had to be there. I remember the day and exactly where I was and what I was doing when I decided that I'd had enough.

We were almost finished with the school, and I was operating a rake, manually, with no motor on it, as all rakes that I've ever seen are, and smoothing out some rocks, preparing to pour concrete over a large area in the back of the school. It was a gorgeous day, with bright sunshine and warm temperature, and I stopped, put my hands on top of the rake, looked around at the mountains that circled around me, and said, "I've had enough! I'm ready to leave Disneyland," and I was, but not before more excitement, a bow, if you will, on what had been a wonderful experience.

Aspen was having a tennis tournament, as it did every year, and people from all over Colorado, Texas and parts unknown always came to play. It doesn't take much to lure people to Aspen and the surrounding area, and there was prize money to be awarded the winner of the tournament.

I hadn't saved a dime from working at any and all of the jobs I'd had while there, and my parents hadn't, and weren't about to, give me a dime to support my habits. I was going to have to play in the tournament and win some money.

The man who won the tournament the year before was returning and he was expected to win it, again. He was a big, tall guy from Texas who had been a basketball player in college and was now a tournament player. I'd never heard of him, and he'd never heard of me. Back then, I always said that if I hadn't heard of a guy, he wasn't going to beat me, so I was confident that I was going to win. So was he.

Worse yet, he had arrived the year before driving a bright red Cadillac with horns across the front, like a Texas Long Horn steer. He had another man with him who made all the bets. They had taken everyone's money the year before and they had plans to do the same thing this year. He was a jerk then; he's a jerk now; and he'll always be a jerk. I really wanted to beat him.

So we were put on opposite sides of the draw, made by my buddy, Tom Peck, and it was a full 64 player draw. We both advanced to the finals, which were played on a magnificent Sunday afternoon, with the whole town out to watch.

I had packed up everything I owned and was ready to leave town once the match was over. Torque was standing, quite happily, in his nice, one horse trailer, and the two dogs were, as always, wagging their tails and happy to greet anyone and everyone.

That morning, I warmed up for an hour with my friend, Jim Wilson, who I'd met in Canada six years earlier, who came out to Colorado to see me and for us to play doubles together. We won the event the day before. This time, we didn't go out for coffee and I went back to the Holiday Inn to shower up, rest, and get ready for the match.

One memorable thing occurred just before it was time for me to walk across the highway to play the match, and that was when these two cowboys wandered in. They didn't belong there, but I didn't say anything. I didn't belong there, either, really. I was no longer an employee, but nobody minded. Everyone knew me.

They were competing in a rodeo somewhere nearby, but one of them was bleeding profusely from his hand. He washed the wound in the sink and then sat down while the other man took a needle and some thread and started to sew him up. I was lying down on one of the benches, resting, just watching what was going on.

When I asked, they acted like it was nothing special. "This kind of thing happens all the time," they told me. "No big deal."

The injured man didn't make a sound while the other man stitched him up. We got to talking and they told me all about the rodeo scene in Colorado, Wyoming, Nevada and the west, in general. They hoped to win a little money later in the day, but that was their life. He rode the bucking broncos. It was a somewhat sobering thought to think about what he was going to be doing that afternoon in comparison to what I was about to do.

So when the designated time arrived, I left the two of them, wishing them well, and headed out the door. When I got over to my truck, I got to thinking that Torque was going to be standing in that trailer for hours and hours and there was no sense in making him stand in that trailer for the next couple of hours while I played the match. I decided to let him out of the trailer and let him stretch his legs a bit.

Then, for who knows what reason, I decided to ride him over to the court, and let someone lead him around for a bit, and I did. I jumped on his back and we walked over to the court, in front of all the spectators, and my opponent, who was on the court, waiting for me. I handed the reins to Tom, and helped him up onto Torque's back. I then walked onto the court.

Unfortunately, Tom decided to waive his racket over his head and let out a whoop, like the Indian that he was – he was part Indian, but I don't know what tribe - which spooked Torque a little, or so I was told. I didn't see any of that. Torque took a step or two to his left and looked around to see what that was all about. Tom fell off, putting his right arm down to soften the fall. In doing so, he injured his shoulder and had to go to the hospital. He had bet heavily on me and did not want to miss the match, but he did.

So there was a man in the chair, calling out the score, and linesmen on every line, just like it's supposed to be, and we were ready to play. He was a good player, and he won the first set 6-3. I played one bad service game. However, I came back and won the next two sets 6-3 and 6-4.

All my friends were jubilant and wanted me to join them at the Holiday Inn bar to celebrate, and there was a beautiful woman in a white dress who wanted me to stay a while longer, too, but I couldn't. I had to be in Pennsylvania in two days for another prize money tennis tournament, and I'd be driving straight through to get there in time.

As the Garth Brooks song goes, "...to sleep would be best, but I just can't afford to rest...I gotta ride in Denver tomorrow night..."

I rode off into the sunset, with people waving me good-bye. Law firms there offered me jobs, wanting me to stay, but I was headed in another direction. I was ready to become a lawyer, but not in Aspen. I really didn't like the cold weather all that much, and I wasn't licensed to practice in Colorado.

As an aside, I met up with the jerk thirty-five years later at the Germantown Cricket Club for the National 55's Grass Court Championships and I asked him if he remember me, which he didn't. Then I reminded him of some details, including Torque. He said, "I remember the horse." He's still a jerk.

In fact, I played him in doubles, and my partner, who was from Oklahoma, also, and knew him well, told me that if he had a chance, the guy would purposefully hit me if it would help him win the match, and to intimidate me. He had a habit of doing that to any and all of his opponents. Unfortunately, he and his partner won that match, but he didn't hit me.

Aspen had been another very enjoyable chapter in my life, but I was ready to move on. As I said before, if I lived to be a hundred, I'd never be a carpenter. I was a good laborer, and a good carpenter's assistant, but I was no carpenter and never would be. It was time to move on. I was, after all, a lawyer, licensed to practice in Florida. I was headed home, but I would do so in a circuitous path.

Chapter Ten

An Assistant Public Defender

I was going to Wilkes Barre, Pennsylvania, where I'd played before and the tournament director knew me. Once I made my decision to head east, I called him and he put me in the draw. I'd won the tournament at least once before, maybe twice, but he told me that he had the best field of players he'd ever had, so I'd better be ready to play.

He asked if I needed housing, and I told him that I'd be fine, but I asked if he could find a place for my horse. Since he knew me, he said, rather non-plussed, "You want housing for your horse … I'll see what I can do," and that was it.

I really needed to win money, because I think I got $250.00 for winning the Aspen tournament, not the $500 I was expecting, and that would barely pay my gas to Pennsylvania, but it did, and I arrived in time for the start of the tournament. When I saw the draw, I was impressed. There were a whole lot of players in there who were really good players, like Peter Fishback from New York; Graham Snook from New Zealand; Terry Moore from California; my friend, Rick Fagel from Miami Shores; Terry Hassell from Pennsylvania; Ben Bishop from New England; Joe Bouquin from New York; and many more.

I'd been playing all summer long in the high altitude of Colorado, on hard courts, where the ball flies. This tournament was on clay, with high humidity, where the balls become heavy and wet from sweat, and don't fly. It was going to take a huge adjustment for me to do well.

The reasons why I was a good player were basically this: I was a tall, lanky lefty with a huge serve; ninety percent of players were righties, and they saw a lefty about 10 percent of the time, but I had a great lanky lefty serve and there weren't many lefties with serves anywhere near as good as mine; I rushed the net at every opportunity, behind both serves, even on clay, which few people did; and I had a great volley and overhead. My serve kept me in matches against better players. Everyone had trouble with my serve and volley game, because few players played the way I did, and not many played it as well as I did. Actually, my game was much like John McEnroe's and we held the racket with the same grip, continental.

My friend had found a nice farm where Torque could stay while I played the tournament. I put down a tent on the outskirts of the club where the tournament was being played and used the facilities to shower and swim in the pool. I ate well, too, and drank as much as they would allow me to. The two dogs were tied to a tree not far from wherever I was. I couldn't let them run free.

I won my first couple of matches, but the slow, clay courts were not my best surface to play on, and it was too much of a disadvantage for me, especially coming from the high altitude and hard courts of Aspen. I played Graham Snook, a Davis Cupper from New Zealand, in the third round and lost, 6-4; 6-4. He was a good, international player who was on his way to the U.S. Open a few weeks later. He had played at Wimbledon and all the big events, so he was a really good player, and he was a nice guy, too.

In fact, after the match, he asked if I wanted to play doubles with him and I readily agreed. We were a good team and we got to the finals, beating a couple of teams with guys who were on their way to New York to play the U.S. Open, also. When we did, my friend, the tournament director, came up to me, singing, "we're in the money! we're in the money!"

I hadn't been able to pay the entry fee, so he was happy and I was ecstatic. I had enough money, barely, to get me to the next prize money tournament, in Macon, Georgia, where the wedding was to be. We played the last match of the tournament and I headed south soon thereafter, "To sleep would be best, but I just can't afford to rest, I got to ride in Macon (sic-Denver), tomorrow night."

My 1974 Dodge truck really was a good vehicle and, unlike my F-150, I didn't have to worry about it not getting me there. It was extremely reliable, and powerful. Torque, who was now a three-year old, weighed well over a thousand pounds, plus the weight of the horse trailer, which was another few hundred pounds, but the Dodge had no trouble pulling it. I could go on the Interstates and drive the speed limit, and not bring attention to myself, for a change, although a horse is always an eye-catcher.

In Macon, I could stay with my brother. Torque could stay at the same place he'd stayed before I headed out to Texas the year before, and I would be there to keep an eye on my vehicle this time. I really wasn't too concerned over losing the F-150. I'd paid a few hundred dollars for it and I'd enjoyed it for a year or two. I wasn't the least bit upset about that, but I didn't tell Chris that. I gave him a bunch of grief over it – still do.

The draw in the Macon tournament was another big one, with a whole different cast of characters. These were all men from the Southern section of the United States Tennis Association, and I knew many of them and they knew me. I think I was ranked in the top five in the South previously, when I won the Georgia State Open, which I won twice, actually. So I was given a seed and had a decent draw.

This tournament was on hard courts, and I got to the finals, beating some good players in the process, like Pem Guerry from Chattanooga, Tennessee, among others. In the finals I played a guy from California, who was leaving to play the U.S. Open the next day. I don't know what he was doing there, but there he was, and he was good, but so was I. I was playing well by that time.

I have met many former players over the years and many, if not most, say that they can't remember matches, let alone points. I remember matches and points, and I remember that particular match well. It's silly, really, but I still remember many of the matches that I've won or lost, but the ones I've lost bother me, still.

Anyone who has ever played sports knows the expression of "choking," which means that you get nervous and you miss a shot, or a putt, or whatever, because of nerves. Just because you miss a shot doesn't mean that you "choked," though. I don't remember ever "choking," but I remember plenty of matches where I didn't play too well.

I remember missing a shot that lost me the match that day and I still can't believe that I missed. I didn't choke, but I missed the damn shot!

It was match point for me on my opponent's serve and I charged the net, after hitting a forehand deep down the line. My opponent hit the ball back down the line and I was right there, ready to put the ball away. My opponent ran to the opposite side of the court, expecting me to go cross-court, and I hit the ball down the line, behind him. He wouldn't have been within thirty feet of the ball, but it hit the top of the tape and bounced back at me.

I stood there in disbelief. I couldn't believe I missed the shot. I hit it perfectly, but it caught the top of the tape and bounced back, not over. He won the point. We went back to deuce, he won his serve and I lost 5-4 in a tie-breaker. Unbelievable! I won some money, but I should have won some more.

That match didn't end my career, but my career as a really serious tennis player was coming to an end. I was ready to become a lawyer, but tennis would be a part of my life for the rest of my life, although I didn't know that at the time, of course. I was still a tennis player, that was my identity – that was who I was, and I had a "name," and I was known all over the country and parts of the world.

The wedding was wonderful, although the marriage would be short-lived. Christopher and Ami would divorce a couple of years later, without any children coming from the marriage. Weddings and funerals are the most frequent times families get together and that was a great family get together.

I have a wonderful family, but my father still wasn't too happy with me and my wanderings, and he wasn't going to help support me financially, so my earnings from the prize-money tournament were going to have to be enough to get me home, and it almost was.

I made it as far as Belle Glade, which is a small city near Lake Okeechobee. I took State Road 441 south from Macon, because I really didn't like driving on the Interstate highways, and neither did Torque. There were just too many tractor-trailers passing us at high speeds, making his trailer shake, rattle and roll.

Also, I knew I might not have enough gas to get all the way back to Miami, so I purposefully went to Belle Glade, because I had my friend, Bill Botts, from the Neighborhood Legal Services office in Washington, D.C. lived there. I knew I could make it that far and I knew that he would loan me some money. I made it to Okeechobee with a few miles to spare.

Bill and I graduated from law school at the same time and he was now working at the Florida Rural Legal Services in Belle Glade. Also, I had worked with him for his father, who was a building contractor in Manassas, Virginia for a few weeks somewhere along the line. He and his wife, Sue, and their daughter, Rita, are good friends of mine to this day. He gladly gave me some money to get me home. I don't think he wanted to let Torque fertilize his front lawn and that might have had something to do with it.

Once home, I found a place to put Torque out to pasture in Davie, Florida, a small community northwest of Miami, but that took a few days to accomplish. Torque was tied to a tree in the side yard. Unfortunately, that tree had my brother's basketball hoop on it.

Torque did what horses do and Bruce hasn't forgiven me yet. "I couldn't shoot for a month!" he told me. Also, Torque got loose one night and was brought home by the North Bay Village police. My father answered the door and assured the officers that the horse would be leaving that very day.

I immediately started to look for a job as a lawyer. Not surprisingly, it wasn't an easy thing to do. I wasn't exactly the ideal candidate. Besides, I still wanted to be a social crusader and I was looking for jobs with a legal services or public defender's office, which didn't pay that well, at all, but that's what I wanted to do.

It takes time to find lawyer jobs. It's a process which usually involves submitting resume's, transcripts from college and law school, letters of reference and writing samples. While I was busily sending out applications for employment all over the state of Florida, I had to find a job. So what did I do? I found a job working at a Shell gas station on Treasure Island, where I could easily walk to and from work. I think my pay was about $5.00 an hour. My father was so proud.

Also, I continued playing tennis when I wasn't pumping gas and learning some things about mechanics. I learned that I had ten thumbs and little aptitude. If I live to be a thousand years old, I will never be a mechanic – or a carpenter.

That Fall, my good friend, Greg Hilley, and I won the Florida State Doubles Championships. He had played at the University of Florida team which won the SEC twice while he was there. I lost to a guy named Van

Winitsky, a very good left-handed player several years younger than me who went on to a long and successful pro career, in a hotly-contested close match that I should have won. I remember the one point that made the difference, but I'll spare you the details.

I had many interviews and several near misses, but no success at finding a job for about four months. Finally, in February of 1976, I received a call from the Public Defender's Office in Clearwater, Florida, and I drove over there to interview. From there, I was going to drive north for two other interviews in Gainesville and Live Oak. I was to meet a man named Robert Edwin Jagger in his St. Petersburg office.

I remember the interview like it was yesterday. I was a bit defensive about where I'd been for the last few years and how I would answer the inevitable question of what in God's name had I been doing for the last several years since graduation. However, Mr. Jagger wasn't all that concerned about it. He told me that I should present myself as authentically as possible and that if prospective employers didn't like me, it was more important that I be who and what I was.

We had a nice, long chat and I felt good about the interview, although he didn't give me any indication of whether or not I'd be getting an offer. He said that he had others to interview and would get back in touch with me. We shook hands and I left Clearwater, heading north.

A few days later, Mr. Jagger called my house, intending to offer me a job, and spoke with my father, as I was not home. According to Mr. Jagger, the conversation went something like this:

"Hello, is Pierce at home?"

"No. He's not here right now."

"This is Bob Jagger calling, from the Pinellas County Public Defender's Office, please have him call me when he gets home."

"This is his father, can I give him a message?"

"No, I need to speak to Pierce. Please have him call me about the job he has applied for."

"If you are offering him a job, he'll take it. Just let me know when you want him to report." (my father was a Navy man and stayed in the Navy Reserve until 1972, when he turned 65 and was formally retired at a ceremony in Guantanamo, Cuba).

"No, just have him call me when he gets home or when you hear from him."

"I know that he's anxious to begin work and I'm sure he wants that job. I'll tell him to be there whenever you say."

"Thank you, but that won't be necessary. Just have him call me."

Reluctantly, my father ended the conversation. He was most anxious to get me out of the house.

Back then, there were no cell phones and there was no way my father could get in touch with me. He had no idea where I was or who I was with. I don't remember where I was or who I was with, but I know I applied to be the managing attorney for the Three Rivers Legal Services Office in the Gainesville area, which serviced a nine county area in North Florida. I interviewed for the job and was told that it was down to me and one other man for the job. I found out the next day that the other guy was offered the job, not me.

When I called home, I heard about the call from Mr. Jagger and called him back. He officially offered me a job and, on February 26, 1976, I officially began my legal career as an Assistant Public Defender. I would be working out of the Clearwater office in the misdemeanor division. My pay would be $12,000 per year and I was delighted.

Mr. Jagger was a great man and he, along with Jack Blair, would become the two most influential men in my life, other than my father and my grandfather Sullivan. He had been among the very first Public Defenders in the state of Florida, as well as the country, as a result of the 1963 decision of the U. S. Supreme Court in the case of Gideon vs. Wainright, which required that all criminal defendants faced with incarceration be provided with legal counsel.

He later became the head of the national Public Defender's Association and remained the Public Defender for the Sixth Judicial Circuit in and for Pinellas and Pasco counties for thirty-five years. He was the longest to serve as such in the country.

He was wonderful mentor and he became one of my best friends. He and his wife, JoAnn, took a liking to me and they welcomed me into their home. Their two sons, Bob and Ed, are two of my best friends to this day.

In fact, not long after arriving in Clearwater, I was out on a tennis court with Mr. Jagger, who was known as "The Boss" by all who worked for him, and his two sons. I introduced them to the sport and began teaching them how to play. Before long, they became tennis players. Years later, the three of us were ranked near the top of our respective age divisions in Florida.

He said to me early on, "Right now you're a tennis player who is becoming a lawyer. Soon you'll be a lawyer who plays tennis on the side. I'm going to do all that I can to make you the best lawyer you can be," and that's what he tried to do with me and everyone else who ever worked for him. He was a great man, a great lawyer and a great employer. He died a year or so ago.

And he was right. I was still a tennis player who was becoming a lawyer. In fact, a month after arriving in Clearwater, I began a program at the McMullen Tennis Center which I called Youth Team Tennis. I had re-associated with Jack Blair and I was, once again, back on the Board of Directors of the Youth Tennis Foundation. With help from Steve Beeland, who knew the Parks and Recreation Director, we were given free use of the courts to create the league. We advertized the program and had nearly fifty kids come to the try-out.

The basic idea, which was mine, was to just let the kids play the game. It wasn't required that they take a whole bunch of lessons, which usually cost a lot of money, to learn how to play. Tennis was regarded as a "rich man's game," or a "country-club sport," and I never liked that. I wanted tennis to be like every other sport I'd ever played – kids went to a park to play a sport, just as I did, no matter what sport it was, and he gets put on a team, and he plays. That's the way it was in every sport – football, baseball, basketball, soccer … everything, except tennis and, of course, golf.

Steve and I gave the kids some instruction, divided them up onto teams, gave them shirts, had an adult "coach" for each team and let them play. We adjusted the rules so that they could get the serves in the court, like allowing them to serve underhand, or to bounce and hit the serve, which was fine. As anyone who ever watched a little league baseball game knows, there were a whole lot of errors - double-faults and missed shots. Just like kids do in any sport, they made lots of mistakes, but they learned how to play and, most importantly, they had fun doing so.

After in ended, two months later, I suggested to Jack that we have a state-wide event for beginning youngsters in the 12 and under category that summer and he agreed. The very first state-wide Youth Team Tennis program was held in August of that year in Clearwater, at the McMullen courts, and we had seven cities participating from all across the state. It was a huge success.

The format was one boys singles, one girls singles, a boys doubles, a girls doubles and a mixed doubles match of one set each. The team with the most number of games won was the winner. It was so successful that Jack agreed to build on it.

We hired a coordinator to go across the state and help develop programs like the one I started in Clearwater and the next year we added a 14 and under event. The state tournament for it was held in Miami at Moore Park, where Bobby Curtis was the park manager. That, too, was a success, as was the 2nd year 12 and under event.

Although we didn't expect it, there was an "unanticipated" consequence of what we were doing. Every kid who signed up to play in any of our leagues across the state was given a free membership to the United States Tennis Association. With that membership came a monthly magazine, some goodies, like a hat and a t-shirt, and some other things.

The unanticipated consequence was that the ranks of the Florida Tennis Association grew with every new member we signed up. The third year, we expanded to a 16 and under division, an 18 and under division, and a 10 and under division, and we added programs at more and more cities across the state. Soon, there were thousands and thousands of new members, which meant MUCH more money from the USTA to the Florida section. That was a huge benefit to Florida.

Over the next five to ten years, every section of the United States adopted its own form of what we called Youth Team Tennis. In 1987, the USTA took over our program and made it the program for the entire country, calling it Junior Team Tennis. It also created a national event for all sections of the country. Bobby Curtis said that they copied us and that our program, my program, was the model. I'm proud of that.

I did a lot more with the Youth Tennis Foundation besides that, and I'm still active with it, but I was becoming a lawyer. Representing people who could go to jail if I didn't do well was a responsibility I took seriously. I worked long, hard hours, including most nights and every weekend. I did my best to become a good lawyer.

Also, within two weeks of starting work, I met a woman who was working as a Judicial Assistant to the Chief Judge for the Sixth Judicial Circuit, and we hit it off quite nicely. She was a tall, attractive blonde and knew all of the lawyers, judges, bailiffs, clerks and everyone else in the courthouse. Everyone, and I mean everyone, was nice to her because of her position. She was a nice person, too, but nobody wanted to get on the bad side of the Chief Judge. His nickname was "Hotdog Harry" and he had a temper.

Working in the misdemeanor division meant that I would be handling cases like DWIs, Petit Larcenies, Bad Checks, Assault and Battery cases, traffic cases involving the possibility of jail, like reckless driving, fleeing and eluding and leaving the scene of an accident involving personal injury or property damage over a hundred dollars, among other things. Also, since I was the new kid on the block, I was assigned to cover the "First Appearance Hearings," where people arrested the night before are brought before the court for purposes of "advising" them of the charges against them and making certain that they had an attorney. If not, if they didn't have enough money to hire a lawyer, one would be appointed at that time.

Usually the office of the Public Defender was assigned to represent those folks. Bail, if any, was set at that time, too. Those took place at 8:00 in the morning, and I still hated to get up that early, but I did. I was never late.

Mr. Jagger truly did his best to help young attorneys, like me, develop. Most importantly, he provided training opportunities and he gave us space and didn't keep us on a tight leash, meaning that we were given the freedom to experiment and learn. We made mistakes, but everyone, in any occupation, will. I certainly did.

In the misdemeanor division, our mistakes didn't put anyone in prison. The maximum penalty for misdemeanors is a year in county jail. For felonies, the minimum sentence involves a year and a day in prison. That's the difference between a jail and a prison.

I was also responsible for what are called "Extradition Hearings." Those are when someone was arrested in Pinellas County on warrants issued by some other state. The accused would be asked if they "waived" the extradition process, or if they wanted to fight it. If they fought it, the governor of the forum state would have to sign papers and send them to the governor of the state of Florida, who would then sign papers directing Florida authorities to return the individual to the requesting state.

More than anything else, though, all beginning public defenders wanted to go to trial. We all wanted trial experience. Most stay two or three years, some a few more, and a few make it a career. The major benefit for young attorneys beginning as either assistant state attorneys, or prosecutors, or as public defenders, was that they would, without any doubt, get trial experience. That meant trials in front of juries. No other area of law provided that kind of experience for young lawyers.

One of the other responsibilities I had was to handle my own appeals. In criminal cases, indigent defendants are entitled to challenge a guilty verdict, or any perceived pre-trial legal mistakes, by appealing the judgment and sentence, at no cost to them. That meant that if something went wrong in any of my cases, I would be required to file an appeal to the Circuit Court, as all misdemeanors are heard and decided in County Courts. Felonies are heard in Circuit Courts and appeals of Circuit Court cases went to the Second District Court of Appeal in Lakeland.

One of my character traits is that I try hard to do the best I can in most everything that I do. I wasn't the best and the brightest of attorneys, but no one tried harder than I did. I know that I tried more cases and handled more appeals than anyone else in the office while I was there.

Also, I was active in the Florida Bar Association and became a member of the Corrections Committee. As such, I visited many prisons in the state and all of the facilities that housed juvenile offenders. I also was the attorney who worked on a major class-action case which challenged the inhumane conditions of those confined in jails across the entire state of Florida. Prisoners had few rights and many never saw the sun shine, had access to a law library, or got any exercise at all, among other complaints. We won that case, although it wasn't because of me.

I remember walking into the Florida State Prison in Raiford, Florida, where "old Sparky," the electric chair, was located. I walked "Death Row," where all the men sentenced to death were confined in individual cells, like animals. I remember quite vividly the sound made by the huge, metal doors to the prison when they closed behind me as I entered. I also remember how relieved I was once those doors closed behind me when I exited the prison.

Guards were not allowed to carry guns, for fear that the prisoners would take them and use them against the guards. Although I was with a group of at least a dozen other attorneys, with escorts, I was uncomfortable, to say the least. I didn't like being there, but the experience made a big impression upon me.

One of the real "perks" of being a fledgling attorney was that "The Boss" sent us to some week long seminars to learn needed skills, some of which involved going to some desirable locations. That summer, I drove out to Denver for one. My two brothers flew out to Denver to meet me and we, together with Christine, who joined us, spent another ten days traveling around out there, doing things like rafting the Colorado River, visiting Mesa Verde, rafting Los Animas river, near Durango, hiking in the Rockies, and canoeing the Buffalo River in Arkansas on the way back, among other things.

The "Boss" also sent me to Washington, D.C. for a seminar, and to Boston, Philadelphia, and other places, as well as numerous one or two day seminars across the state of Florida. He also had us report on what we had learned, video-taping us in the process. Once cameras were allowed in the courtrooms, he was one of the first to provide access to his assistants, so that we could "see" how we did, which was sometimes painful to watch. We were novices.

He was, truly, a great boss, and many of his former assistants went on to become judges at the circuit court and appellate levels. Also, he became a great friend, but it wasn't just me. He treated all of his employees, especially the support staff, like the secretaries, investigators, and administrative staff, with the same degree of courtesy and respect. He was genuinely loved, admired and respected by all who knew him, and especially all who worked for him.

I must say, however, that few came to know him and his family as well as I did. I enjoyed many nights and weekends at his home, with enjoyable dinners and conversation, though his dog, Tippy, never did like me, and always barked at me whenever I walked through the door. His two sons really took to the game of tennis and both became excellent players. His wife, JoAnn, was like a mother, sister and best friend, and she still is.

During the summer months, he hired law students to clerk in all of the various offices in St. Pete, Clearwater, New Port Richey or Dade City. Both of my brothers went to law school and both came to work with me. Christopher came in 1977 and Allan came in 1978. Both learned that they didn't want to do criminal law when they graduated, and both became successful attorneys in other areas of law.

After a good, long "stint" in the misdemeanor division, I was transferred to the felony division in Pasco County, in the New Port Richey office. I stayed there for over a year, before being transferred to the Juvenile Division of the office, where I became the managing attorney. I caused trouble wherever I went.

Mr. Jagger told me on multiple occasions that he received more "fan mail" about me than any one else in his office - ever. Whenever a public defender does his or her job, the entire court system has to work – clerks, bailiffs, court reporters, deputies, judges, state's attorneys – everyone, and I made everyone work and made more than a few people unhappy with me. Again, there were better and brighter attorneys, but no one tried harder than I did.

I also made some good friends while there. I started a Public Defender softball team; we played in a basketball league; we played football against the Clearwater cops regularly, and we even had a golf tournament with teams of judges, state's attorneys, bailiffs and public defenders. I have always been an organizer of such things, plus I started a mixed doubles tennis league for adults. My team was aptly named the "Ballbusters."

After I worked long enough to save a little money, I bought a 1 and a half acre piece of property in Palm Harbor and put Torque in the pasture behind the house. I raised a few pigs and had several "pig-picking" parties with bluegrass bands. Teenage daughters of Rosemary and Angie, two secretaries from the PD's office, came out to ride Torque regularly.

I also met a man who became one of my best friends and remains one to this day, and that was Patrick Doherty. He was one of the best criminal defense lawyers in the state and had left the PD's office shortly before I arrived. His father was born in Ireland in 1906 and Patrick was a first-generation Irish-American.

We began to run 5ks together. In 1978, we ran the Miami Marathon together, after preparing by doing 10ks, 15ks and a couple of half-marathons. We became life-long friends.

I'd never run that much before meeting him and it took me about a month to get to the point that I could run a 5k. For tennis, running sprints, jumping rope, running lines of the court and running no more than a mile was the best conditioning for me, not running a long distance. I remember well the day we drove to south St. Petersburg from Tarpon Springs, a drive of almost an hour, to run our first 5k.

It was a terrible event. All we did was run around a block four times. It was ridiculous, but we made it. It was for a good cause, though I have no idea what the cause was, and they gave us a t-shirt.

Before the race, just as we were getting there, Patrick says to me, as I'm driving and we pass by a donut shop, "Let's just go have some donuts and tell everyone we did this, okay?" I refused. To this day, I don't know if he was serious or not. He's that kind of guy – hilarious, actually.

I was still playing tennis at a high level, being one of the best players in the area, and I was working with the best high school players in the county, as well as beginning players. The Youth Tennis Foundation, at my behest, with the approval and endorsement of Jack Blair, our president, put on a tournament for teams of high school players from across the state. We paid all of the expenses, including all of the expenses to send the winners to the National City-Team Championships.

`Surprisingly, the only teams which won that annual event prior to that were my 1965 team from Miami, on which I played number 1, and Chris Evert's team in 1967, before she turned professional at age 14. She was that good. My passion for the game of tennis has been a constant in my life.

In April of 1979, Christine and I were married at the Light of Christ Catholic Church. Our reception was at the Seminole Lake Country Club. It was the social event of the year for our circle of friends. Life was good, but I still had some wild oats to sew. I don't know why, but the pasture was always greener somewhere else. I still have that problem.

A month or two later, I celebrated my greatest accomplishment as an assistant public defender, one which few others could say that they have ever done, and that was to successfully argue a case before the Supreme Court of the State of Florida. I took a per curiam opinion of a decision by the 2nd District Court of Appeal to the highest court in our state. It wasn't a case that I had tried or had anything to do with at the trial level. It was assigned to me after the man was convicted and the attorney who had tried the case had left the office.

I filed a Petition for Writ of Certiorari and won on a rather obscure procedural issue involving the exclusion of a witness due to the failure to timely list that witness prior to trial. The expression per curiam means that the lower court didn't issue a written opinion. The word certiorari means that the higher court will hear an appeal, even though there is no automatic right to an appeal. Those Writs are rarely issued.

Lawyers will understand how rare that is. The appellate lawyers in the Public Defender's Office in Bartow, who handled appeals for all Public Defender offices in the 2nd District, had filed what is called an "Anders Brief," which basically says that there was no merit to the appeal. I disagreed. Few attorneys would have taken on that case, but for whatever reason, I did, and I won. I'm proud of that.

As I look back, I really don't know why I had to leave the Public Defender's office and Pinellas County. Everything was good there. I could never, ever, find a boss who was more supportive. I had everything a man could want, but for whatever reason, I decided to move on.

Looking back from my advanced age of 75, it now appears obvious that I had "wanderlust," but there's more to it than that. I just don't know exactly how to explain it, other than to say that I wanted to live on a farm in a rural setting, closer to nature, not in a big city as I was.

Trust me when I say that Mr. Jagger was disappointed to see me go, as were some others, but certainly not all. However, how it came to pass is another story. The next chapter involves a move to "Heaven," ... almost.

Chapter Eleven
West Virginia

As everyone who works for someone else knows, employees usually get a week or two off every year for vacation. After a few years, you might get three weeks off. Some people could "buy back" vacation days and just keep working, essentially getting paid twice to work instead of taking a vacation. I always took my vacation days.

In the summer of 1978, Christine and I went to West Virginia and spent two weeks camping at various state and national parks in what John Denver famously called "Almost Heaven." We canoed rivers and hiked in Bluefield, Harpers Ferry, Wheeling, Blackwater Falls and a couple of other places, camping all the way. Somewhere along the road I saw a sign for the West Virginia Legal Services Plan and I decided to make a call and see if they needed any lawyers.

I had won the West Virginia Open, held at the Oglethorpe Park in Wheeling, in 1971 and I had good memories of the state. I liked the fact that the largest city in the state had less than 100,000 people in it. It was a rural state with rolling hills, navigable rivers and back roads – it was called "Wild and Wonderful" West Virginia.

To my surprise, I was immediately passed through to Jim Martin, the Director of the program. After introducing myself and giving him a brief description of my background, he said that he was always looking to hire lawyers and asked what part of the state I was most interested in. I told him that I'd give it some thought and get back to him.

I had enjoyed my year-plus in the nearby mountains of Virginia five years earlier and, I guess, looking back, I really wanted to live that life style. I was still a "city boy" and knew very little of what life on a farm would be like, but I wanted to try. I was definitely encouraged by my conversation with Jim Martin and the thought of living in the "country" intrigued me.

Christine's parents were both from Illinois and both had been raised on farms. They operated a business in Largo, Florida, called Garden Hardware, which catered to growers and farmers. She was receptive to the idea.

WVLSP had offices all over the state and we looked over maps and read all about the various areas of what is called the "Mountain State." It is the only state that is completely within the Appalachian Mountain range, and its average elevation is higher than any other state east of the Mississippi River. We were most interested in the area called the "Eastern Panhandle," because it was less than two hours from the Washington, D.C. area.

By that time, my youngest brother, Bruce, was in college at Catholic University, where he played on the basketball team, and my sister, Carol, was firmly esconced in the Maryland suburbs. She was, at that point, an extremely successful tax lawyer, making a whole lot of money. Since I had gone to school there, and played tennis there, I had many friends there. That, too, was an attraction.

Also, that part of West Virginia had rivers running through it, like the South Branch of the Potomac River, and the Cacapon River, with the Cheat River not too far away. I liked that, too. I decided to give Jim Martin a call.

When I did, Jim told me that they had an office in Romney, located an hour west of Winchester, Virginia, which covered a five-county area of Hampshire, Hardy, Mineral, Grant and Pendleton counties and the attorney for that office was leaving, so there was a vacancy. Plus, he said that if Christine was to come, she could have a job as a paralegal. That was a very appealing offer, one that I had trouble refusing.

Leaving the Public Defender's Office was not an easy decision. I was happy there and my "boss" was happy with me. His two sons, Bob and Ed, were now excellent tennis players. Bob went to Florida Southern University in Lakeland and was on the tennis team. Ed, who was a few years younger, would earn a scholarship to Western Carolina a year or so later.

The Youth Tennis Foundation was doing extremely well. I was playing tennis regularly at a fairly high level, and was playing in softball leagues, a team tennis league that I had started for adults, running 5ks and other events with Pat Doherty, and I had a nice acre and a half of land with a pasture for Torque. Life was good, so why did I have to change all that? I don't know, but I felt "compelled" to do so.

Christine and I decided to take the offer extended to us by Jim Martin and move to Romney, West Virginia. We both gave notice to our respective employers and we decided to move to West Virginia! I sold my "farm" to a fellow softball player and we started making plans. In July of 1979, we packed our bags, loaded Torque into his one-horse trailer and headed north. My brother, Christopher, accompanied us on the journey to help us with the move.

The managing attorney for the Romney office had left and there was no one working there, so when we drove into Romney, a town of about fifteen hundred people, with one red light, we went straight to the office. That was where we would live until we found a place, which was fine with Jim. He really did everything he could to help us.

So I had money to buy a place and the prices were a whole lot less in West Virginia than in Florida. We found an old, colonial-style house, built in 1801, on 22 acres, with a two acre pond, a huge barn, a silo and a stream running through it for about $80,000. It was located in between two one-lane bridges and there were only two houses anywhere nearby. We looked out over an open mountainside in the distance. It could not have been more picturesque.

The house, which was two stories high, had an attic I could stand up in. It had huge tree trunks over a foot thick to support the structure, with lath and plaster on the walls, fireplaces and water-fueled radiators in every room, plus a somewhat modern kitchen. That was an add-on.

Torque had a huge pasture, and I had an extra ten acre parcel a neighbor had been using as a hay field. He agreed to continue to do everything necessary to make hay on that field and give me one-third of the hay. Also, we had an acre next to the house that was perfect for a garden. We immediately bought a roto-tiller and put some things in the ground after having our neighbor till the ground with his tractor. We absolutely loved the place.

It was July, though, and that was the summer-time. Summers are beautiful up there. The days were warm, not too hot, and the nights were cool, not cold. I swam in the pond and watched deer run by. Christine's parents bought us some cattle, and we had our farm!

I officially opened the office in Romney right after buying the house and started the process of staffing it. I began by making a big mistake. I interviewed absolutely everyone who applied for the secretarial position – all twenty-three of them. I thought I was doing them all a favor, giving them some experience with interviewing. I was wrong. All I did was make twenty-one of them very unhappy with me.

However, I found two secretaries, one of which I later put in a satellite office in Keyser, which was the biggest city in the five county area. Most of the cases WVLSP handled in that part of the state were family law cases, like divorce and child custody issues. Christine became a paralegal and she handled the Social Security cases, which don't require a lawyer in the administrative process, unless a lawsuit is filed in Federal Court, and if that happened, a lawyer would need to get involved. She also worked up all the divorce cases.

To qualify for assistance the applicants had to be financially eligible. West Virginia was, and still is, the second poorest state in the country. A disturbingly large percentage of its citizens were, and still are, on public assistance, like Social Security Disability, SSI or Black Lung. There was no shortage of requests for assistance.

We also handled consumer matters, landlord-tenant issues, mortgage foreclosures and public benefits, like unemployment compensation or welfare, among other things. The Legal Services Corporation, developed in the late '60s during what was called a "War on Poverty" by the Johnson administration, funded all legal services programs across the country. The intent was to provide the poor with legal assistance in civil matters. The Public Defender's offices around the country provided legal assistance in criminal matters. The two programs are not related, though they service the same general population.

We also handled appeals, as well, and I had the opportunity to argue several cases before the Supreme Court of Appeals for the State of West Virginia. It was a long drive from Romney to Charleston, the state capitol, and I was allowed to fly on a two-seater airplane on a few occasions, which was a treat. There was an occasion, however, when the fog was so thick the pilot couldn't see the airport and had to fly around until it cleared. I barely made it to the courtroom on time.

My brother, Christopher, graduated from law school in May of 1980 and he agreed to come up to West Virginia and work with us for a year. He came up to live with us shortly after he graduated, but he really had no interest in doing any of the farm chores, like milking the Guernsey cow, Betsy, I had acquired. She required two milkings a day and Christopher refused to avail himself of the opportunity to experience that, despite my persistent pleas that he do so. He said if he learned, he was sure I'd have him do it all the time, so he never learned.

He is always good company, but he said that living on a farm was like having a 365 day a year job. You work like hell and pray for leap year. That was Christopher.

In October of 1980, not long after he arrived, Patrick Pierce Kelley was born, and that was a major highlight. We hoped that he would be born in the house, with the assistance of a mid-wife, under the supervision of a medical doctor, but after twenty-some hours of labor, Christine was exhausted and couldn't "push" any more.

We had to go to a hospital in Cumberland, Maryland, half an hour away, for his arrival. His cranium was a bit too large for a home delivery, but a C-section wasn't required, fortunately. He was a healthy and happy little baby, and we were two delighted parents.

My sister, Carol and her three children came to visit every so often, as did our youngest brother, Bruce, especially during that year Christopher was there. Bruce came one time with TEN of his basketball teammates. They went through all the milk Betsy could provide, as well as all the eggs the dozen chickens could lay per day, with no trouble whatsoever, and most of the meat I won at a local raffle. It was a side of beef, as I recall. Those boys could eat.

They rode Torque, swam in the pond, and went canoeing down the South Branch of the Potomac from Petersburg to Romney, a trip of about 20 miles, among other things. I drove them down to the put-in spot, gave them the canoes they needed, plus all the gear and told them exactly where I would meet them. I didn't go with them because I didn't have enough canoes for a group that large.

However, they lost track of time and didn't arrive to the take-out until about midnight. I have no idea how they made it down the river in the dark, but they did. I sat there and waited for them for hours, and then went home, not knowing what to do.

There were no cell phones back then. They had enough alcohol to sustain them through what was a long day and night, and didn't complain. They were tired puppies when they arrived. I never did get a good explanation of what took them so long. I received a phone call from someone who lived near where they came off the river, and that's how I was able to find them.

The winters in West Virginia were something else, though. I remember one night when the temperature got down to 22 degrees below zero, and the furnace stopped working. Fortunately, I had purchased a wood-stove, and as long as we had enough wood, we would never freeze to death. That thing put out some heat!

Fireplaces send most of the heat up the chimney, and the wood burns out quickly, whereas the woodstove, which sat inside the room, kept the heat in the room. Sometimes it got so hot that you had to get out of the room. It was hard to regulate.

Christopher never liked the cold. Christine and I got used to it, but I can't say that we ever grew to enjoy those long, cold winters. I learned that farmers up there didn't plant crops like corn until the first of May, as a general rule, and the freezing temperatures usually arrived in early November, making for at least six months of winter.

I remember coming home from work one day and finding Christopher sitting in a chair pushed right up next to the woodstove. His feet were on top of the stove. I noticed that the rubber on the soles of his shoes was melting, and I told him so. He responded by saying, "I know. I'm never living further north of Fort Lauderdale ever again," and he hasn't, to date. He still lives in Miami Shores, where my brother, Allan, also lives.

Life was good. Together, Christine and I were making enough money to allow us to do whatever we wanted to do, as far as the farm was concerned, and she began taking riding lessons. We purchased a nice mare for her to ride, and somehow acquired another horse and a pony from friends who needed a place to pasture their horses.

Having a milk cow was an eye-opening experience. I knew little of all that was involved prior to buying Betsy. She gave over four quarts of milk per day, which is a lot of milk! Holsteins, which are a much bigger breed of cow, give twice as much, and that's what most dairy farms have. Guernseys give much more cream in their milk, however.

So I'd bring in a full bucket of milk in the morning and then again in the afternoon. Christine would put the milk in large glass jars and leave it on the counter for several hours, allowing the "cream to rise to the top." That was an expression I'd heard many times, but never understood the significance of until then.

Once the cream rose to the top, she would scoop it out and separate it from the rest of the milk. Then, she could make butter, ice cream, or whipped cream – all sorts of things, but it required work. She did all of that. Then, we put the milk in a separate refrigerator. We sold quarts of milk to our neighbors for years.

However, in January of 1981, Ronald Reagan became the 40th president of the United States. He had been the governor of California prior to that and he absolutely despised the Legal Services Corporation because of all of the lawsuits filed by the Legal Services programs in California against him over the working conditions of farm workers out there, many, if not most of whom, were illegal immigrants. Reagan voted to abolish all federally-funded legal services programs each and every year that he was in office.

Fortunately, Congress wouldn't allow him to totally eliminate the Legal Services Corporation, but they did drastically reduce the funding. They did, however, cut our budgets to the tune of about one-third of what it was prior to the time Reagan took office. It was devastating to the entire legal services community all across the country, including WVLSP and us. Programs "re-trenched" in the major cities and our office, which covered a five-county rural area, was eliminated. We lost our jobs that summer.

Christopher went back to Miami after his year was up and took a job with a firm in Coral Gables. I opened an office out of my home, which was a mistake, as I soon learned. People in need of a lawyer wanted to have a lawyer who had a "brick and mortar" office. They didn't want to drive out in the country to find me, and I really didn't like having them in my home, for the most part, especially since Christine soon became pregnant with our second child, Marjorie Meagan Kelley, who was born in July of 1982, about the same time I was opening the home-office.

Not long after, I opened an office in Keyser, directly across the street from the courthouse. I hired a secretary, as Christine was too busy caring for the two kids and all the chores relating to milking Betsy. It was an exhilarating time of life. I began handling criminal cases again, and I did quite well, if I do say so myself.

In fact, I won so many cases that the local police wanted to hire me to represent them, thereby preventing me from defending criminals. I refused. I liked doing the jury trials, not administrative things, as that job would have required. I wasn't making much money, though. People up there just don't have that much money to spend on lawyers.

Life in West Virginia was everything I hoped it would be. It was difficult. It was a challenge, but it was a very pleasant adventure for me. I wanted to live on a farm and lead a "country" kind of life, and I was doing exactly that.

There is nothing like getting vegetables straight out of the ground, or off of the vine, and eating them fresh – nothing. I have never had anything better to eat than the things I got from the ground in that garden of ours. It was way too big for our needs and we put up a bunch of things, canning many of them to do so.

Peas, carrots, potatoes, corn, beans, tomatoes, onions, cucumbers – everything, was absolutely wonderful. There was no comparison between what I had ever eaten before or since to what we grew back then on that farm. However, being a farmer, even a "Gentleman Farmer," as I was, was hard work. It was a 365 day a year job, with no time off, as Christopher aptly observed.

He always had a funny quip to make people laugh, but it was no laughing matter. I'd walk outside the house and see dozens of things that needed to be done, all of which involved work, but I wasn't complaining. I loved those days, especially with the young children. I wanted children and now I had two of them, both healthy and happy little ones.

Those were good days, some of the best of my life, but the house was, as my father told me several times, a "white elephant." I didn't know what the expression meant. It is defined to mean a "property requiring much time and expense and yielding little profit." That it was.

I spent days upon days sanding the floors, repairing broken pipes, and replacing old electrical wires, among many other things, and that was on the inside of the house. The barn and "grainery," as it was called, required much work, too. The house hadn't been lived in for years before we bought it and there was work to be done everywhere.

I didn't mind it, but I just didn't seem to have time to do all the things that needed to be done, and run a profitable law office. Things were difficult from a financial perspective.

Being a "Gentleman farmer" basically means that you own the place but you get others to do the work. There were lots of things I was simply unable to do, like the electric, plumbing and anything to do with carpentry that required an extra pair of hands. Trying to put sheetrock up on a ten foot high ceiling with Christine holding the other end was a formula for failure, and there were many such projects which I just couldn't do myself.

I had to hire someone to come out and trim Torque's hooves and replace his "shoes" when they fell off. The Veterinarian had to come out every so often to take a look at him, as well as Betsy, especially after she calved, as she did one year. I'd taken her to a "real" dairy farmer's farm to have that happen.

"Real" farmers know how to do all of those things and they absolutely hate to have to spend any money whatsoever hiring help. I have the utmost respect for farmers as they know how to do so many things, like repairing tractors. I bought a small Farmall tractor and it was a chore just to change the various attachments, and God forbid something went wrong with the engine, as it did on occasion. As one banker told me, when I went looking for a loan, horses are not assets. They are liabilities, and that was true. Everything cost money and I needed help to do most everything that needed to be done on that farm.

Also, back then, there was no internet, and we didn't get any reception from an antennae, because of the mountains. The closest stations were out of Pittsburgh and Washington, D.C., a long way away. However, that was when the big dishes came into existence, and I bought one. That was before everything was scrambled, and we got unlimited access to all sorts of channels for years.

I bought one with a ten foot diameter dish. It was a bit of an eye-sore, but it worked great, surprisingly. I had to crank a handle to change the direction of the dish to change a channel, which wasn't all that easy, but we were so happy to be connected with the rest of civilization.

In September of 1984, a new member of the family arrived, namely Robert Brendan Kelley. Just as with Meagan, everything went perfectly, with a midwife by Christine's side and a medical doctor on his way. He, too, was a healthy and happy, little baby. Patrick would turn 4 a month later, and Meagan had just turned 2 a month earlier.

Late summer and early Fall is a beautiful time of year in West Virginia, and so it was every year we were there. By the first two weeks of October, the full colors of Fall were abundant. I had maple trees on the property and those are the ones that produce the most colorful leaves.

There was an Apple Harvest Festival in Burlington, ten miles down Beaver Creek Road that was fabulous. Apples are a huge crop for that part of the country. Again, there is nothing like getting apple cider straight from the source, plus all of the other delights, like apple pies and pastries.

We lived in a small community that was called Headsville. It is significant only because, according to the United States government, the very last Post Office and general store combination was located there. In fact, that building was removed and taken to Washington, D.C. and now sits in the Smithsonian National Museum of American History.

I had begun teaching classes at two of the local colleges a few years earlier and I was still doing so. Shepherd College, with its main campus in Shepherdstown, W.Va., not far from Harpers Ferry and Berkeley Springs, hired me to teach a class on Economics in its Petersburg, W. Va. Branch, and I was teaching Political Science at Potomac State College, located in Keyser. Adjunct professors don't get paid much money, but every little bit helped.

Also, I had started tennis programs in Romney and Petersburg, much as I had done in Clearwater. There were dozens of youngsters playing in both locations. I had them on teams and then had an end of season tournament for the kids, just as I had done before.

I started a tennis tournament for the kids in both cities, too. Also, there was an indoor court about a half hour away and I'd go play there once a week or so. The guys up there put up a hundred dollars apiece for the first guy to beat me, but that never happened. I won the local tournaments in

Maryland, too, so tennis was still a part of my life up there, too, and I met a man who would become one of my best friends, Paul Sullivan.

There was an Irish bar just outside of Cumberland, Maryland, and it was starting a dart league, so I decided to play. I formed a team and we went up to play against three other teams of four. This guy on one of the other teams had a white sweatshirt on that said "Sullivan." That was my mother's maiden name.

I walked up to him and introduced myself and he told me that his first name was Paul. One of my mother's two brothers is named Paul. We became friends instantly and we remain so to this day.

The winters, however, were long and brutal. The problem with cold weather for me, a Florida guy, is that you spend so much time indoors. I'd get outside to milk Betsy and do some chores, but I'd always end up back inside before too long in front of the woodstove, that seemed to constantly need feeding.

I learned all about cabin fever during my time up there, and I also learned that if I lived to be a thousand years old, I'd never be a farmer. Like I just said, the thing about farmers is that they have learned how to do absolutely everything that needs to be done around a farm. That was not me.

I am a hard-headed Irishman, but I learned that just as I would never be a carpenter or a mechanic, I would also never be a farmer. I had to learn that for myself, by experience. It took a while, but I figured it out.

One good thing about Betsy calving was that I didn't have to milk her for a while. I took that opportunity to take the family down to Miami to see my family and enjoy the warm weather during February of 1985. February is the coldest month of the year. January is when we would get the most snowfall.

My father was still alive at the time, though he was now an empty nester. Bruce was off at college, and both Allan and Christopher were married by then. Pop was beginning to show signs of having some cognitive difficulties, though, and he was about to retire from the practice of law. We stayed with him at our home in North Bay Village.

While I was standing on the beach at the Bath Club one afternoon, with Patrick by my side, he said, "Dad, I like wearing a bathing suit and swimming in the ocean. I don't want to go back to West Virginia."

He was four and a half years old at the time. It made me laugh because Christine and I had talked about doing just that. It was pretty clear that Pop was going to need some help, and I missed my brothers and my family.

Allan and his wife, Kathleen, had just had their first child, a boy, who was the same age as Brendan. My financial situation wasn't as good as I wanted it to be, and it didn't appear likely to improve dramatically anytime soon. West Virginia is a poor state under the best of circumstances and it was an even poorer state under less than desirable circumstances. The economic situation in the country at the time was none too good and it was that much worse in West Virginia, and that was definitely the case for me.

However, the biggest reason to leave West Virginia was because I would always be an "outsider" there, even if I lived to be a hundred years old. As the John Denver song goes, "Life is old there, older than the trees … younger than the mountains blowin' in the breeze." Families have lived in those "hollers" for centuries.

I'd made some good friends there, like David Webb, who was married to the daughter of Harley O. Staggers, who had been a congressman for nearly forty years. I also became friends with Harley's two sons, Bucky and Danny, and some others, like Paul Sullivan. Bucky was the Congressman from that part of the state, taking over his father's position when he retired.

I was liked well-enough by some, though not all. In fact, the Democratic party asked me to run for the position of circuit judge. I turned down the offer.

I had volunteered at a number of organizations, including the Mineral County Parks and Recreation Board, where I came up with some revolutionary ideas. I received much criticism, though, for supporting soccer programs, in addition to the tennis leagues.

Many people up there told me that boys were supposed to play football and the girls were to be cheerleaders, and that was it. Anything to detract from that was a bad thing. One thing for certain about that was that Friday nights in the Fall was all about high school football games. That was Americana. That's where all of the communities all over that state can be found – watching those high school football games. That really was something to admire and behold.

So it was with mixed emotions that I sold Betsy and all of the other livestock, put the house on the market, and made plans to move back to

Miami. I even found a good home for Torque with a summer camp for kids where he could be used on trail rides. I began the process of looking for jobs in Miami, as well as a place to live in Miami Shores, where my two brothers were living.

As much as I enjoyed my time in West Virginia, and I absolutely did, although not all of it, I was ready to leave. I'm not so sure about Christine, though. She didn't complain, but she was very happy up there. That was, by far, the best time for the two of us and our marriage. I moved in April of 1985. I was 37 years old at the time.

Chapter Twelve

The Federal Public Defender's Office

I left Christine and the kids in West Virginia and traveled down to Miami in search of a job and a place to live. I had neither when I left. However, within a relatively short period of time, I found both and the family came down to join me and start a new chapter of life.

I bought a nice, small, three bedroom, one bath house in Miami Shores, just a couple of blocks from St. Rose of Lima Catholic Church and school. It was a perfect location. The kids could, quite literally, walk to school. Both brothers lived within a few miles and Pop was about five miles away.

Also, I was offered a job with the Federal Public Defender's office, which seemed perfect for me, given my background, although the salary was less than desired. At that point, I had almost ten years of experience as a lawyer, with many criminal trials under my belt, plus a substantial amount of successful appellate experience, so I was a veteran. Usually, assistant Federal Public Defenders come straight out of law school with no experience, and then they leave after a few years. Most of the other attorneys in the office were in that general category.

Because of my level of experience, and because I had no cases assigned to me as of the moment I entered the office, I was assigned to handle what was known as the Sunshine State Bank case. The government described it as "the largest marijuana smuggling conspiracy in the history of the United States" up to that moment in time, that being the summer of 1985. It would be the only case I would work on for the next six months. It was a monster.

The case was set for trial in October and it was anticipated that the trial would last six months. Nearly 200,000 documents were produced by way of mandatory disclosure. Nothing had been done on the case as of the moment I entered the office. That was, apparently, the reason I was hired. I was given no secretary, no paralegal, no legal assistant and there was no money to hire anyone to assist me.

The case was called the Sunshine State Bank case because there were five defendants named in the indictment, two of which were officers of the Sunshine State Bank, namely Rafael Corona and his son, Ray. They were the president and vice-president of the bank. Their lawyer, Manuel Lopez Castro, was also a defendant, as was one of the drug defendants, and my client, who will remain nameless, was the fifth. He was accused of operating the "front" organization through which the illegal drug monies were deposited into an account with the bank.

Essentially, it was more of a "money-laundering" case than it was a drug smuggling case, although the government had to produce evidence of the drug operation and prove that over a million and a half pounds of marijuana were illegally brought into the United States by the drug defendants. All of the members of the drug conspiracy had pled guilty, except for the one man, who preferred to go down on his sword. He wasn't going to testify against anyone else.

I met my client soon thereafter and found him to be an older man, in his late sixties, bald-headed and a somewhat odd-looking gentleman, but he was very polite and unassuming. He told me that he was completely innocent of any wrongdoing. No one in the office believed him. Everyone was certain that he was going to be convicted and that there was little chance of mounting a successful defense.

He explained to me that the crux of our case was to involve the concept of what were euphemistically called "offshore corporations." They were, and they still are to this day, legal, he told me. Much to my surprise, he was right - they are legal, although they definitely push the boundaries of legality and can definitely be used for illegal purposes.

There are not many countries in the world where they are legal, like the United States, but there are several, many of which are in the Caribbean, where they are. Switzerland is the prime example. Any readers unfamiliar with "offshore corporations" should research them to find out what they are and what they can legally do. It will surprise you, I assure you.

The essence of these off-shore corporations is that they are kept as confidential as is humanly possible. The countries that allow off-shore corporations are usually tax-haven places like the Cayman Islands, Panama, Bermuda, the British Virgin Islands and, of course, Switzerland, as I mentioned. In fact, not too many years ago, banks in Switzerland were forced to reveal the ownership of accounts dating from the second world war which belonged to Jews who were exterminated. Since there was no one to claim the money, the banks simply kept the money. That wasn't quite kosher, was it?

The way they work is that people create a corporation in those "tax friendly" countries, hiding the true owners identity, at times, and never revealing who the owners are or what the assets of the corporations are to anyone. They are as "fishy" as they sound but, in those countries, and others, they are entirely legal until proven otherwise. Switzerland is famous for that.

Husbands have been known to use them to hide assets from wives in divorce proceedings. Legitimate U.S. corporations use these "off-shore" corporations to reduce or, in some cases, eliminate any tax liability. In this case, drug smugglers were alleged to be using the "off-shore corporations" to hide their identity, their assets, and launder money.

Months later, one of my first questions to the prospective panel of jurors was if they ever heard of off-shore corporations. None had and some laughed when I explained that our defense to the charges involved a few off-shore corporations. I told the jury that the corporations my client was involved with were entirely legal, and that was never dis-proven, because they were.

My client insisted that he was a legitimate business man operating a business as an employee of one or more of those off-shore corporations. He said he was a salaried employee and that he had a secretary or two to help him run the business. He also said that he had plenty of business associates in Panama and the Cayman Islands to support his version of events and corroborate his testimony. He was insistent that I needed to go down to Panama to meet his "witnesses" and investigate his case to the fullest extent possible.

I met with the man several times a week for an hour or two every day, for months, trying to figure out a way to create an argument that a reasonably-minded juror might actually believe, but I was not having much success. One of the most significant decisions a criminal defense lawyer must make in any criminal case is whether or not to put the defendant on the witness stand. How that person would be able to withstand a vigorous cross-examination from an effective prosecutor was always the issue. I was having a hard time making sense out of anything he was telling me, but I kept trying to make sense of it all, because I was the one who was going to have to "sell it" to the jury.

The co-defendants all had excellent lawyers representing them. The father, Rafael Corona, had a man named Don Bierman as his lawyer, and he was reputed to be one of the best, and most experienced, criminal defense lawyers in Dade County. The son, Ray, had Ted Klein as his lawyer. Teddy, as his friends called him, went on to become a Federal District Court judge a few years later. I was told that both men were being paid a million dollars apiece to handle the case. I was being paid a salary $35,000.

The lawyer who was a defendant in the case, Manuel Lopez Castro, had an excellent lawyer by the name of Tom Sklafani representing him. Tom was a graduate of Notre Dame du Lac and very proud of it. I have no idea how much he was being paid.

The drug defendant, whose name I can't recall, was being represented by a former United States Attorney for the Southern District of Florida by the name of Bill Meadows, who was an extremely well-respected member of the bar. He had been appointed by the Court to represent the man. He was well-liked by the trial judge, James Kehoe, who had been on the bench for well over thirty years. He was a seasoned jurist who wouldn't put up with any nonsense.

No one knew me, because I'd never practiced in Dade County, so I was kind of the wild card of the defense team. They weren't sure what to make of me. None of them wanted to see me messing up their cases. They didn't give a damn about my client, as long as he wasn't going to say anything bad about their clients.

In fact, by the time trial had arrived, I learned that Bierman and Klein hired a jury consultant for $100,000 to help choose a jury. They didn't want me doing anything to upset or contradict what that expert had to say about who should sit on the jury. To them, I was along for the ride.

I asked them to just do me the courtesy of explaining to me why a prospective juror was either good or bad for the defense, including my defendant, so that I could understand the decision-making process. I wasn't going to just roll over and play dead. I had a client to represent, but I was going to defer to their collective experience and judgment wherever possible.

Clearly, my client was not the "target" defendant. This case attracted national attention and was the subject of many CNN reports and was front-page news in Miami. Rafael and Ray Corona were the targets, and their lawyer was accused of being intimately involved with the entire scheme. Jose Fernandez, the primary drug defendant, had, allegedly, bought his way into an ownership position in the bank with profits from his drug enterprise.

That was a time when marijuana smuggling was rampant and Miami, the Keys and South Florida were said to be the hub. I wanted to distance myself and my client from the others and fly underneath the radar, but I didn't know what evidence the government had against my client. The government wasn't going to make it easy for me, and they weren't about to explain anything to me.

Since this was my only case, I would go into the office every day and pour through the documents provided by the government. I had never worn glasses before but, after spending day after day, week after week, month after month of going through documents, I had to buy the "reader" glasses, because my eyes were adversely affected. It was an extremely difficult case to handle.

Because of his persistent demands that I travel to Panama to meet with the people who could be witnesses on his behalf, I was able to convince my employer to send me to Panama to meet these people. I think he had to do it. If my client was convicted, he could argue that the Public Defender's office failed to provide him with an adequate defense because they didn't bother to investigate his case and that I had refused to travel to Panama to meet with those witnesses. So I was going to Panama, whether I wanted to or not, and I didn't really want to go.

Not only that, but I was going to have to go by myself. I asked for someone to accompany me who actually knew how to speak Spanish fluently, but that request was denied. I had studied Spanish in high school and in college, but I was nowhere near conversant, let alone fluent. I was barely conversational. For me, it was more like pig-latin. I knew some words, and some vocabulary, but nothing close to adequate. It was truly ridiculous, but that was the decision.

Meanwhile, while all of that was going on at the office, my family was flourishing in Miami. The kids delighted in going to the beach, swimming in the ocean and the pool at the Bath Club, and seeing their uncles, aunts and cousins. I started another tennis program at the Miami Shores Community House, I was playing a lot of tennis, and I was in two softball leagues with my brothers. I was still in the prime of life. I hadn't turned forty yet. I was young!

On top of that, I had to pay my way down and back to Panama and advance all of my expenses while there. I would be reimbursed, but that was a lot of money out of my pocket at a time when I didn't have all that much money. Despite that, I was obligated to do it and I did.

I flew to Panama City sometime during the late summer of 1985, while Manuel Antonio Noriega was the dictator. Four years later, he would be arrested by the United States Army in what was called the largest military operation since the Vietnam War on charges relating to drug trafficking. It was called "Operation Just Cause," and it was ordered by President George H. W. Bush.

13,000 soldiers were sent to support the 12,000 U.S. soldiers already there at a military base, because we were still in control of the Panama Canal. Hundreds of U.S. soldiers were either killed or wounded in the battle that ensued before Noriega surrendered. Noriega was the "king-pin" of a huge drug enterprise.

I, of course, had no knowledge that I would be investigating drug smuggling in a country where drug smuggling was part of the fabric of the society. The fact that there were uniformed Panamanian police officers or soldiers on every street corner, armed with machine guns and other weapons, as well as military jeeps with four armed men patrolling the streets, gave me a false sense of security. I had no idea of the danger I was in.

Despite that, I dutifully located and interviewed each and every one of the people my client told me to contact. They would, he assured me, support his defense. Needless to say, those men, some of whom were very credible and decent people, such as an editor of a local newspaper, albeit one that represented an opposition point of view from the Noriega government, didn't provide any evidence which would exonerate my client. They did, however, explain some of the "facts of life" in Panama.

They all explained to me the off-shore corporation situation, as well as the reality of drug trafficking in Panama. More importantly, to the extent that any of them had any good or helpful things to say about my client, NO ONE would voluntarily submit to a deposition and absolutely NO ONE would even think about traveling to Miami to testify in a court of law on his behalf.

Everyone was polite, and courteous, but our conversations were very private and were not overheard by anyone. They fully understood the situation and the danger they were in if the police knew what we were discussing. I, of course, was totally oblivious of it all.

Looking back on that week of total and complete futility, I realize how lucky I was to come back alive. I cannot say that I gained any knowledge or information that I was able to use at the time of trial. I did, however, do what the client asked me to do and I explained to him why no one would risk their livelihood, their reputation, or their lives to come forward and say that he was an innocent man who was hood-winked into being involved in a major drug smuggling enterprise.

So, sometime around the last week of August, the trial began. There were motions to continue filed by some of the defendants, but Judge Kehoe would hear none of it. Hundreds of prospective jurors had been summoned to appear. In Federal Court, a twelve-member jury is required for felony cases and, most significantly, the jurors were told that the trial could last six months, because that is what the prosecutors told the judge.

Needless to say, there weren't many people who wanted to sit in a courtroom for six months and listen to the grisly details concerning a drug smuggling and money laundering case. Nowadays, jurors are paid $50 per day. Back then, it was much less, but I can't remember how much it was.

You can just imagine how people with jobs, a family, a business or even being in school, would react when told that they might have to sit for up to six months, if selected. Remember, all jurors were summoned to appear. They didn't do so voluntarily, and if they failed to appear, they were subject to arrest.

Furthermore, Judge Kehoe didn't accept many pleas to be excused as being sufficient. If he did, no one would have been on the jury. He was ruthless, and I guess he had to be. I couldn't imagine what some of those people would do if they had to serve for six months, as they were told they might have to do. I'm surprised that we were able to select a jury. We would have several alternates, too.

Once the judge had questioned the jury to "qualify" them for service, and get rid of any who had a legitimate or lawful basis to be excused, then the attorneys began the questioning. By that time, I'd had dozens and dozens of trials, both civil and criminal, though most were criminal, and the "voir dire" portion of a trial, or jury selection, usually lasts a few hours and maybe, on extremely rare occasions, a full day. This one lasted well over a week.

Back then, attorneys for both sides were allowed to excuse at least three jurors for just about any reason whatsoever. Since then, it has become much more difficult to do that, due to racially motivated behavior on the part of many prosecutors. If the defendant was black, for example, the prosecutors would routinely excuse any and all prospective jurors who were black, without explanation. Since one in ten Americans were black back then, that usually meant that a black defendant would go to trial with a jury that had no blacks on it.

Since none of the five defendants in this case were black, that wasn't a problem. Everyone else, besides my client, were Hispanic, however, and the issue of potential prejudice was raised quite frequently, however. The "Marielitos" had left the port of Mariel in Cuba five years earlier and the city of Miami, Dade County and many parts of the state of Florida were still reeling from the problems that caused.

For those who don't remember, Fidel Castro opened his jails and mental hospitals and said all could go to the United States, with his blessings and no problem whatsoever. Our president, Jimmy Carter, who was and is a wonderful and compassionate man, welcomed them. Most of us who lived in Dade County did not share President Carter's benevolent attitude.

Doctors, lawyers and wealthy businessmen left Cuba in 1960 and fled to Miami after Fidel overthrew Bautista, and they assimilated into the American culture quite easily. Not so with the Marielitos. They were, for the most part, criminals and mentally ill persons, which is why Castro was willing to get them out of Cuba.

Regardless, and in any event, after over a week of seemingly endless inquiry, a jury was selected. The juror consultant basically told the five lawyers who to select, and we did. I had the least to say about all of that, but I had to develop a rapport with the jury, just as the others did, and I did the best I could. I didn't have any ethical problem whatsoever in that regard.

Once the jury was selected, and there were an additional eight alternate jurors selected, too, in case any juror had to be excused during the trial for any reason whatsoever, including illness or emergency. The attorneys then made opening statements. The defense attorneys were given two hours to do so and the prosecutors, and there were two of them, were given four hours to give the jury an "overview" of what the case would involve.

Following that, the government presented its case. To do so, they had maps and graphs which showed the route of about a hundred boats that had each brought in 30,000 pounds of marijuana, on average, over the previous five years or so. They presented law enforcement officers, bank examiners, records custodians, investigators, some people who had previously been convicted in this Jose Fernandez conspiracy, and many others to prove their case. That took over a month for them to do so.

One interesting, and unusual, aspect of the case was that the government was given permission to travel to the Cayman Islands to take depositions of some banking officials and then it was allowed to play those video-taped depositions in front of the jury. There were some offshore corporations with accounts there. Although the government said that no testimony would be elicited that would be harmful to my client, my client wanted to go. Again, I had to pay, in advance, for myself AND for him, and we went.

The main witness for the government was Jose Antonio Fernandez, the leader of the conspiracy. He had plead guilty to fifteen felonies and been sentenced to fifty years in prison before testifying. He told the jury that he knew my client and called him "hombre calvo," or the "bald-headed man." That was about it, nothing more damning than that came out of his mouth, which was good for my client. There was other evidence, of course, but his testimony could have been fatal, and I didn't know what he was going to say before he actually said it.

Once the government rested its case, there were a multitude of motions submitted by the defense attorneys, all of which were denied. After that, it was the defendants opportunity to present a defense. As in all criminal cases, the burden of proof to prove a case beyond and to the exclusion of a reasonable doubt is on the government. However, if the government presents a "prima facie" case, or sufficient evidence, in the opinion of the trial judge, to let a jury decide guilt or innocence, then the defendants have an opportunity to present a defense, or not.

In many criminal cases, defendants choose not to testify and, instead, they challenge the sufficiency of the evidence, arguing that the evidence was insufficient to convict and that a reasonable doubt existed. The question of whether or not to call the defendant to the witness stand was a huge decision for the five of us to make. The other four lawyers wanted to know if I intended to call my client as a witness. Some were afraid that his testimony might hurt their case.

I decided, after months of talking to my client and going over and over what he would testify to and how he would answer questions posed of him by the prosecutors, NOT to call him as a witness. Fortunately, he agreed. The other defense lawyers were relieved to hear that. Sometimes defendants "turn state's evidence," or become a witness for the prosecution. That wasn't going to happen in this case, at least not with my client, fortunately.

As I recall, only one of the defendants testified. I could be wrong about that, but I don't remember any of them taking the witness stand other than the attorney, Manuel Lopez Castro. He testified that all he did was prepare legal documents and that he had no involvement with either the drug smuggling operation or the banking issues. That shortened the case dramatically.

I called one witness, a woman who had been the secretary for my client's business. She had moved to Valley Forge, Pennsylvania, and I had flown up there to meet her and find out what she had to say, at my expense. Fortunately, she had some favorable testimony to provide and she agreed to fly down to testify.

The Public Defender's Office paid her expenses to do so. She explained to the jury what the business involved, what she did, what my client did, and, most importantly, she testified that she had no knowledge of any criminal activity. She also testified that she and my client were paid a salary, nothing more. She wrote the checks for the office and my client signed them. That was my case.

Once all defendants rested their cases, motions were again submitted, all of which were denied. There was some rebuttal testimony, but none of it involved my client and I don't remember what it involved. After that, it was time for closing arguments by the attorneys.

There was a lengthy process outside of the presence of the jury regarding what instructions were to be given to the jury, but those were all legal issues and I won't go into any of that. There are "standard" jury instructions for all criminal cases in the Federal courts, and then there are always some "special" instructions that apply only to the facts of the specific case before the court. I had little to do with that because most of those issues didn't involve my client.

My strategy throughout the trial was to fly under the radar. I tried hard to limit my questioning of witnesses as much as possible. I sat at the end of the table, furthest away from the jury, and I tried to hide from their sight as much as possible. The clients sat behind the five lawyers.

The government was given six hours to present its closing arguments and all five defendants were given three hours each. That took a couple of days. I was the last to go.

I argued that my client was an innocent man, as well as stressing the fact that the government hadn't proven its case against him, and that, at the very least, the jury should have some "doubts," to which they could attach a "reason," and, therefore, that they should have a "reasonable" doubt as to whether or not my client was guilty of the charges against him.

The Eagles had released the song called "Smuggler's blues" shortly before the trial began and I remember using lines from that song in my closing argument. It was the verse that went "it's the lure of easy money, it's got a very strong appeal." I argued that my client wasn't getting any easy money. He wasn't reaping rewards from the drugs. He was getting paid a salary, like his secretary, and they didn't know that the money came from drug sales.

My father, together with my brother, Allan, attended the closing arguments and heard what I had to say. Afterwards, my father asked me, "Pierce, where did you learn how to talk like that?" I guess I had found my "voice" as a lawyer. My father didn't recognize it. He meant it as a compliment and I knew it. I was proud to know that he was proud of me.

The jury was "out" for eight days, deliberating. That was a long time. Oftentimes, a judge will declare a mistrial if a jury deliberates for a long time and says that they were "impassed," and couldn't reach a unanimous verdict. Judge Kehoe wouldn't do that. He told them on a few occasions to keep deliberating. He said that there was no reason to think than another jury wouldn't have the same problems they were having. He told them to keep trying and reminded them of their oath to do their jobs as citizens and do the best they could.

On the ninth day, the jury returned a verdict of guilt against the drug defendant and the attorney, and said that they could not reach a unanimous decision as to the two Coronas. My client was found "Not Guilty." I, literally, "walked" him out of the courtroom, out of the courthouse, and onto the street, where I congratulated him, wished him good luck, and said good-bye. I have never seen him since.

I had won a major case that was reported on CNN national news. Of course, no one came to interview me. My client wasn't important. The mistrial of the two bank officers and the conviction of the lawyer was the big news, and it was big news. Drug trafficking in the United States was a major problem in the country at the time and it still is, although marijuana is quite tame compared to drugs, like fentanyl, that now are causing so many problems.

One somewhat comical side note to the case, although it's not funny at all, is that Judge Kehoe allowed the lawyer, Manuel Lopez Castro, to remain released on bond pending sentencing, rather than have him taken into custody and put in jail immediately. The lawyer absconded and remained at large for over twenty years before finally being captured. That rarely happens.

However, although I had achieved a significant victory, I made a decision that forever changed the course of my career, and I must say, if I had it to do over again, I would not have done what I did. It was a mistake.

Chapter Thirteen

Medical Malpractice

The mistake I made, after successfully defending my client in the largest marijuana smuggling conspiracy in the history of the United States, up to that point in time, was to submit an application to become the next Federal Public Defender for the Southern District of Florida. I shouldn't have done that, and I wish that I hadn't done that, but I did.

I did so at the urging of many, but not all, of the attorneys in the office at the time. The man who had been the Federal Public Defender for several decades was up for reappointment and he was not, in my opinion, doing a very good job. The staff turnover was incredibly high, morale was low and there were many deficiencies, especially when compared to the office of Robert E. Jagger. Of course, Mr. Jagger was voted the best Public Defender in the country at one time.

For example, none of the secretaries had been there longer than a year, and most had only been there for a matter of months; the lawyers all had much less experience than I had, and I don't remember any being there over two years; the salaries were the lowest in the country for Assistant Federal Public Defenders; the office hadn't appealed many cases to the 11th Circuit in decades, and had only appealed one case to the U.S. Supreme Court during his tenure, although it had the highest volume of cases in the country at the time; and they weren't taking cases to trial.

Also, it had no "feeder" program, as Mr. Jagger did, whereby law students from the several local law schools could work in the office while in school and, in all likelihood, join the office upon graduation. That had been the primary way Mr. Jagger found his attorneys. It gave him an opportunity to see the prospects perform and choose the very best of applicants.

The justices on the 11th Circuit Court of Appeals were the ones to make the appointment, and it was a critical mistake on my part not to be fully aware of the significance of that fact. I failed to realize that the composition of that group was such that I had about as much chance of getting the appointment as a snowball has a chance of existing in hell. That is where I made my mistake, and it was of colossal proportions.

Furthermore, the people in the Clerk's office, to whom I submitted my application, immediately told my employer what I had done. Once my employer found out that I had applied for his job, I had to leave the office, and I did, but I had nowhere to go. That, too, was a mistake.

I didn't have a contingency plan, and I couldn't afford to be without a job. I had a wife, three children and four mortgages, two on the house in West Virginia, which hadn't sold yet, and two on the house in Florida. I was in trouble. Needless to say, I didn't get the appointment.

Fortunately, my brother, Christopher, was able to be of assistance. He had two classmates from Archbishop Curley High who were successful lawyers in the Miami Area – Charlie Curran and Kevin O'Connor. He talked to the two of them and Kevin offered me a job to work with him in the office of Lanza, Sevier and O'Connor, an insurance defense firm located in Coral Gables, which specialized in medical malpractice cases.

I gladly accepted the job, although I didn't know what I was in for. That is an extremely difficult area of law and I had little knowledge of it, having been a criminal defense lawyer and a poverty lawyer for my entire ten year career up to that point in time, but I had trial experience, and that was a huge plus.

South Florida, and that includes Dade, Broward and Palm Beach counties, was the area of the country from which the largest verdicts were coming in medical malpractice cases. Some of the best attorneys in the country were practicing in that part of the state. The whole area of law was really just beginning to expand at the time. The idea of people suing their doctors over mistakes those doctors made was truly revolutionary at the time.

Kevin was one of the very best insurance defense lawyers in the three county area and he was called upon to try cases, all of which lasted a week, at the very least, in all three counties. His partners were excellent defense lawyers, too, but I would be working primarily with Kevin. He would be the one trying the cases in front of a jury, but I, and other non-partner members of the firm, would work the cases up for him.

That meant that I, and the others, would be the ones taking or attending depositions of doctors, both for and against our clients, as well as other things, like attending hearings, responding to discovery requests, filing motions and so forth. It was extremely challenging. Some call insurance defense work a "sweat-box," because the days were long and many weekends were spent in at the office, due to the high volume of work. Plus, there was a lot of driving involved to get to the various courthouses, attorneys' offices, court reporters offices, doctors' offices and the rest. It was a tough job from that perspective, too.

However, handling a medical malpractice case takes a lot of skill. You had to know the medical issues, too, and I didn't, at first, but I had to learn. That took time. No one can "teach" experience.

Handling a medical malpractice case costs a lot of money to do, both from the plaintiff's side, and from the defense perspective. I was told by attorneys representing people injured as a result of alleged malpractice on the part of doctors that the injuries had to be substantial because they would be investing upwards of $50,000 on each and every case. Therefore, the verdicts and settlements in each and every case had to be extremely high for the injured plaintiff to get a sizable amount of money, after costs and attorney's fees were paid. Attorney's routinely recover 40% of a verdict or settlement, before costs are paid.

Again, the largest verdicts in the country were coming out of South Florida. It was a hot-bed of activity. Legislatures all over the country, but especially in Florida, were debating whether or not to limit the amount of recovery a plaintiff could get. That issue was actually on the ballot in Florida.

The verdicts were so high, at times, that insurance companies, the doctors and even the general public had become alarmed. The main bone of contention was over the calculation of "pain and suffering." Insurance companies, and the doctors themselves, wanted to put a limit on the amount of money that could possibly be awarded for "pain and suffering," aside from the actual "out-of-pocket," or "economic," expenses.

When a patient filed a lawsuit against a doctor, the claim almost always includrd claims against a hospital, a medical group, any and all other doctors who treated the patient and anyone else, like anesthesiologists, radiologists or other specialists who might have any possible liability for the incident, no matter how small, so long as they had a "deep pocket." The result of that was that there were six or eight defendants in each case, with each defendant having a separate lawyer defending. Also, each defendant would, more often than not, get an "expert witness" to testify on their behalf in their specific specialty.

In most cases, the "expert witnesses" were from somewhere other than South Florida. As a result, scheduling anything was a monumental problem. Because of that, after I gained some experience, I was thrown into the fire. I might be called upon to jump on a plane and fly to New York; Washington, D.C.; Portland, Oregon; Boston, Massachusetts; or anyplace else in the country on a moment's notice. I would be expected to read and learn about files that might be a foot thick overnight or in a matter of hours. It was extremely difficult and it was enormously stressful.

On top of that, those depositions were never pleasant. There was a whole lot of money at stake and these lawyers weren't friendly with each other. Even lawyers who were on the defense side didn't always get along well with each other. They would routinely fight with each other over who was responsible for what. It was a dog-eat-dog environment, and there were plenty of big dogs in the neighborhood.

On top of that, defense firms would fight over who gets the business from the doctors or their insurance companies. Beginning sometime in the mid to late '70s, law firms were allowed to advertize. That had never been allowed prior to that time. As a result, lawyers representing injured plaintiffs began advertizing on television, billboards, bus stops, the back of taxi-cabs and everyplace else, and they were doing so with much vigor. It was the hey-day for lawyers seeking to get rich quick and South Florida was the main battlefield.

The really "big" law firms, such as Morgan and Morgan, had yet to come into existence and advertizing was still seen as a "no-no" by many of the better law firms. However, when those firms that did so much advertizing began making huge amounts of money, even when they weren't even close to being the best lawyers in court, things changed. Many, many law firms began to advertize, including many of the good ones. Morgan and Morgan began to dominate the field and it began spending millions upon millions to attract the business. It continues to do so to this very day, perhaps even more so, with more "big" firms competing with them.

After a while, I became quite proficient at doing whatever was required of me, but I really grew to hate what I was doing. The stress was enormous, and I really didn't like the way insurance companies approached each and every case. It was always with an attitude that the plaintiffs were either lying about their injuries or grossly exaggerating them, which was true in many cases, but not everyone was lying. Not everyone was exaggerating their injuries.

I found myself changing from a person who had become a lawyer to help people, like the poor and downtrodden, as a public defender or a poverty lawyer, to a person who questioned everyone, and I mean virtually every plaintiff, with a jaded view. I didn't like that, even in those cases where the claim was questionable and the injuries seemed to be grossly exaggerated. I didn't like the person I had become or was becoming.

The lawyer for the plaintiff was supposed to get as much money as possible for his client. The lawyer for the defendant was supposed to do everything possible to see that the plaintiff got the least amount of money possible, or no money at all. That was the game. I just didn't like the game. I didn't like what I was being asked to do and I didn't like what it was doing to me, but I had to do what I did. I had a wife and children to support and I still had four mortgages to pay.

I have to admit, however, that the many of the cases were interesting, exciting and challenging. I remember many of them quite well, like the one where a man broke into a home, trying to steal property and rape the woman occupant, who shot him. The ambulance took the injured robber/rapist to the closest hospital, but that hospital refused to accept him as a patient, knowing that he had no money to pay for the medical services.

The hospital staff told the ambulance driver to take the man to Jackson Memorial, which accepted such patients. The man died en route. I flew to Portland, Oregon to depose one of the world's leading experts on trauma medicine in that case. Doctors without Borders was involved with that case, too, on behalf of the doctor who was threatened with the loss of his license for failing to render care.

Another case involved the birth of two twin girls. The first child born wasn't breathing, but the second child was delivered without any problem. For some reason, the first child was left to die, because the doctors felt that since the child hadn't begun to breathe in such a long time after efforts to resuscitate her had failed that she would be severely brain-damaged. Half an hour later, the first child began to breathe, spontaneously.

I flew to New York City on short notice, together with six other lawyers, to depose a doctor who charged $1,000 per hour for his testimony. I couldn't believe the amount of his fee at the time, but he was one of the best experts in the country. Surprisingly, the child's injuries weren't too severe, but the case certainly had value and the question was, as in all such cases, what was the likely jury verdict. What would a jury do if the case was taken to trial? That was always the question and no one knew what that number would be. It was like a high-stakes poker game in many ways.

The firm handled some cases other than medical malpractice, and one case that I tried, among several others, involved representing the City of Coral Gables on a claim of excessive force against one of its police officers. The deputy, who was male, had arrested a woman on a charge of DUI, or driving under the influence of alcohol to the extent that her normal faculties were impaired. There weren't many female officers on the force at the time and the offense occurred late at night when no female officers were on duty.

The preferred policy was to have a female officer involved whenever a female was being arrested. Since there weren't any female officers available, the male deputy decided not to handcuff her, as he should have done, after arresting her. Instead, he placed her in the back of his vehicle, which had a cage separating the front seat, where he sat, from the back seat, where she sat. He also locked the doors so she couldn't escape.

As he was driving the woman to the station to book her, she took a bottle of mace from her purse, which the officer allowed her to hold on to, and proceeded to spray the officer, cursing him for arresting her. She also began kicking at the windows and the cage. He immediately stopped the vehicle and pulled her from the vehicle. She forcibly resisted.

At that point, a scuffle ensued. The officer, who was not much bigger than the woman, put her right arm behind her back and forced her to the ground. In the process, the woman suffered a rather serious injury to her shoulder. The plaintiff's attorneys told the jury that he pulled the woman's arm from its socket.

That was an interesting case, and I could clearly see both sides of the argument. That was a case that needed to be decided by a jury, because the two sides couldn't agree on who was right and who was wrong. That is why we have juries to decide cases. I had no problem with that case, except the woman was a very pretty woman, who was as nice as nice could be when she testified before the jury. That made things a bit more difficult for me.

Being a lawyer isn't an easy occupation. It requires a number of skills, especially when you're a "trial lawyer," as I had become. I always enjoyed the opportunity to argue before a jury. It was like being an actor on stage. The curtain went up and your every move was observed by a multitude of people, including the seven or eight jurors. That was the best part of being a lawyer, for me. That was the part I enjoyed the most.

In fact, that case was tried twice. The first trial ended in a mistrial due to improper comment by the plaintiff's lawyer. The second trial resulted in favor of the plaintiff for her medical bills, but not much more. The verdict was nowhere near what the plaintiff asked the jury to award her, so I "won" that case, as far as my employer and the City of Coral Gables was concerned, although they would have preferred a "zero" verdict.

There were hundreds of cases like that, most of which settled before trial. From the defense attorneys' perspective, the best case was one which was worked hard for as long as possible, for as much money as possible, and then settled right before trial. If it went to trial, the chance of an adverse, or really bad, verdict, could affect future assignments. Statistically, less than 3% of civil cases actually go to trial.

However, I still found time on weekends to continue with the tennis program I had started in Miami Shores, which involved as many as forty or fifty kids. Both Patrick and Meagan, and later, Brendan, participated and all have favorable memories of those days. I took teams to the state championships, which were now being run by the Florida Tennis Association, which had taken over our Youth Team Tennis program and called it Junior Team Tennis by then.

In 1987, the last year that the Youth Tennis Foundation operated the Youth Team Tennis program that I had started way back in 1976 in Clearwater, I went to New York and met with Billie Jean King, who gave us $10,000 and thousands of Domino's Pizza t-shirts of all colors for all of the kids across the state who participated in our program to wear.

Also, in 1987, the Youth Tennis Foundation held its annual meeting at the Doral Country Club in Miami at a $100 a plate dinner. Arthur Ashe was our featured speaker. Hundreds of people turned out for it. Later that year, the Florida Tennis Association cut off our funds, saying we should be giving them money, not the other way around.

I was also playing in adult tennis leagues with my brothers, as well as U. S. Tennis Association tournaments, softball leagues, other things. Once the house in West Virginia finally sold, I was able to put a pool in the backyard of our home in Miami Shores, so my kids could swim every day. That was a luxury I probably couldn't afford at the time, but I did it anyway. It cost about $20,000.

Also, I was involved in my local community, serving on the Parks and Recreation Advisory board and being a member of the Kiwanis Club. Swimming was our main family activity back then. We attended Mass regularly, as a family, as required by the school. Attendance at Mass was required for all students and it was taken by the Nuns.

After three years with Kevin, I'd had enough. I think Kevin was going to offer me a position as a junior partner in the firm, but I wanted out. The stress was really more than I wanted and the demands of the job would only get worse, much worse, not better, as my responsibilities increased, especially if I became a partner. I didn't want that. Again, it wasn't the "smartest" decision, or the most pragmatic, but that's what I did.

That was at the end of 1988. Patrick was eight years old by then, Meagan was six and Brendan was four. Also, in September of 1987, another child joined the family – another girl, Caitlin. I wanted to be actively involved in their lives, especially when it came to sports. Schoolwork was, obviously, important, as was good conduct, but I felt that they should all be athletes and I was especially hopeful that they would be tennis players.

I began looking for another opportunity and I really didn't have anything other than what I was doing in mind. I wasn't going to leave Kevin until I found myself another job. I was a trial lawyer with experience in criminal law and medical malpractice and insurance defense work. I really didn't want to do either one at that point, but I had no other options.

I was still teaching paralegal students at a couple of junior colleges and universities in the area and I tried to find a position at a school where I could teach in a paralegal studies program and coach the tennis team, but I was never able to find an opportunity to do so. I was forty-one years old.

Chapter Fourteen
Commercial Litigation

An opportunity arose at the end of 1988 when a man named Howard Setlin, who was a partner in the law firm of Therrel, Baisden and Meyer, Weiss, offered me a job. They had an office on Lincoln Road in Miami Beach, which I knew well. I would no longer be handling any personal injury cases, nor would I be handling any criminal cases. I would be representing people and businesses in commercial matters.

Again, I was entering into a new area of law. My years of trial work were expected to be of importance, but Howard, who was a friend of my parents, was having some health problems and needed assistance with his cases. I would be working primarily with him and for him. He was a very nice man and an excellent lawyer. I was happy with the opportunity he was giving me, but I was truly ecstatic not to have the stress and pressure of Kevin's office on my shoulders any longer.

Kevin was wonderful to me, and I have nothing but good things to say about him. He was an excellent attorney and a very nice man, but the stress of his job was more than I wanted. A few years later, the stress got to Kevin and he had some serious physical problems which were, without a doubt, related to all of the stress he was under. He's fine now, but it took its toll on him.

My eyesight had worsened and I was sure it was because of all the reading I had to do of medical records and reports, as well as deposition transcripts and pleadings, not to mention legal texts and cases. Also, my hair was beginning to turn gray. I had been a blonde as a child, which gradually turned to what is called "dirty" blonde, and was no darkening and becoming sprinkled with more than a few gray hairs. I didn't like that. I was now a middle-aged man. Turning forty was a milestone. I was no longer a "youth."

About that time, I found out that my eye problems were worse than I imagined and involved more than reading too much fine print. I was diagnosed with early stage glaucoma. My father had glaucoma and I wasn't surprised when I was told that by my friend, Dave Sime, who was possibly the best athlete I've ever known in my life. He was the world's fastest human being in the early '50s and was favored to win gold medals at both the 1952 and 1956 Olympics in the 100 yard dash and was deeply disappointed to only win two silver medals.

He was also a good tennis player and we played together often. I always admired him for his athletic abilities, but he didn't pursue a professional career in sports because, as he told me, he'd rather save people's sight than hit home runs. He was a great guy, and a good eye doctor.

I began taking prescription eye drops morning and night at that time and I still do to this day. Years later, I developed cataracts in both eyes, as my father did. I'm sure that all the years of playing tennis didn't help with my eye problems, but they were the result of both genetics and the punishment I put them through.

When I was playing my best tennis, I had to put that black stuff underneath my eyes to lessen the glare. There were days when my eyes would start watering when I walked out of the clubhouse into the sun, before hitting a ball. I can attest that the non-glare stuff you see athletes put under their eyes really isn't just a cosmetic thing. I couldn't have played without it.

On top of that, stress can kill. I was under a whole lot of stress and I didn't like that. I now had four children. When I first got married, the main reason to be married, in my mind, was to have children and I wanted about ten of them. I learned that each child requires a large investment of time, and you can't lump them all together. I found out that each one is a distinct, unique person. I was determined to spend more time with my burgeoning family.

Therell, Baisden and Meyer, Weiss was actually an unusual combination of two highly successful law firms from the Miami Beach area of Dade County. The Therell, Baisden part of the firm was all about the non-Jewish element of Miami Beach, meaning the wealthy Christians who were members of the exclusive clubs on the Beach where Jews were not welcome.

The Meyer, Weiss part of the firm was all about the Jewish population in Miami Beach, which was considerable. There was much anti-semitism in the early days, and Jews were discriminated against quite openly for decades. The city was formally founded in 1915. Jews were, apparently, "required" to live south of Fifth Street, which is now South Beach, one of the premier destinations in the world.

The joinder of the two law firms was an attempt to bridge the gap between the gentiles and the Jews in Miami Beach, and to make more money in the process. However, non-Jewish members of the firm were given a paid membership to clubs, like the Bath Club, where Jews weren't allowed to be members. It was a strange marriage. For me, however, it was an attractive perk. My family and I were now members of the Bath Club. My parents had been members since the mid-1950s, but now I was a member in my own right.

As I look back on those days, I'm not proud of being a member of a club which discriminated against Jews and African-Americans, but that was a system I didn't create, nor did I embrace. I had attended Nautilus Jr. High School, where I was in the minority, but I made friends there that I have remained friends with my entire life. I have nothing but admiration for how the Jewish people have accomplished so much despite thousands of years of discrimination. Also, much of my legal career has been devoted to helping the poor and less fortunate in our society, so I don't think I have too many problems in that regard, but that is my history.

I had some very interesting cases while working at that firm. They truly catered to people with money, unlike the criminal defendants or poor people I had represented for most of my career up to that point in time. I was representing bank presidents and well-to-do people, including multi-millionaires. What I didn't realize was that hardly any commercial litigation cases actually go to trial and, when I discovered that, I didn't like it. I was a trial lawyer.

People with money, or own businesses which make lots of money, will fight and fight over whatever the subject of the lawsuit is up to the point when both sides realize that they're spending way too much money on lawyers and costs and it made more business sense to resolve the matter. Usually, after several years, at times, they would come to that conclusion. That happened in every single case I had while working there. I had many cases in litigation, and some on appeal, but not once did I actually get in front of a jury to argue a case while working at Howard's firm – that was what commercial litigation was for me.

However, the best case I ever had during my entire legal career, aside from the largest marijuana smuggling conspiracy in the history of the United States, came during my time with that firm. I had the opportunity to fly to Australia, and go to the Barrier Reef, for a two hour deposition in a case involving an extremely interesting set of facts. If you draw a line from Miami Beach through the center of the earth, you will end up in Australia. It was half-way around the world.

I was assigned to represent an heir to one of the original oil tycoons in the United States. He was worth millions upon millions of dollars. Money was no object and the case was fascinating. It was, as I said above, the best case I ever had in my 48 years of practicing law, by far.

Here are the facts – my client had bankrolled a company that was owned by one of his best friends who asked to borrow money in order to build Bangsticks. For those of you who don't know, a Bangstick is used, primarily, to kill sharks. That was the original intent. I'm sure it has other uses, too, but that is why it was invented – to kill sharks.

Again, my client bankrolled the venture. He didn't create it, nor did he participate in its marketing or sale, and he may never have used one, but since he had put his money in the business, and may have been associated in some way with the corporation, he was named as a defendant in a lawsuit brought by a seventeen year-old boy from Miami Beach who was injured while using the Bangstick. The boy lost three fingers on his right hand when he put his hand over the business end of what was a hermetically sealed shotgun and the gun discharged.

The friend to whom the money was loaned was an absolutely brilliant marine biologist, with incredible chutzpah, courage, bravery or "balls," for lack of a better word. He is the one who created the Bangstick. He did so at the demand of his companions who accompanied him on what can only be described as an unbelievably frightening foray into the depths of the Atlantic Ocean off of Key Largo to study marine life at night. He, being a marine scientist, wanted to learn what the nocturnal aquaculture was like on the coral reefs. There really hadn't been much attention given to that issue at the time. He was a student at the University of Miami. This was in the early 1960s.

His companions, who were not scientists, accompanied him and held lights so he could see what was going on. Needless to say, it was pitch dark under the water and the men, quite understandably, were scared shitless – excuse my French. As an aside, do the French really talk like that? Why is it always "excuse my French"?

After a few uneventful, but still harrowing, adventures, the companions insisted that they be given some sort of weapon to ward of sharks and other aggressive creatures, such as barracuda, snakes or whatever, should they suddenly appear. The scientist, quite brilliantly, created this "gun" which worked incredibly well. It still does, to this day.

A shark, no matter how big or ferocious, when hit with what was a shotgun shell, anywhere on its body, rolls over and dies, almost immediately. The gun, dubbed the Bangstick, was simple to use and extremely effective. To my knowledge, anyone who has ever used the Bangstick, to this day, marvels at its effect on sharks, even the very big ones.

However, the "gun" must be used properly. It must be loaded properly, and it must be fired properly. In this case, the seventeen year-old was by himself on the waters off of Miami Beach "chumming" for sharks. That means he had put bloody fish parts, or the bloody remains of some other sea creature, into the water, hoping to attract sharks.

On this occasion, as a big shark approached the bait, the boy hurriedly went to load the Bangstick by putting a shotgun shell in it. In his haste, he was having difficulty getting the shell loaded and he accidentally caused the gun to go off, thereby taking off three fingers. He filed suit, claiming that the Bangstick was defectively designed and manufactured.

Unfortunately, my client failed to respond to the complaint filed against him. He never even talked to a lawyer about it. I have no idea why he did that. I never asked. Without there being any defense offered whatsoever, a jury returned a three million dollar verdict against the man.

I was assigned the case after the verdict was returned. Fortunately, I discovered that the trial judge had made a mistake and the verdict was set aside. In other words, the judgment was set aside and the plaintiff was going to be required to prove that the Bangstick was defectively designed and manufactured. Also, a defense of "contributory," or "comparative" negligence could be raised at trial. If successful, the plaintiff's attorneys would then have to prove what amount of money the teenager was entitled to at that new jury trial.

Years before the incident took place, the brilliant marine biologist had moved to Australia. I heard, but it was never confirmed, that he did so to avoid paying alimony to an ex-wife. I don't know if that was true or not. What was true was that he was still studying marine biology, this time in the waters around the Great Barrier Reef. The lawyers, and all of us, would have to go to Australia and question him regarding how he came up with the design, among other things.

He wasn't going to voluntarily return to the United States, so we were going to have to go to him. At that point, an insurance company was involved and the legal issue was, among all of the other things, whether or not my client's Homeowner's policy would protect him against the claim. I was not representing the insurance company now. I was representing the man in his individual capacity. My client authorized me to fly Business Class for that 26,000 mile round trip.

I flew from Miami to Dallas; then Dallas to Denver; then Denver to Los Angeles; and then Los Angeles to Oahu, Hawaii. That trip took nearly twenty hours. When I disembarked, I thought I was going to spend a night in Hawaii and then fly to Sydney the next day. I was informed that my plane was to leave in an hour. My Travel Agent had failed to take into account the differing time-zones. I was way beyond exhausted!

The flight to Sydney took over ten hours. Once I arrived, there was a delay of several hours, and then I flew from Sydney to Brisbane, in Queensland, where I boarded another plane to Cairns, at the northern tip of the continent. When I got off the plane, I'd been traveling for nearly two days.

To make matters worse, I was the one who was transporting the Bangstick. It is a weapon and it had to be inspected at various points along the journey. That was a royal pain, too. I was actually somewhat surprised that they let me do what I did. It was taller than I am and I am 6'3" tall, and it was in a big metal case.

Fortunately, I had allowed time for me to spend some time in Australia. That, too, was approved by my client. I had time to take a hydro-plane to the Barrier Reef and snorkel. That was an adventure in and of itself.

The boat was actually a huge trimaran, which means it had three hulls, with several powerful engines to propel it. I, along with about a hundred other passengers, traveled for over an hour at a speed in excess of sixty nautical miles per hour to a spot in the middle of the Coral Sea, where a relatively small wooden platform sat, all by itself, bobbing up and down in the water.

I thought that the Great Barrier Reef was just off the coast, as the reefs off of Key Largo are, where our brilliant marine biologist conducted his experiments, but I was wrong. The Reef extends for over 2,900 kilometers, or about 2,000 miles, around the northern border of the continent, and it sits quite a ways off of shore.

Some of the other passengers had brought scuba equipment with them, and most were part of a guided tour group. Others, like me, were there to sight-see. I had a bathing suit, a mask and some fins. I just dove in and swam around.

I confess that I didn't have anywhere near the same degree of confidence that our brilliant marine biologist had, and I didn't go too far from the platform, nor did I dive too deep, nor stay too long in the water. I saw plenty of small white-fin and black-fin sharks darting all around me, but I didn't see Bruce, the iconic shark from the movie Jaws, which had come out twelve years earlier, in 1975, and I wasn't too thrilled with the prospect that I might meet up with Bruce, or one of his distant relatives. I returned to the boat somewhat quickly, but I wasn't the first one back.

I also took some time to travel by train up a mountain, on what seemed to me to be a seriously perilous route, to an Aborigine village. It seemed as if the train went up at about a 45 degree angle and it hugged the side of the mountain. This wasn't a tourist attraction and I was, quite obviously, a tourist. There were no friendly, smiling faces to greet me and sell me some trinkets.

The people weren't unfriendly, they just weren't used to seeing people who were different from them. And I wasn't used to seeing people who were like they were. I didn't feel uncomfortable, but I was a stranger in a strange land. These were aborigines.

The deposition itself was a dud. Nothing of any value came from it at all. It had to be taken, just to provide the narrative as to how and why the Bangstick came into existence, and the scientist had to be the one to do it. He confirmed that my client had nothing to do with any of that but that testimony, unfortunately, wasn't going to get my client off the hook.

The most striking and memorable part was when the witness, our brilliant marine biologist, told of some other visitors who had come to visit him at his home and had failed to heed his warning about the crocodiles. He said that two men saw a twenty-some foot long croc sitting on the side of a river, sunning itself, and they thought that was a fantastic photo op. The crocodile thought it was feeding time, and he ate them.

The other most interesting part of the trip to meet the biologist was when he explained that he no longer carried a Bangstick with him when he went into the waters. I knew that the Great Barrier Reef was home to the biggest sharks on the planet and I asked him about that. He said that he wore a specially-designed wetsuit that made him look like a sea snake and that warded off any threat of a shark attack.

When I persisted, he explained that sharks don't bother sea snakes. If they do, they will die, and sharks have, somehow, learned about that. His wetsuit had the same coloring as that of a sea snake.

Sharks supposedly don't have good eyesight, so when they saw the colors of the wetsuit, they avoided him. That was truly hard to believe. As I said before, this guy was fearless. He really was something else.

I took it upon myself to do some research into sea snakes and I learned that what the biologist had told me was, indeed, true. There are legends from that part of the world to the effect that sea snakes are the "kings" of the seas. They have no natural enemies, other than mankind. No creature in the sea will dare attack them.

Furthermore, when sea snakes from the Pacific find their way into the waters of the Atlantic, the same thing happens. The sharks die and, after a while, sharks in the Atlantic learn to avoid sea snakes, too. Check it out. It's true.

When I got back home, I felt dizzy and my equilibrium was out of balance. I'd never had anything like that happen to me ever before in my life, and it worried me. I saw a neurologist, something I'd never done before, and I submitted to an MRI.

Anyone who has ever had a full-body MRI knows what that is like, and it's no day at the beach. You're put in a cylinder that is about as long as you are tall, and your nose is about an inch from the top. Your arms have very little room on the sides. At first, I couldn't do it, and I had them pull me out. I convinced myself that I had to do it, and I went back in. It was as unpleasant a half-hour of my life as I can remember.

The neurologist told me that I had probably contracted what is called a "South Sea virus," and it could return at any time. There is no medicine to combat it. He wished me good luck and sent me home. Fortunately, the symptoms went away and they have never returned – yet.

Before I left for Australia, I promised my son, Brendan, who was four years old at the time, that I'd take him to Australia with me the next time I went. After returning, I told him I was going to take him to Ireland, instead. The trip to Australia was just too long. I gave him a koala bear that I had bought. We named it Kevin. I don't think he still has it, but he might.

I had other interesting cases while working for Therell, Baisden and Meyer, Weiss, but none could compare to the Bangstick case. Another memorable one was when the owner of Capital Bank in Miami wanted the penthouse suite of his bank building, where his office was located, tiled with pure white Italian marble. A relatively small tile contractor agreed to provide the tile.

However, once it was installed, there were plenty of tile with what are called "tiger stripes" in them. The owner refused to accept the tile, saying it did not conform to the contract. The contractor said it was impossible to have that much tile, and it was a huge area atop the large building, one of the largest in the Miami skyline, that was all white. This was <u>after</u> the tile had been installed.

There was a huge legal battle over that issue – did the finished job "substantially" conform to the contract, or was the work sub-standard? Neither side would budge. After years of litigation, the case somehow resolved. I can't remember exactly what happened, but I think the little guy declared bankruptcy and his insurance company paid the limits of the policy. Neither side was happy and, again, the case never went to trial.

Compared to working for Kevin handling medical malpractice cases, working for Howard was truly pleasurable. However, two years after I got there, Howard sustained a life-threatening heart attack, rendering him unable to work. He underwent successful open-heart surgery, but the firm fired him, because he was no longer able to perform his legal duties to their satisfaction.

That was the wrong thing to do, and it certainly wasn't a kindly thing to do, but that's what they did. He filed suit against the law firm, and won, but it took years to accomplish that result. Another result of the firing of Howard was that I was let go, too. I came in because of Howard, and when he was no longer there, neither was I.

I wasn't all that displeased with what had happened to me, and very relieved to know that Howard would recover, except for the fact that I no longer had a job and, therefore, no income, which was a fairly catastrophic situation since I now had four children. I really didn't like the work all that much. In commercial litigation cases, you push a whole lot of paper, and then settle. I was a trial lawyer. It really wasn't a good place for me.

During the two years from the time I left Kevin's office to the time I left Howard's office, which was from early 1988 until early 1990, a very significant event occurred, and I had no idea at the time that it would lead to an enormous change in my life in the years to come, but it did – I authored and had published a book about tennis. It was called <u>A Parent's Guide to Coaching Tennis</u>, and it was published by a company called Betterway.

It's actually quite ironic how all of that came to be, and it really was a matter of finding a silver lining in what was an unfortunate situation. I broke an ankle while playing softball in our North Miami league and was laid up for eight weeks because of it. I was able to go to work with a cast on my foot after a week or so, but I was on crutches and had to keep my leg up to prevent further swelling while it healed.

I was a first baseman my whole life, being left-handed, but I became a pitcher on the team during those years. I would always run around the infield, wherever a play was being made and I would routinely cover the plate when there were plays at home. So a runner was trying to score from second base on a single to center field, but our center fielder, Larry Zolot, had a powerful arm and he threw the ball to me in plenty of time to get the runner out.

However, this guy from the other team thought he could leap over me, as I was down on one knee, fielding the throw, and avoid the tag, but he was wrong. He didn't make it over me. He landed on top of me.

The force of his body hitting my upper torso caused me to be thrown backwards over my right ankle. I was not even close to being in the basepath, but he thought that was his best chance of avoiding the tag. I was wearing cleats and my right foot was stuck in the clay.

The result was my ankle was broken. I continued to play and finished the game, moving around like a mummy, dragging my right foot behind me. I knew something was seriously wrong, but I didn't know how bad it was. The ankle continued to throb through the night and when I went to my doctor the next morning, the diagnosis was confirmed.

Fortunately, it was a non-compounded fracture and all they had to do was immobilize the ankle and put a cast on it – no surgery. They gave me some pain pills, crutches, and sent me on my way. I was told to come back if the pain worsened but, otherwise, he'd see me in a month, as I recall.

So I'd been teaching tennis to children at the Miami Shores Community Center ever since we moved back to Florida from West Virginia, and I decided to write down things that I routinely told both the parents and the children – the simple things, like racket back, turn to the side, step in and hit; how to hold the racket; how to swing the racket – things like that, the basics, and so I began what became a much more involved process than I thought it would be.

I don't think that the idea of writing a book was even my intention, at first. I think I envisioned writing a pamphlet, something short and to the point, that I could hand out. Also, I don't believe that the thought that I would become an author ever entered my mind at that point in time. This was something about tennis and I was a tennis player who knew what I was talking about.

A father of one of the children in my tennis leagues, a man named Victor Quinaz, operated a printing business and I talked to him about what it would cost to create a pamphlet like that. He gave me an idea as to what it would cost, but told me that it depended upon how many pages the pamphlet would be. He also said that it would depend upon how many pictures were in the book, whether they were color or black and white, and a bunch of other things that I hadn't given much thought to.

Also, my good friend, Von Beebe, who I had met back in 1973 at Moore Park, when I first met Bobby Curtis, had just written a book entitled <u>Bilingual Education and the Miami Experience</u>. He was the principal at Coconut Grove Elementary School at the time and he was at the forefront of the problem educators were having in educating children in the Dade County public schools who didn't speak English. Many, many Spanish-speaking children from South and Central America were flooding into South Florida at the time. I sought his assistance, too.

It wasn't anywhere near as easy as I thought it would be. I knew the game of tennis better than anything else in the world. I truly thought it would be a piece of cake. I was wrong.

When Victor read my first draft, his initial response was how many big words were in there and how difficult it was for him to understand. He was Portuguese by birth, but spoke English fluently. I realized that I needed to simplify things to the lowest denominator. Still, it wasn't all that easy.

When I was able, even before the cast came off, actually, I was back on the court, hitting balls. Obviously, I couldn't run, or move much at all, so it was mostly drills where I could hit from a stationary position. Von would get out on the court with me and we'd hit for an hour or so, and then we'd go drink a beer and talk about my book. He became my editor.

After many months, and after creating what I thought was a decent draft, I began the process of finding a publisher. I looked at other books about tennis to see who published them, and bought books on how to find a publisher. There's a lot to that, as I soon discovered. I sent out the "query" letters, as required.

Also, I set about finding someone to write the Foreword to my book. My first choice was Jimmy Evert, father of Chris and four other children, all of whom became champions. The Youth Tennis Foundation had created an "Evert Award" in honor of the family. He was a friend and a very nice man.

Anyone who knew Jimmy, and he's now long gone, knew that he was a humble, gentle, soft-spoken man. When I asked him to do it, he said, "I don't that kind of thing, Pierce. Get Nick (Bollettieri) to do it." I told him I didn't want Nick to do it. I wanted him.

Somewhat reluctantly, after reading my book, he told me to prepare a draft of what I wanted him to say and he'd think about it. However, he said that I had to change a significant part of the book before he would do it. He didn't like the continental grip which I advocated, since the children wouldn't have to change grips to hit different shots. He was adamant that the Eastern forehand and backhand was the <u>only</u> grip to teach a beginning youngster.

Chris was married to John Lloyd from England at the time and he hit with a continental forehand, as I did and as John McEnroe did. Jimmy went on and on about how John Lloyd couldn't generate enough power with that grip and how flawed it was. In hindsight, he was right, it was a flawed grip, and I don't think anyone uses it now, but McEnroe did pretty well with it, and I didn't do too badly, either. I was only concerned with what to teach a beginning player. I agreed to make the change.

Essentially, what I had done was just have a beginning youngster hold the racket with one grip and not have to constantly change grips from forehand to backhand. My feeling was that it complicated the process for the little kids I was working with. If they showed interest, and promise, I thought it would be an easy thing to change to the eastern grips once the child grew a little. I still do, but Jimmy didn't agree, so I made the change in the text.

Jimmy revised my draft and signed off on the Foreword. I was, and I will always remain, grateful to him for doing so. In fact, the Youth Tennis Foundation still has an "Evert Award" to this date. We pay the tuition for a boy and a girl to attend a one week summer camp at the Evert Academy, which costs us about $2,000 for each child.

The male receives the Jimmy Evert award and the female receives the Collette Evert award. One thing I learned from Jimmy, or maybe it was his oldest child, Drew, who told me, and that was that after Jimmy gave a lesson to each of his five children every afternoon, the child would go over to the next court and hit with Collette for half an hour. They were a team. She was a wonderful person, too.

There was no doubt that my book had a much better chance of being favorably received by prospective publishers because of Jimmy's endorsement. It gave me instant credibility. Chris' career officially began in December of 1972 and it ended in 1989, the year my book came out. She was, and still is, an international celebrity.

Chris was born in Fort Lauderdale, Florida, in 1954 and she is seven years younger than I am, but I was playing in the juniors until 1965 and I had met Jimmy, Colette and their children during those years. She is the second oldest in the family, and her older brother, Drew, was the doubles partner of Ricky Fagel, who was the son of Herman Fagel, the tennis pro at the Miami Shores Community Tennis Courts, where I played a lot of tennis way back when.

My book was a good one. It's now "old school," because just about everyone on tour hits semi-western forehands and two-handed backhands nowadays. Hardly anyone hits with either of the Eastern grips or the continental grips anymore.

I was pleasantly surprised to receive a favorable response almost immediately. Betterway Publications wanted to publish my book and I was to be given a $5,000 advance to do so, but the publisher told me that I had to add some more pages. I gladly agreed to do so.

While I was doing that, and before formally accepting his offer, I received a phone call from the head of Simon and Schuster, who expressed interest in my book. He said, "I like your book, but many on my staff don't like it as much as I do. I'm not sure about it, so that's why I'm calling you. I can do it whether they approve or not. I'm just not sure."

The man from Betterway was pressuring me, saying that I had to let him know within so many days or else he would withdraw his offer. He had a "Parents Guide" series and he wanted my book on tennis. He had books on baseball, basketball, football, golf and so forth already in print or in production.

I made a mistake. I took the "bird in hand" and that's what I told the man from Simon and Schuster. I should have flown to New York and met with the man, but I didn't. I wish I had, but I didn't. I regret that. I had four children and not that much money for me to fly to New York with hope and a prayer.

So the book came out a few months later, after I added more chapters and made edits. Not long after, I received a telephone call from my sister, Carol, who told me that my book had received a favorable review in Tennis magazine, the premiere world-wide publication for tennis players. Although she wasn't an athlete, she always followed my career and supported me in every way she could.

Tennis magazine called my book "THE perfect introduction and primer for parents of beginning players." I couldn't have said it better myself if I was allowed to write the review. I couldn't have asked for more. I couldn't have BOUGHT that kind of review. I hadn't even submitted my book to them and asked them to review it. The publisher must have done that.

The success of my book came out of the clear blue. I was shocked. Needless to say, I was delighted to actually see it in print, when I was able to locate a copy of the magazine and saw it with my own eyes.

However, if only I had stayed with Simon and Schuster, I am absolutely certain that my book would have become an international sensation. Unfortunately, I hadn't done that, and it didn't. Betterway did absolutely nothing to promote my book.

However, the United States Tennis Association also reviewed it and called it the "Perfect Introduction and primer for parents of beginning players," too. Bill Colson, a senior editor from Sports Illustrated, who had been on my team that won the National City Team event back in 1965, favorably reviewed it, as well, as did several newspaper sportswriters and tennis luminaries.

Despite my mistake, my book did sell, and it did reasonably well, just not nearly as well as it could have. I think that I've sold over 20,000 copies, but that didn't translate into too much money. I didn't write the book to make money, but I sure would have been happy to make as much as possible.

Regardless, it was a success and I was proud of it. I still am, although it's now out-dated. Tennis is an entirely different game nowadays due to the change in the size of the racket face, the composition of the rackets (no more wooden ones), and the strings, among other things.

Also, during that period of time, I continued to work as an adjunct professor at colleges in the Miami area, teaching paralegal students, as I had done in West Virginia for several years. I needed the money, and I enjoyed the work.

Patrick was now ten years old and he was becoming a good athlete. He was tall for his age, which was predictable, since Christine was 5'11" tall, and I was 6'3". Meagan was eight, and she, too, was tall for her age. Both were playing in the tennis league I had created, as well as soccer, baseball/ softball and basketball, and both were good swimmers.

Brendan was six, and still a little young for any organized sport, but he was always around, participating in one way or another. Caitlin, now four, was a water bug. The problem with her was that she was totally fearless at first, unafraid, or unaware of the fact that she might drown. She was now old enough that she knew how to swim and would, before too long, become an excellent swimmer.

However, I had lost a job and I had to feed those growing children. Someone once asked me what I fed them to make them grow so much. I told them it was hamburgers, french fries and cokes, which wasn't too far from the truth. McDonald's "Happy Meals" and pizzas were always on the menu. I had to find another job, and fast. That was 1991 and I was 44 years old.

Chapter Fifteen

1991-1994 – Years of Transition

It was about that time that I began to think that I should move the family back to the west coast of Florida. That was where Christine's family was from, and I had many good friends in the Clearwater/St. Petersburg area, like the Jaggers and the Dohertys, together with many tennis playing friends. Miami had changed dramatically over the years and there were now more people who spoke Spanish as their native language than there were those who didn't.

Please don't misunderstand, the city of Miami and Dade County were then and they still are vibrant communities. Coconut Grove was a huge attraction to the rest of the country in the late sixties and into the seventies, and then South Beach became the "mecca" for the new culture that had emerged. Money was pouring into the area from all across the globe but, primarily, it was coming from Central and South America.

The last time I walked around the downtown area where the state and federal courthouses are located, there were seventy (70!), or more, large cranes all around me, as new high-rise buildings were being constructed. The area was, and still is, booming. Miami was becoming a metropolis, much like New York City had been at the turn of the prior century.

Since I was out of a job at the moment, it was an opportune time to look for employment in Pinellas County. My Legal Services background came into play, again, and I was offered a job with Gulfcoast Legal Services in their St. Petersburg office.

It was located directly across the street from the airport and less than a mile from Al Lang field, where major league teams such as the St. Louis

Cardinals, Baltimore Orioles and New York Yankees had been playing spring training games since the early 1900s. It was a nice location and I was to be the managing attorney.

As with every other Legal Services program I had been with, the office provided legal assistance in the areas of landlord-tenant, consumer, divorce, social security, unemployment compensation and child custody cases, among other things, but this office also had attorneys who specialized in matters relating to senior citizens. St. Petersburg was renowned as a desirable destination for retirees, because of the warm weather and beautiful beaches.

Since my employment predicament arose so suddenly, I didn't have the time, or the money, to find a home for my family. I couldn't afford to buy a new home until I sold the house in Miami Shores, where we were living. Plus, the kids were in school and it was going to take some planning to figure things like that out.

So I would get up at 4:30 in the morning on Monday mornings and drive across Alligator Alley towards Naples, and then up I-75 to get to south St. Petersburg, just over the Sunshine Skyway Bridge, a notoriously high and large structure. That was a four and a half hour drive and I would arrive by 9:00, ready to go to work. I'd drive back to Miami Shores on Friday afternoons and spend weekends there. During the week, I stayed at Christine's sister's house. She and her husband, Joe, had a large house with an extra bedroom.

After my days at the Federal Public Defender's office handling that huge trial, and then the days with Kevin O'Connor, handling major medical malpractice cases against some of the best lawyers in the state, and then the two years of commercial litigation involving some large corporate clients and some extremely wealthy individuals, Gulfcoast Legal Services was a much different legal environment, to say the least. It was going to take a major adjustment on my part. John Cunningham, the director of the program, was hoping that I could help develop the legal skills of his attorneys and paralegals. No one in the office had ever tried a case in front of a jury.

Attorneys who work for Legal Services programs have a different skill set from all other attorneys, actually. They do what they do because they have a social conscience and they truly want to help the poor and underprivileged. The clientele is, by definition and according to Federal mandate, poor. There are, without any doubt whatsoever, some major psychological and sociological issues which the poor in our country confront on a daily basis, one of which being self-esteem.

Clients would routinely fail to show up for appointments, or for hearings in court, due to one catastrophe or another. A car breaking down, a sudden and unexpected illness, an eviction, an arrest, a domestic dispute – the list goes on and on – were all reasons for that. Money can't solve all problems, but it sure can help. None of the clients had any of that – money, that is - and that was, almost always, the root cause of their problems.

My job, as the managing attorney, was to supervise the work of all of the attorneys and the paralegals, as well as the support staff, which consisted of secretaries, receptionists and clerks. I think there were over twenty-five people in the office, including the director and an attorney who specialized in appeals. It's not easy being a "boss," and I struggled with the responsibilities I'd been given. It wasn't easy to criticize people who simply didn't have the same background and experience I'd had in my legal career. I rubbed some people the wrong way, but others were very happy with me.

While there, I successfully tried a case before a jury in Circuit Court, which was a rarity for the office. It involved a disabled woman, who was in a wheelchair. She carried an oxygen cannister in her lap. She was also a smoker, too. The judge wasn't happy with her and made her sit outside of the courtroom at times, which really wasn't appropriate, but that's what he did.

I solved one of her problems, but she had a multitude of other problems to deal with that I couldn't help with. That was a typical result. Poverty isn't pretty.

I also filed a major housing discrimination case in Federal Court in another case. A landlord refused to rent to an African-American woman who had a large number of children. While understandable, perhaps, since the landlord was receiving federal funds under a special housing grant, he couldn't simply deny the woman housing because of the size of the household, but he did. We won that case at the trial level, but it lost on appeal, after I left.

I was missing my family and I tired of the drive after six months. The four kids were a bit much for Christine and I wasn't there to help. Nor could I watch and participate with their athletic activities, although the Saturday tennis clinics were still going on. I wasn't happy with my circumstances and started looking around for another job.

Another unfortunate aspect of being a Legal Services lawyer was the pay. It was much less than attorneys receive in virtually every other area of law. Though I was being paid more than anyone else in the office, except for John Cunningham, it wasn't enough. I was going to have to find a job in the Miami area and move back home.

I found a job with an insurance defense firm that had an opening in its office in Islamorada, at mile marker 82 on U.S. 1 in the Keys. My years of working with Kevin O'Connor helped me to get that job, but it was a different type of law. This firm dealt mostly with auto accident cases, slips and falls, and personal injury cases not involving any medical malpractice claims.

Also, Islamorada is about an hour and a half from Miami Shores, and I had to drive right through the heart of Miami to get there. I commuted back and forth for a while, but that was grueling. After a while, I found a place to sleep down there during the week.

It was a small office, with two attorneys and two secretaries, and I was the senior attorney, even though I had no experience handling some of the cases. I inherited some cases that were set for trial but hadn't been properly developed, and that was a problem. Also, that office was responsible for all cases in the Keys from Key West to Key Largo, a distance of over a hundred miles on a two lane road, one in each direction. Traffic was always a problem.

Insurance companies don't pay their lawyers too well, but they give lawyers a whole bunch of cases, so law firms make their money by handling a large volume of cases. In other words, it was a "sweat shop," and I knew it, but I really had no choice. I wanted to get back to being with my family.

I had some interesting cases to work on while there, though, and one of my favorite of all time involved a lawsuit arising from a "swimming with the dolphins" incident. At the time, there were only four places on the planet which allowed people to swim with dolphins, to my knowledge.

That is what I was told by Jayne Rodriguez, the owner of the facility located in Marathon.

A couple from Philadelphia came down to swim with the dolphins but the adventure ended badly when the dolphin swam between the two and broke the woman's ribs and the man's wrist. The dolphin "trainer" told the two to fully extend their arms so that they would be about five feet away from each other. The dolphin would swim between them, and one would hold onto the dorsal fin and go for a ride of about a hundred yards in a fenced area. Those were the instructions.

However, these two didn't follow directions and left only a couple of feet between them. The dolphin, which weighed about six hundred pounds, and could travel at speeds up to thirty some knots, did what it was told to do and made contact with both swimmers due to the small area between the two. The dolphin did nothing wrong. The swimmers did and, maybe, so did the trainer. That was their claim, that the trainer didn't properly train them how to behave.

The legal issue in the case was whether or not the "release" which the couple had signed before getting in the water was valid. Both signed documents saying that they "accepted the risk" of swimming with a dolphin and released the facility from any liability if they were injured. If the release was valid, as it appeared to be, they couldn't bring a lawsuit. They would have "released" their right to file a lawsuit and they would have "agreed" to accept the risk that is inherent in swimming with a dolphin.

It was much like the ones people must sign to go on a trail ride, or jump out of an airplane, or do any number of somewhat dangerous activities. Except this particular release did not specifically mention the word "negligence." Normally, the release will say that the individual "releases" any claim which he or she might have as a result of the "negligence" of the operator. Most people sign the documents thinking that they won't hold up in court, but they do.

However, the Third District Court of Appeal ruled that since the release these two people signed didn't specifically include the word "negligence," the release was ineffective. In doing so, that sent the case back to the Circuit Court for trial. That's where I came in. I had nothing to do with anything that happened before I got there.

As far as the claim of negligence was concerned, there was a problem because a dolphin, and all dolphins, are considered "wild animals." The owner or keeper of a "wild animal" is <u>strictly liable</u> no matter what the circumstances surrounding any injuries caused by coming in contact with a "wild animal," as a general rule. Therefore, Jayne Rodriguez and the Dolphin Research Center, or their insurance company, to be more exact, would be liable to the Philadeldphia Couple.

Again, it was an extremely interesting case. As I began to investigate the case, I learned that this particular dolphin had been one of the dolphins used on the television show, Flipper, which everyone in the world was aware of. Over the years, there had been about half a dozen dolphins to do that.

Furthermore, I was provided with a reel of film showing this particular dolphin in a pool with some severely handicapped children who could do no more than float, with flotation devices holding them up. This dolphin swam right up to those young children, who looked to be no more than seven or eight years old, and stuck his rostrum, or snout, right in the children's face, inches away. It was an incredible thing to behold.

I was convinced that, while it may be true that dolphins are wild animals, this particular dolphin was <u>not</u> a wild animal. He was as gentle as could be. Also, I wasn't convinced that dolphins are wild animals. True, they weren't friendly farm animals which are kept in a barn, but had any dolphin ever hurt any human being ever in the history of mankind? Not to my knowledge. Besides, the dolphin did nothing wrong in this particular case.

I really enjoyed meeting that dolphin, Jayne Rodriguez and her entire staff. It was, and still is, a wonderful place doing special work. Dolphin are magnificent creatures, even if they are considered to be "wild animals" by the legal world.

However, she was afraid that any adverse publicity would be bad for her business. Plus, she was dealing with the Federal government and they were all worried about the efficacy of the entire concept of swimming with dolphins. It was still an experimental project, to some extent. In the end, the insurance company paid for the couples medical expenses and that was the end of the case.

Another interesting case involving animals which I handled while in that office had a baby elephant as the alleged culprit. A baby elephant can weigh up to two hundred pounds and stands about three feet off the ground not long after birth. As they age, they put on a whole lot of weight and can grow to weigh as much as fifteen thousand pounds and as high as thirteen feet tall. The elephant in this case was still a baby, but it weighed a few hundred pounds and was about three feet high.

A man was transporting this elephant from Texas to Florida to its new owner, who lived somewhere in the southern part of Dade County, right at the Monroe county line. Monroe County was established in 1823, while James Monroe, our fifth president, was in office (1817-1825). The "Keys" are Monroe County. I was given the case.

Again, the holder and keeper of a wild animal is strictly liable for any injuries caused by the wild animal. However, in this case, the man who was transporting the baby elephant was hitting the elephant with a club, trying to get the elephant to load in a trailer. There were witnesses to corroborate how the incident happened, but after several minutes of beating on the elephant, it turned on the man and rammed him up against one of the posts to the fence in which it was contained, killing the man.

I felt like this case should have been an "exception" to the general rule under those facts. Also, since the man died, the case for wrongful death was brought by his wife, but they were in the midst of a nasty divorce proceeding. Further, the person I was assigned to defend, who was the man who had purchased and paid for the elephant, had never officially "received" the elephant. It was being delivered to him when the incident occurred. If the purchaser, my client, was found liable, a jury would have to assess how much money the woman was entitled to.

I wanted to try that case, but the insurance company was afraid of a large verdict, so it settled the case for a couple of hundred thousand dollars before trial. Only about three percent of civil cases filed actually go to trial. It's not easy for an attorney to get trial experience, except in the criminal arena, where trials are more common. I had much more trial experience than most civil attorneys at that stage of life, because of all of the criminal cases I had tried.

I really didn't like working for insurance companies, but I was pretty good at doing the job of being a trial lawyer. I was as nervous as anyone could be when I first began, and I used to have to write out and then read my closing arguments to a jury. It took a long time to cultivate the skills necessary to be a trial lawyer, but I had paid my dues and I wasn't too bad at it.

I liked working in the Keys and I liked the "Conch Republic." It was a fun place to practice law and the food was outstanding, what with fresh caught fish being sold everywhere. I represented the "Sloppy Joe's" restaurant, too, which is a landmark in Key West because it was one of Ernest Hemingway's many "haunts" from his days there. I have many funny stories to tell from those days.

For example, the chief judge at the time was a woman, and she was a very nice woman and a good judge. However, I confess to being more than a little surprised when she was on the front page of the local newspaper leading the parade, appearing to be naked. Actually, she had the spray on paint thing going on, but I don't think you'd find that happening anywhere else in the country, other than San Francisco, I'll bet.

Another example of that was when I met the Federal Magistrate for the Southern District of Florida. I walked into his chambers, inside the courthouse, all dressed up in coat, tie and wing-tipped shoes, as all lawyers do when appearing before a judge or magistrate. When I walked in I was shocked to see him in blue jeans and a polo shirt. It was somewhat rare for judges not to have the black robes on, even in chambers. Again, that could only happen in the Keys.

Another Key West story, which I had absolutely nothing to do with, but it is the "lore of the land," involved the former sheriff of Key West who was said to be "swimming with the fishes." That was before I got there, but it was still legendary stuff. His name was Bum Farto. It was. You can look it up. He was, allegedly, selling drugs out of the trunk of his police car. Apparently, he ran afoul of the wrong group of criminals and hasn't been seen in decades.

Yet another time I was trying a case for the Monroe County School Board, but we ran short of jurors. We had a venire of fifteen people, but after picking jurors and kicking some off, we were left with five. The clerk went out on the street trying to find someone to come sit on our case. That wasn't kosher, but it was funny.

The Keys are a place to eat, drink and be merry – and fish. I've never been a fisherman, and I was just more interested in my children and their athletic endeavors. I never really fit in with the "Conchs," as they were called. They are a different breed. They eat, drink and fish, and they are a merry band of people.

There were tennis courts and tennis players in the Keys, too, and I knew them all. After work, I'd be out on the tennis courts. The only time I went fishing was when one of my clients took me out. It was and it still is a fisherman's paradise. One of my idols as a child was Ted Williams of the Boston Red Sox, and he fished in the Keys for decades after his baseball career ended.

Some lawyers assigned to work the Keys would think that they died and went to heaven. That wasn't me. After I showed the owners of the firm that I could try a case, they transferred me up to the Miami office, which was just fine with me. They had a whole lot more cases in Miami than the Keys, that was for sure.

Just before I left the Islamorada office, however, hurricane Andrew struck. That was August 24, 1992. I was in the Keys office that very night, hours earlier, trying to protect the office and my files from what was projected to be a category 5 storm. I'd been there the whole day before it struck and even within a few hours of when it actually made landfall. The eye of the storm hit Florida City, 25 miles south of downtown Miami, at 4:52 a.m. I left the office at about 10:00 the night before.

Fortunately, the storm spared the office and most of the Keys, except for the uppermost part, just north of Key Largo. Homestead and South Dade bore the brunt of the damage, which was catastrophic. I felt guilty about it because I was still working, being a lawyer, while the whole community was reeling, and humanitarian aid was being rushed in from all across the state and country. The law office just kept pushing out paper and doing its job. It was a "sweatshop" and I was required to keep pumping out the work.

The Miami legal scene was and still is much different from the court system in the Keys, by a long shot. Several million people were living in Dade County, and millions more in Broward and Palm Beach counties, which I was also required to cover, whereas less than a hundred thousand people lived in the Keys back then. The number of cases, judges, lawyers, people and cars in Miami made things much more difficult. The commute to the office was shorter, but I had to go through heavy congestion both to and from work, as I was now in traffic jams both in the morning and the afternoon.

Representing clients on behalf of their insurance companies was difficult, and stressful, but I enjoyed many of the courtroom battles and the legal challenges. I had many interesting cases and a number of jury trials. When asked what type of law I practiced, or what kind of lawyer I was, I continue to say that I was a trial lawyer, and I was.

One of my favorite cases that I tried in Miami involved representing a man who was an officer in the Florida Department of Law Enforcement, or FDLE. He was a co-defendant, along with a City of Miami police officer and two Dade County Sheriff deputies who were alleged to have violated the rights of an African-American man in a drug bust that went bad. Some people were killed and the claim had racial overtones to it. It was a high profile case in the community.

After two weeks of trial, my client was dismissed from the case by the plaintiffs' attorneys, who said that they didn't want to hear me say another word. That was a high compliment, and I appreciated it. I wasn't the best defense attorney by any means, but I was competent and I always tried to do the best I could on every case.

By 1993, I had proven myself to the powers that be in the law firm, that was expanding to more parts of the state and now had ten offices scattered around Florida, and I convinced them to open an office in Clearwater. They told me that I was the best trial attorney in their firm and that I would be asked to help try cases across the state, where necessary, while the Clearwater office built up its caseload.

We moved in the summer of 1993, and this time we did so with some forethought and planning. I was able to sell our house to some friends and buy a house before actually moving. As anyone who has ever moved knows, it's a long, hard process to pack up everything you own and then move everything into a new house.

I left Miami Shores, driving a rental truck with all of our earthly possessions, in late August, headed for the Tarpon Springs/East Lake area of Pinellas County. We would arrive in time for school to start and the kids were already enrolled when we arrived. Unfortunately, I didn't make it. On the drive over, the truck broke down and we had to be towed the last 200 miles. That was an omen of things to come.

By that time, Patrick was 13 and would be 14 in October. Meagan had just turned 12. Brendan was about to turn 10 and Caitlin was 7 years old. It was a big move for them, and leaving behind their friends and the only home that they really knew, was difficult for them, I'm sure. I wanted to make the move before they got too much older, when it would have been even more difficult for them, and they would have been much more vocal about their opposition to the move.

Also, there were some excellent schools in what was a relatively new section of Pinellas County. A brand-new high school had opened up the year before, where the children of Christine's brother, Kenny, were enrolled, and it was outstanding. I thought it was a perfect place for them, and for us, to live.

At first, I opened an office in Tarpon Springs, not too far from the house, in an office-sharing building with other lawyers. There was a common area for meetings or depositions, plus a photocopier and fax machine, and a receptionist who answered calls for all of the attorneys. Not long thereafter, the firm bought a building in Clearwater on a golf course, which was much nicer.

It took some time to develop a case load, and that gave me time to spend watching my children play sports. Patrick had become quite good at basketball and baseball, and he had grown to be over 6' tall early on. Meagan, too, had above average height, and she liked soccer and tennis. Brendan was good at everything, while Caitlin had become an excellent swimmer. She liked soccer, too.

As is evident, it was a challenge to get to all of the events. Every now and then, soccer games would be at the same facility but, usually, they were all over the place. Nothing, with the exception of watching very young girls playing softball, is as difficult to watch as a swimming meet. You wait for hours, seemingly, for your child to swim, and the race is over in less than a minute. I became a professional spectator, but I enjoyed those days.

I re-acquainted with some tennis playing friends and found time at odd hours to play. Before too long, I became a coach of at least one of every child's teams. That was a difficult, and thankless, job. Everyone thinks that their child will be the next super-star in whatever sport it was. If a child doesn't excel, it was the coach's fault.

However, things began to unravel between Christine and me. We had been a really good match while living in West Virginia, because she was so good at living life on a farm, and she wasn't too happy when we left. She had made good friends in Miami Shores, and wasn't too happy when I decided to move back to the west coast. That was my decision, and though we talked about it, she didn't agree with me on that, even though that's where all of her family was, and where she grew up.

There were other problems, too. We didn't agree on many issues relating to raising children, and we didn't present with a unified approach to the children, which wasn't good. Also, when differences arose, we didn't handle them well.

I can't blame them all on her, and I don't, because I can definitely be hard-headed about things. Regardless, for whatever the reasons, which I won't go into, I left the house and found myself an apartment not far away. That was in late 1994.

I made more money during my last year of work in Miami than at any other time in my life, before or since. I made a fraction of that during my first year of work in Pinellas County. I couldn't afford two houses and my financial situation worsened quickly. All of the children took Christine's side in what had occurred, blaming me, and my relationship with all of my children deteriorated dramatically.

As I look back on my life, that period of time, from 1994 until 2000, was the worst, so far. Things could still get worse, right? I'm not dead yet.

I was miserable at work, miserable at home, and unhappy in almost all aspects of my life, except for tennis. That was my only release. I had made a few friends, who weren't all that good, who I began playing with, and that was my only release from all the stress that I was under.

I really didn't want to get divorced, because of how it affected my relationship with my children, but Humpty-Dumpty had fallen and there was nothing that could put Humpty-Dumpty back together again. There was no way to salvage the relationship, or the marriage, and no way I could repair the relationship with my children. They were all teenagers by then and that didn't help matters at all. I would go to watch all of their sporting events, but they wouldn't even acknowledge my presence at times. That was an extremely difficult time of life, as I said before.

Being so miserable and unhappy as I was had a positive side effect – an unanticipated consequence, if you will. I began to run – a lot, and for a long time. I'd always run just to help me be a better tennis player, but I'd run sprints, jump rope, run the lines of the court, and then do a mile, at most. Now, I started to run 5ks.

My friend, Patrick Doherty, had a New Year's Eve party in December of 1994 and I went, solo. At the party, probably in some degree of insobriety, we made a pact to run a marathon in Dublin, Ireland in October of 1995. Patrick had continued to run religiously, ever since we ran that marathon in Miami in 1978, but I hadn't.

As I recall, it was my idea, and that's what we agreed to do. I began in earnest to get ready. He had done an Ironman in Hawaii a few years earlier. That was quite an accomplishment. If I was still around, I'd have run it with him, I'm sure.

Over the next nine months, we ran dozens of 5ks, several 10ks, a 15k in the Gasparilla event in Tampa, plus a half marathon in Miami. Also, every Saturday morning, I'd get up at 5:00 or so, drive an hour to meet Patrick, and we'd run 18 miles.

He would always leave a bottle of Gator-aid at the half way mark, under a bus bench. After running the 18 miles, we'd go to Bob Evans and eat a breakfast that absolutely surpassed whatever amount of calories we had burned, and it tasted great. I wasn't worried about my weight at the time, but I often wondered about the wisdom of what we were doing. It seemed to me to be self-defeating.

In October, Pat, his wife, Marlene, and I, flew to Dublin to run the marathon. We had a great time. He still had relatives there, in the area of Cashel, and we visited them, too, before the race. We took a ferry out to the Aran Islands and did all kinds of things, that being my first time on the "auld sod."

Unfortunately, on the morning of the race, I walked down the stairs and saw Patrick, in street clothes, looking like death warmed over. He'd gotten sick overnight and couldn't run. That was a disappointment for both of us. I would have to run the race by myself.

One humorous anecdote from that race, which was more like a "survivor" challenge than a competition, occurred at mile eighteen of the event. That part of a marathon is called "The Wall" by those who run marathons. Running by myself, I wasn't talking to anyone, and I was feeling tired and depressed.

So I walked into a bar, and there were many along the route, and asked the bartender for a beer, though I had no money. He gladly gave me one and, as I exited the bar, I saw a red-haired Irish girl run by. I immediately ran after her and ran the last eight miles with her. That's the truth. Thank you God!

I filed for divorce in early 1998 and we were divorced shortly thereafter. I gave her the house, so she could keep the children in the home I had bought for the family, and I kept all of the debt. That made my financial situation that much worse, but I was making more money. Still, it was a very difficult time of life from every aspect of life, and there was no other woman involved, either. My only friends were my buddies from tennis.

However, my eye-sight was worsening and I was swinging and missing high forehand shots. I didn't understand what was going on. My eye doctor, James P. Gills, who was one of the best opthalmologists in the country, told me that I had a cataract in my right eye. That's the eye that had been hit with a ball back when I was a senior in high school, and I was sure that was why the cataract had developed.

Dr. Gills had performed such procedures on the Reverend Billy Graham, as well as former president George H. W. Bush and other distinguished people. He was not only one of the best eye doctors in the country, he was a friend. He assured me that all would be well.

I was awake for the entire procedure, which involves removing the lens of my right eye that was clouded over by the cataract and inserting a clear artificial lens. Dr. Gills told me that if I felt anything at all, I should immediately let him know. My eye had been numbed, and I didn't feel a thing. When the surgery was over, Dr. Gills told me that I could go out and play that very day.

I didn't do that, but I played the next day and the difference was miraculous. I could see as well as ever. My left eye was fine, and I had a lens put in my right eye that was best for medium distances. I did that with tennis in mind. Within weeks, I was back to playing high quality tennis again.

Because I no longer had a family life, I began playing more tennis. I began entering tournaments again. I traveled to Pennsylvania to play the over 50 National Grass Court Championships at the Germantown Cricket Club, a magnificent facility which lived in the early 1900s and was a showcase of the opulence of those days, when only the rich could afford to be members and play there.

I stayed with my friend, Mike Mullan and his wife. He was still the coach of the Swarthmore men's team, and I did reasonably well, losing in the quarter-finals of both the singles and doubles events. There were several other senior divisions there at the same time, and I knew most of the players, but not all. Some were guys who hadn't played back in the juniors, college or beyond, but they were good athletes and had become good tennis players.

I also played the National Clay Court tournament, held in Sarasota, Florida later that year and did well there, too. I ended up being ranked in the top 25 players in the country and the top 5 in Florida. I had gained about forty pounds over my playing days, but I could still serve and volley as well as anyone.

Skinny guys who could run all day, hit drop shots and lobs and keep me on the court in long points were too tough for me. My style of play didn't age well. Nobody could serve and volley and do too well in the older divisions, except on the fast grass courts. I played at a high level for the next five years of so.

I didn't really care all that much about winning, since this was truly deja vu for me. I enjoyed seeing old friends and talking about the "old days" as much as anything else. I also enjoyed drinking beers at the end of the day, just as I did back when I was a young man. It was my "happy place." Don't get me wrong, I tried hard to win. I just wasn't as good as I had been, that's all.

Tennis had been the passion of my life from the time I started to play at age ten or eleven and it continues to be a huge part of my life to this day. At that time of my life, it was my salvation. My best friends in the world are from my tennis days.

The other main passion of my life, although it was dwindling a bit, was the legal profession. I had become a lawyer to help the less-fortunate in our society, and I had become both a public defender and a legal services, or legal aid, lawyer to do so. Both had disappointed me to some degree, and I had lost much of my naivete about being either a criminal defense lawyer or a legal services lawyer.

As far as the criminal arena was concerned, in the beginning, especially while working in the misdemeanor division, the crimes were much less serious than they became, once I advanced to the felony division. Some of the criminals I was being called upon to defend were truly hard to understand. Their problems stemmed from a number of different things – cultural, familial, genetics, nurturing, or a lack thereof, and a whole lot of societal issues, none of which could I, or anyone else, satisfactorily address.

It was difficult to truly embrace the idea that justice was being served or, more importantly, that I was doing a great service to the country by doing what I was called upon to do. I put my shoulder to the wheel and did my best. I don't know that I made any dent in the "war on poverty" that I joined way back in the late '60s. I certainly didn't make a "name" for myself in that regard, though I had my share of success stories.

In the civil arena, after Reagan's two terms in office from January 20, 1981 until January 20, 1989, followed by a four year stint with George H. Bush, ending in January of 1992, the entire Legal Services community had been decimated. Congress not only dramatically reduced funding for the programs, it also reduced the areas of law legal services attorneys could practice in. The "war" was being lost and there was nothing I could do to turn the tide of battle.

No fee-generating cases were permitted; no fee awards were allowed; there was no way for legal services programs to make money the way that private attorneys do and thereby generate money for the program and, thereby, improve it. Basically, legal services programs were given crumbs and told to make the best of the situation.

For the most part, attorneys in legal services programs helped people with divorces. Family law is just not an exciting area of law, it just isn't. It's life and death to those who are in the middle of the divorce battles, but for the lawyers it's just painful. People don't think with their brains, they think with their hearts, and it's almost always a heart-breaking process, especially for the children involved, with few legal issues of any consequence to argue about.

In the area of family law, there just wasn't much "meat" to sink your teeth into as a lawyer. Legal services attorneys did make some ground-breaking law in the areas of landlord-tenant and public housing, though, and, to a lesser extent, civil rights issues. Still, it wasn't all that rewarding for me on a personal level, and I had very few jury trials. As I have said several times now, trying cases before a jury was the most enjoyable part of being a lawyer for me, and being a legal services attorney didn't provide me with that opportunity too often.

So there I was, not happy about doing insurance defense work, no longer enthused about criminal law, or legal services work, or commercial litigation, either. So what was left? What was I to do?

I was still the managing attorney for the Clearwater office of the firm I was working for and I still enjoyed the opportunity to go to court and get in front of juries. Also, I enjoyed doing appellate work, especially when oral argument was involved, but I was still representing insurance companies no matter how you slice it. That wasn't why I became a lawyer. It wasn't satisfying what I saw to be my purpose for being a lawyer. I was unhappy with the practice of law, and my life, post-divorce, was still a mess.

A "silver lining," if you will, from those post-divorce days was that I had more time to myself. I was playing more tennis, as I've indicated, but I also found time to write another book. This time, it was about law.

I was teaching at the Tarpon Springs campus of St. Petersburg College, as I had for several years, in the area of Paralegal Studies, which was a growing industry. I taught Civil Litigation, usually, but I also taught some of the other subjects offered to paralegal students, such as Legal Research and Writing, Investigations, Business Law, and some other topics. I really didn't like the text that was provided to me by the school for my Civil Litigation class, so I decided to write my own text book.

As it so happened, I tried a case in Highlands County, which is located in the middle of the state, several hours from my office, in 1999, as I recall, while working for the insurance defense firm. Sebring is the county seat and it is most famous for its twelve hour endurance race for sports cars. The race has been held there at what is called an "International Speedway" since 1950.

The case involved a simple trip and fall at one of the large department stores. The woman fell and sustained some serious injuries to her neck and back and sought a substantial amount of money because of the alleged negligence of the store in failing to keep the aisles free from debris.

The case lasted for a full week and was hotly contested. I argued that the cause of the incident was the failure of the woman to watch her step. The attorney for the injured plaintiff argued that the store had left a box in the aisle and failed to properly maintain their place of business in doing so. It was a "premises liability" kind of case.

The jury returned a verdict in favor of my client, which pleased both my employer, the department store (client), and the insurance company. Needless to say, the injured plaintiff was devastated. It is a cliche', but "I was just doing my job." I didn't take pleasure in beating her or her attorney, who was a very nice man and a good lawyer.

There are several things that I remember quite vividly about that case that I think are worth sharing. First, while the jury was out, deliberating, the client and I walked down the hall to another courtroom where a man was on trial for a serious felony, and I can't remember what the charge was. I remember thinking that if the jury found that man guilty of the crime he was charged with, he was going to prison. If they found him innocent, he was going home to have dinner with his family. It put the differences between a criminal trial and a civil trial in sharp contrast.

Another memory is of the juror who was almost excused from the trial during the middle of my case. There are always a few "alternate" jurors who are selected and they sit with the rest of the jurors, listen to a case, and substitute in when a regular juror is excused. So there was someone who could take his place, but I didn't want to see him go. He was a rancher, and I knew that he was a man who had to be careful every minute of the day on his farm, where he had a large herd of cattle. I was sure that he, more than any other juror, knew all about being responsible for his own actions.

After returning to the courtroom from our lunch break one day, that juror told the court that he had to leave the courthouse and go back to his farm, because he had an emergency situation at the farm. When the judge asked what the emergency was, the man told him that one of his prized bulls was stuck in a culvert and couldn't get out. It was raining heavily that day, and the rancher said that if he didn't get the bull, which weighed about two tons, out right away that the bull was going to drown and he was going to be out of a whole lot of money. He said he would need to use a big tractor to get it out. He was as serious as a heart attack.

Fortunately, the judge agreed to recess the trial for the day and told everyone to come back at 8:00 the next morning. When we did, the rancher told us that the bull survived and everything was fine. As it turned out, he was elected the foreman and he was the one to sign the verdict.

Most importantly, for me, however, was that this case became the basis for the text book I would write on civil litigation. The case was a perfect example of how a civil case is litigated, from the time of injury to the time of trial and verdict. Since so many cases settle before trial, about ninety-seven percent, this case came along at exactly the right time for me.

After I wrote the book, which is entitled "Civil Litigation: A Case Study," I did as I had done with my tennis book and pitched it to publishers of text books. Again, I received a favorable response, together with a sizable advance and, within a year or so, the book was in print. It became the text book for my classes on Civil Litigation. Also, it was used by other colleges, as well.

Needless to say, I was delighted. The director of the program at St. Petersburg College was, too, since I was the first of their professors to publish a text book. I received many compliments for that effort and I am proud of that accomplishment.

I must admit that the success I enjoyed with the tennis book and the legal text book made me think, for the first time, that I had some talent. I had never really thought of myself as an author prior to that. These were two non-fiction books and I was writing about topics I knew well – tennis and law. I was inspired to start writing more, and I began to write some short stories.

At first, I just wrote some stories from my tennis playing days, like the one about Torque and that match I played in Aspen. I also wrote a story about my friend, Jim Wilson, drinking too much coffee that time in Denver. I wrote an article about what it was like being a player when the game opened up and players, like me, were allowed to compete for prize money. That really was a huge moment for the game of tennis, and for me.

Before that, everyone was an "amateur," unable to play for money as athletes were doing in football, baseball, basketball and golf, especially golf, among other sports, like bowling. There was the Jack Kramer tour, and the so-called "Handsome Eight" group, but for guys like me, when the game "opened up," it was an exciting time to be in the game.

The Vietnam War had diverted me from pursuing that dream of mine, and so did the tumultuous scenes playing out all over the country during those anti-war days. The country was changing. People were changing. It wasn't all that "cool" to be a professional athlete.

All of those various factors distracted me and caused me to lose focus. I no longer wanted to be a champion. I no longer was willing to pay the price necessary to become a champion. As Brian Gottfried and others had told me, and as I well knew, to be a champion you had to "eat, sleep and breathe it."

In fact, I wrote a short story on what it took to become a champion at about that time, which was in the early 2000s. My friend, Jim Martz, put the article in his Florida Tennis magazine and told me that it was one of the best pieces he had ever published. That, too, encouraged me into thinking that I had some talent as a writer.

Before I knew it, I had dozens of stories, some of which weren't all that good, but some were pretty good, or at least that's what others were telling me and that's what I thought. I wrote a story about that left-handed foul shot my college roommate had made to tie the NCAA record, and I wrote a story about my trip to Australia and sea snakes. I wrote another one about the swimming with the dolphin case, and one about being at the Grateful Dead concert with my tennis team. Stories were pouring out of me. Half a dozen of them were published in various magazines.

That's when I decided to write my first novel, and I decided to write it about a DUI case. Both of my two sons were now driving, as was my oldest daughter, but both sons were drinking more than they should have. I had no control over the situation and my now ex-wife didn't want to punish them for fear of losing them as "friends." She wanted them to "like" her. She refused to force them to go to counseling, even after one of them was arrested for excessive drinking.

I wanted both of them to understand the potential consequences of driving while under the influence of alcohol, which included not only the punishment, but the possibility of death or great bodily harm to themselves or others, not to mention the damage to vehicles, insurance premiums and the rest. I contrived a story of a high school football coach who was involved in an accident in which a man was killed, after the coach had a few drinks, but not that many. I wanted them understand the legal issues

175

and what a DUI trial is all about, and how a .08 reading comes about from consuming just a few beers, not a dozen, like they were doing.

I bought books on how to write a novel, how to develop characters, how to create a plot, how to find publishers, how to market books – all kinds of things. I read where an author should "write what he knows," and I knew all about those issues. I included the trial, and all parts of a trial, including picking a jury, opening statements, the prosecutor's case-in-chief, the defendant's case, jury instructions, closing arguments and jury deliberations. I wanted them, and everyone else who might read that book, to understand what a DUI trial was all about.

I had no idea what I was getting myself into. I thought I would breeze through the process, much like I had with the tennis book and the text book on civil litigation. I was wrong, but the process had begun and I was determined to see it through.

I was still working at the same place, for the same employer, as I had been for nearly ten years now. I'd spent over a year in the Keys office, a couple of years in the Miami office, and now I'd been in the Clearwater office for over seven years. I wasn't happy there, as I have explained, but I had no other options that could pay me as well.

I truly was unhappy with virtually every aspect of my life, except for tennis and my newly-found passion for writing. I had no meaningful relationship with any of my children; I had no other woman in my life; I still had a mountain of debt; and I was miserable. Playing tennis and writing were my only sources of pleasure, although both required a great deal of effort and work.

To make matters worse, my ex-wife was working with me in the office. She needed a job and I needed a well-qualified paralegal. She had become an excellent paralegal. We still had our differences, not the least of which was child-rearing, but I could not afford for her <u>not</u> to be working.

Unbeknowst to me, other things were going on behind the scenes at the office at that time. My employer wasn't paying me what I was entitled to. I was constantly complaining about being under-paid and, as a result, I had become a persona non grata in the firm because I was being told that I was wrong and they were right. I had successfully developed the office for them, from scratch, and made them a whole lot of money, but now I was expendable. I was fired.

I brought a lawsuit against the firm to recover what I claimed was owed to me immediately thereafter, and hired an excellent firm to represent me. By the terms of the settlement, I'm not allowed to discuss all that was involved, or the amount of the settlement, but let's just say that it was well above the six figure threshold. I was right, they were wrong, but I was out of a job, again.

Christine was fired, too. I immediately began a job search for both of us. I found a job at the Pinellas County Attorney's office for Christine, with Robert Jagger's son, Bob. He was a senior attorney at the County Attorney's office, and he was very happy to have her with him. She was an excellent employee and ended up working there for the next twenty-five years.

After a short while, I was able to find a job with another defense firm in the downtown Tampa area, through a tennis-playing friend. Another chapter of my life was about to begin. My tenure with the Miami law firm was over, and so was my time in Pinellas County. I was moving on. It was now the year 2000, and I was 53 years old.

Chapter Sixteen

Tampa and Four Green Fields

I found a nice, little one bedroom apartment on the fourth floor of a building on Harbor Island, just outside of downtown Tampa. It sat right on the Hillsborough River and the big cruise ships passed right by me on a regular basis. It was a sight to see those big ships being pulled by the tug boats through that narrow channel, which fed into Tampa Bay. From there, the ships went under the Sunshine Skyway Bridge and out into the open Gulf to various ports in the Caribbean.

My office was less than a mile away. I hate to think about all of the hours I spent driving to or from my various offices over the fifteen years or so I'd been practicing in Florida, beginning in 1985 when I returned from West Virginia. It was tedious. Now, the commute was nothing – a matter of minutes.

Plus, there was an Irish bar, called Four Green Fields, between my apartment and my office. All of the bartenders were from Ireland and still had the brogue, and they knew how to pour a pint of Guinness the right way, using the spoon and all. The musicians were usually Irishmen, too. I became a regular.

And to top it off, there were public tennis courts a few blocks from my apartment, with a public pool in between. It really was a good place for me to land. My children were all still in what had been the marital home, and I still made all of the athletic events, even though I wasn't welcomed at them. Otherwise, my new "digs" were ideal in many ways.

My oldest child, Patrick, was turning 20 in October, and in college. Meagan was a star cross-country runner and track athlete, specializing in the 800 meter run. Her relay team set school records which still stand. Brendan was playing five different sports for his junior high school, and Caitlin excelled in swimming. Meagan and Brendan were playing in tennis leagues. All were athletes and everyone was healthy, popular and doing reasonably well in school. None wanted anything to do with me, however.

So I still had plenty of time to myself, except for the legal work I was required to do. It was still doing insurance defense work, but the firm I was now with had some excellent clients and some big cases. For example, I was assigned to represent the owners of several of the biggest office buildings in all of Tampa. Those were million dollar cases, at times.

My office was on the eighth floor and looked out upon the Hillsborough River, with Tampa Bay in the background. The law firm even had a van to take me to and from the courthouse whenever I needed to go. It was a first-class organization.

I was playing tennis regularly, going to Four Green Fields regularly, watching my children play sports, still teaching at St. Petersburg College, and eating most of my meals at any of the several restaurants within walking distance from my apartment. I did no cooking whatsoever. Also, I began to have more of a social life. Although I was still unhappy, things were better than they had been in years.

I had been playing quite a bit of tennis at the nearby Harbor Island Club, where the best players in Tampa were members, and I was playing USTA tournament events, as well as in a couple of leagues. During the years 2000 and 2003, a couple of those teams I was on won the local, district, regional and then the state championships, and we went to Palm Springs, California and Tuscon, Arizona to compete in the national championships.

Tennis was, and still is, a passion for me. I have loved the game from the time I first began playing it. One of the best parts of being a tennis player is the friends you make. In tennis, for a variety of reasons that are, most likely, self-evident, the people who play tennis are, with few exceptions, first-class people, regardless of what country they come from, their ethnic background, or their financial status. The game engenders that.

In my tennis book, Jimmy Evert wrote that he taught all five of his children how to play tennis so that they could learn social skills that would help them throughout their lives. Of course, all five of his children became champions, but the point was that children who play tennis learn some things that will help them in life, like playing fairly, calling the lines correctly, not cheating to win, being a good sport, whether you win or not – character building traits. I met a whole lot of wonderful human beings over the years through the game of tennis.

For example, my doubles partner in one of the leagues I was playing in was Paul Reilly, who was, and still is, the CEO of Raymond James Financial, a multi-national bank and investment services firm. The chief financial officer of Raymond James was also on the team. Paul is, like me, an Irishman, and he was a graduate of Notre Dame. Three of his brothers were on the team with us.

He was a great tennis player, too, and we went undefeated through all of our district, regional, state and national events. People say that you can judge a person by the friends he keeps. Paul, and the others, were good friends to have.

I was still working on my first novel, which was nowhere near ready for publication, and I was still writing short stories. I was getting more serious about being an author and I took a class at the Hillsborough Community College on creative writing to help me along. I also started a writer's group with a few of the other students, so that we could share ideas and collaborate.

As usual, I tried several cases while at that Tampa firm, some of which were extremely challenging and interesting. One such case, which later became a novel, although the novel had nothing whatsoever to do with the case, involved an absolutely awful car accident in which five people were killed. It was one of the worst cases I ever handled, almost as bad as the case involving the Canadian nurse from Nova Scotia. That was the worst. It still saddens me whenever I think about either of those two cases. They were tragic.

In that case, a young teenage boy, who had just obtained his driver's license, was following an older adult on I-75. He had never driven on an interstate highway at a high rate of speed before. He was not driving improperly in any way, but he was driving at the speed limit and it scared him, I believe, and that is what caused the accident.

However, that's not what the lawyers for the five decedents claimed. When the boy lost control of his car, it veered over a fifty foot grass median and collided head-on with a car carrying four people, three of whom were teenagers themselves. All died. It was an absolutely awful case. The mother of the boy was disconsolate and wanted nothing to do with the lawsuit.

A lawsuit was filed on behalf of the occupants of the car headed south on I-75, who were totally blameless. They claimed that a tractor-trailer had changed lanes suddenly, causing the boy to lose control of his vehicle and, thereby, caused the accident. Needless to say, the demand for settlement was astronomical. I was assigned to represent the two people, who were from Oklahoma, who owned and operated the rig.

The two men denied that they ever made a lane changed. They stopped to render aid as soon as they saw what happened. However, two Florida State Troopers who investigated the crash, found some evidence in the roadway and on the vehicles which led them to believe that there had been a very slight collision between the car the boy was driving and the tractor-trailer and they cited my clients for careless driving and improper lane change.

A woman driving right behind the tractor-trailer testified that the tractor-trailer did not change lanes and there was no collision between the tractor-trailer and the boy's vehicle, so there was a significant dispute as to the facts of the case. Regardless, it was a tear-jerker. Innocent people died in a horrific car accident and the legal system had to sort out the problem. That was my job, and I was assigned to represent the two Native-American Indians who owned and operated the rig, who were a father and son from the Osage Nation.

People have asked me how I can divorce myself from the tragedy and immense sadness which some cases involve in which people have experienced incredibly horrific injuries such as in that case. The same issue arises in some criminal cases where death or great bodily harm is inflicted upon someone and a lawyer must defend the accused. I uniformly respond by saying it's like a doctor who can't stand the sight of blood – that person just isn't suited to be a personal injury trial lawyer or a criminal defense lawyer. Some people just can't do it.

I am able to do it, but it certainly doesn't mean that I take any joy in doing so. This was one of those cases where it really hurt me to have to deal with the family members of the deceased people. Four teenagers and one adult died. There is no way to sugar-coat the problem. It is an awful situation to have to deal with.

However, that case gave me the opportunity to meet two people who I never, ever, would have met but for the fact that I was assigned to be their lawyer. Their last name was Tallchief, and they were full-blooded Osage Indians. It gave me the opportunity to enter into a world I had known very little about.

As is apparent from things I've said so far about being a lawyer, there is much to dislike about it. However, just looking at the cases I've related to you, the readers, you can see that the practice of law offers those willing to take on the challenges and the difficulties involved with being a lawyer an opportunity to do things that other occupations simply can't do. There is so much diversity to the types of cases to be handled and so much variety to the areas of law to be explored that there are many who welcome the challenge.

It's not easy, and I seriously question if I'd do it again, but I am grateful for the opportunities I have been given through the practice of law. This awful car accident is a perfect example of that. It was a horrible case that I hate to think about, but I had a wonderful experience as a result of my involvement in the case that enriched my life greatly.

Without going into anymore details regarding the case, other than to say that it settled after two weeks of trial, <u>after</u> the jury knocked on the door, indicating that they had a verdict. The most memorable part of the case for me was befriending my two clients. I didn't know any full-blooded native-American Indians before meeting them.

After the case was fully concluded, I asked them if I could write a book about them. It was not to have anything to do with the accident or the aftermath. They agreed to allow me to do so, but I wasn't quite ready to begin doing so. I told them that I'd get back in touch with them when I was. That was in 2003 or so. I was still working on my first novel, which still wasn't ready for publication. I was, however, somewhat aggressively trying to find an agent and a publisher.

I was continuing to travel a fair amount because of the nature of the work I was doing, and I always tried to schedule out-of-state depositions for a Friday. That way, I could take a child with me, take the deposition on Friday, and then spend the weekend with a child in whatever place the deposition was taken. Taking them one at a time was, by far, the best way to go, for a variety of reasons.

I took then to a number of desirable locations. For example, I took Patrick to Denver and New Orleans; Meagan to New York and Denver; Brendan to Seattle and Cleveland; and Caitlin to Philadelphia and Boston, plus many others I can't remember at the moment. Despite all of the problems I was having with them, and there were many, those trips were the best way for me to enjoy their company and them mine during those years.

In 2001, after I began working with the Tampa law firm, Patrick was still in college, enjoying the party atmosphere. In fact, he left Valencia Community College, located in Orlando, and transferred to Santa Fe Community College in Gainesville, because the party life was better in Gainesville, next to the University of Florida. He wasn't playing sports at the collegiate level, but he enjoyed playing intra-murals and was very good at them.

Meagan was in her last year of high school and doing reasonably well academically and excelling in track and field. Brendan was attending a Catholic school in Dunedin, where he was very popular, but he was going through some growing pains, mostly associated with his age, that being a teenager, and getting ready to drive. Caitlin was still in Middle School, and actively participating in sports. All were going through changes in their lives, but none of them had much to do with me.

By late 2003, Patrick had decided not to pursue his education any further, deciding, instead, to go to work for a neighbor's father, who owned a construction business; Meagan was attending the University of South Florida and was running cross-country and track, doing very well academically, plus she now had a boyfriend, which was the primary reason she stayed in Florida to go to college; Brendan was graduating from high school, but had started to drink alcohol and was experimenting with drugs; and Caitlin was in an all-out revolt. She was failing classes, drinking excessively, abandoning her sporting activities entirely, and she, too, was experimenting with drugs.

I had absolutely no control over the situation and Christine refused to seek professional help for any of them, though I begged her to do so. Of all the problems relating to parenting children after the divorce, this was, by far, the most perplexing. The problems with the two youngest children came to a head when Brendan was arrested for two separate criminal offenses and Caitlin was arrested for a criminal offense that caused both to be expelled from their high school at different times. Both were placed in a school at the very southern end of St. Petersburg for children like them, an hour away from their home in Tarpon Springs.

Still, Christine would not require either one to go to counseling. Brendan was able to drive himself to and from the school in south St. Pete, but Caitlin would have to take a bus. There was no way she could take a two hour bus ride to the school, and then take a two hour bus ride from school back home every day.

I had to do something about the situation, or else Caitlin would have flunked out of high school. So, I quit my job in Tampa, left my spectacular situation on Harbor Island, found a job with an insurance company as an employee, or what is called "in-house counsel." I then found an apartment in south St. Petersburg where Caitlin and I could live, and I moved.

Also, I bought her a dog, at her request, since she would need company while I was at work. I bought her an 8 week old Golden Retriever. She named her Bailey.

The absolute worst time of my life, I believe, was the four month period of time when I was "in-house counsel" for an insurance company. They treated me like dirt. When I was a defense attorney in a private law firm, I always developed a good rapport with the adjuster assigned to whatever case I was handling for them, and, usually, I had been selected by the adjuster to be the attorney to handle a specific case.

Not so with "in-house counsel." I was an employee, just like the adjusters were, and just as the secretaries were, and the clerks, and the rest, but I was being paid more. They resented that. I was given more cases than I could possibly handle, because the more cases I was assigned to meant that fewer cases were sent out to insurance defense lawyers, who would charge money by they hour and bill excessively. That's how it works. I was absolutely miserable.

However, I was there for Caitlin. She had flunked so many semester classes, that she was, literally SIX entire courses behind the rest of her class, not six week grading periods – semester long classes, and she was miserable. She was taken away from all of her friends; she had no social life, except when she went somewhere with me; she was doing poorly in school; she had low self-esteem; and she had no athletic activities – she had nothing going for her, and she was in danger of worse things happening.

The first thing I did was to find her a mental health counselor. The first person I found was a man, and that didn't go well. He told me that she was, most likely, on her way to prison with the anti-social attitude she was displaying. I found a female counselor to replace him. That worked much better.

Gradually, over time, things began to improve. I enrolled her in an after school program whereby she could make up a failed class. We found a night class she could attend and make up two other failed subjects. We enrolled her in summer classes, though they were months off, and she made up the other failed classes. As one of her teachers said, "she found her smile again." She began making "A"s and a few "B"s.

However, at the end of the semester, she went back to live with her mother. Bailey, who was a wonderful dog, went with her. She completed the summer programs and made up all of the necessary classwork, allowing her to graduate with her class. In fact, she enrolled at St. Petersburg College in the Fall and was making "A"s while there. Bailey was returned to me. Christine didn't like her.

However, after the Spring semester ended, and after Caitlin went back home to live with her mother, I quit my job. They weren't unhappy to see me leave and I, most definitely, wasn't unhappy to leave. It was the worst job I would ever have in my life, even worse than sweeping sidewalks in Plano, Texas for $4.75 per hour.

At about that time, that being the late spring of 2003, my left shoulder began to give me a lot of trouble. I thought it was a torn rotator cuff, but my friend, Hugh Rutledge, who was one of the doctors for the Toronto Blue Jays during spring training days in nearby Dunedin, told me that it was more than likely a torn labrum, which would require surgery to repair.

I didn't want to have surgery because I knew that there was a six month process of rehabilitation. Unfortunately, the best part of my game was my serve, and I wouldn't be able to serve with a torn labrum. That meant that my playing days were likely over. I'd hit enough tennis balls in my life and I reasoned that I could deal with it. As you can imagine, that was difficult for me.

Another chapter of my life was about to begin, and this new chapter would represent another significant departure from pragmatism, much like a couple of other periods of my life, as you have seen and will soon see, again – maybe there's a theme there. What is it?

Chapter Seventeen

Cedar Key

In 2000, during the days when I had so much time to myself, I took some time to look around the state of Florida to see if there was anywhere in the state I'd like to live, other than in a big city. I had traveled all over the state during my tennis days, and as a lawyer, too, to a lesser extent, having tried cases all over the state, and knew it pretty well. If you look up and down the east coast, everyplace has been developed. That wasn't the case on the west coast of Florida.

From Naples, up through Fort Myers, Sarasota, Bradenton, Tampa/ St. Pete, Clearwater, and as far north as New Port Richey, it's pretty well developed, but from there it thins out. That is what is called the "Big Bend" part of Florida. I knew the Homosassa/Crystal River area, and Yankeetown, to some extent, but not much about anything north of there until you get to Tallahassee.

I began looking at that part of the state and saw this little town way off by itself, right on the Gulf of Mexico, called Cedar Key, and I decided to pay a visit. It was about two hours north of Tampa on a newly-created road called the Suncoast Parkway, which was a toll road. U.S. 19 is the main thoroughfare, but there is a whole lot of traffic and plenty of stop lights.

Cedar Key, I discovered, was a small town of about 850 people, according to the latest census, and it actually consists of a whole lot of little islands. I drove up the parkway to Homosassa on the Suncoast Parkway, then up U.S. 19, past Crystal River and Yankeetown, until I reached State Road 24, where I turned west, and headed towards the Gulf. I then drove 24 miles with hardly anything on it to get to Cedar Key.

I crossed over the Number Four bridge, entering the city limits, and then drove another three miles, crossing over a few more bridges, to the "heart" of this small little town. There were hundreds of small islands scattered about wherever I looked on both sides of the water.

It had a small, downtown area, with a street running along the water called Dock Street, where there was a fishing pier, much like the one featured in the movie "Body Heat," starring Kathleen Turner, William Hurt, Ted Danson and others. That was one of my favorite movies.

Also, since I visited on a weekend, I found that it had at least six bars/restaurants with live music. Where else, outside of Ireland, would that be possible, I asked myself. There were at least a dozen restaurants and/or coffee shops in town, too. I wandered around the town, on foot, for a couple of days and absolutely fell in love with the place. I immediately began looking for something to buy.

I didn't have a place to live, other than my apartment, and I wanted a little more stability than that. Also, it looked like a perfect place for me to pursue my writing ambitions, much the way Hemingway had chosen Cuba, Key West, and then Idaho. In fact, back in the mid-nineteenth century, New Orleans, Cedar Key and Key West were a triad of points on a trading route, when sailing ships dominated the maritime industry, before Tampa became what Tampa is now.

Furthermore, it was said to be an "Artist's haven," as more than 80 people called themselves "artists" and were actively creating works of art. There were two stores where artists owned and operated a business as a collective, where the artists would take turns running the stores. It seemed to me to be an "undiscovered" treasure and I was smitten.

I had some money to spend from the settlement with my former law firm and I found a one bedroom condominium for sale for a little over a hundred thousand dollars, which I thought was a bargain. I felt like this was a place - Cedar Key, that is – that was going to be discovered at any moment, like maybe tomorrow. I bought it.

It was at the Old Fenimore Condominiums and I had an unobstructed view off of my balcony to the open Gulf of Mexico. Also, and it puzzled me, at first, as to how that could be, but I could watch the sun rise in the morning. How could I look out over the Gulf of Mexico and see the sun rise, you ask?

It's because the collection of islands comprising the Cedar Keys bend back around so that you're actually looking south and east. It still perplexes me, and I shake my head in disbelief every time I see the sun rise there. I still do, but I loved being able to watch the sun come up over the horizon, despite my geographic conundrum.

I began staying out there on weekends and holidays, whenever I didn't have any tennis matches or other commitments. I even bought a boat, with the help of my friend, Steve Beeland, a nice 17 foot Mako. It was a "flats" boat, perfect for the waters off of and around Cedar Key, and I kept it at the Marina.

I could call ahead and they'd have the boat in the water, all gassed up and ready to go, when I arrived. When I returned, after an afternoon of fruitless fishing misadventures, they'd clean the boat and put it away for me. It was perfect – a little expensive, perhaps, but I didn't know any better and I thought it was a bargain. I truly loved the place, and wanted to become a better fisherman, but that never happened.

I really loved getting up to Cedar Key back then. It was much like when I moved to West Virginia, so much different from living in a big city, as I was. Also, it was a great place to write and I was doing so as much as possible, although I was pretty busy during that period of time. I decided to write a book about Cedar Key, and I began doing so.

My first novel, about the DUI, was finished, except for the interminable process of editing. Also, I was submitting it to agents and publishers, doing all that needed to be done to meet their rather strict requirements. I had read books on how to properly submit a proposal to agents and publishers and each one was a little different, but all were time-consuming and required much thought.

For example, I had to submit a "query" letter, and there are specific instructions on how to do that. Plus, I had to do a detailed "synopsis" of the book, as well as provide sample chapters, and some other things. The publishing industry has requirements on how to go about its business and you, as an author, must do exactly what they say.

Furthermore, I learned that most publishers of novels would not accept any proposed novels that didn't come through an agent. There is a book called "The Writer's Market," which is now in its 100th year of publication. It is the "Bible" for people like me. It provides would-be authors with names and addresses for all of the publishers and agents in the country, with a breakdown of what types of books they will accept.

I dutifully followed the instructions provided and sent out batches of "query" letters for months and months to agents. That was the way it had to be done and there is a definite stigma attached to not doing things in the publishing world the traditional way. I had to go through an established agent, who then would get me placed with one of the premier publishing houses, like Simon & Schuster, Penguin, Random House or HarperCollins, to name a few. That's the procedure to be followed and I was doing my best to follow it.

As all of you know, no doubt, authors are told to expect rejection. People like John Grisham, Stephen King, and even J.K. Rowling, plus countless untold others, received rejection after rejection. I was in good company, but they were, eventually, "discovered." I was prepared for the rejection letters.

For my tennis book and the legal text, it had been a breeze. Not so with novels. I began to receive rejection letter after rejection letter from agents. Every now and then, I'd get a favorable reply, asking for more information, but it never ended well.

I really didn't want to give up and go to the "alternative" way of getting published, which was by doing it myself, or self-publishing. I didn't, and I struggled mightily not to do so. In fact, I began writing my next novel, about Cedar Key, while doing me best to find an agent and get A Very Fine Line into print, but I was not having any luck in doing so.

Three of my best friends, all of whom were excellent criminal defense lawyers, gave "rave reviews" about A Very Fine Line, and those were on the back cover. I had a graphic artist put an excellent drawing on the front cover. I was still doing everything I could think of to make that book a success, without success.

I was enjoying Cedar Key, though, and I was as busy as I could be during the week between the practice of law, tennis and visits to Four Green Fields. However, after almost two years there, I decided that I really didn't like living in a condominium all that much. I didn't like having neighbors around me all the time. I wanted to be outside of town, but not too far outside of town. I began to look around.

I found an acre of ground a few miles outside of the city limits on State Road 347, just before the turn for the Shell Mound park, that I could buy for about $5,000. It needed to be cleared some, but it looked like a good spot to build a home, and I wanted to build a log cabin. I didn't have enough money to have two homes, and why would I need more than one, so I decided to sell the condominium and build a cabin, but first I had to find the cabin I wanted to build.

I found a log home supplier in Crystal River and then began looking for a builder. Once I'd found the builder, then I needed to get financing, and I applied for a loan. Everything fell into place and I began construction sometime in early 2003. I had to sell my condominium, though, to make it all work, and I did, making a nice little profit of about $50,000 in the process.

Once construction began, I couldn't stay away. I wanted to be there during all stages of construction, although I wasn't able to do much of the work. Mostly, I just watched and was a "go-fer." A man named Carl Colson was the carpenter and he had a full crew. It actually took longer to get the loan and make all the arrangements for the financing than it did to build the cabin once we got started.

All that took place at the time I had moved to St. Petersburg and had Caitlin with me. She went home to be with her mother every weekend, so I went to Cedar Key to work on the house when she did. She had absolutely no desire to see what I was doing or to visit Cedar Key, go fishing or do anything with me, nor did any of the others. Cedar Key was all about me.

People call the log home packages that I bought a "kit" home, which isn't accurate. Yes, I picked out the style and all, and they delivered all of the wood to complete the project, but every piece of wood had to be cut and many, if not most, of the logs had to be drilled. The problem with log homes, which many people don't realize until they do what I did, was that, with a log home, things like electric wires and plumbing lines have to go INSIDE the logs, so that they're not exposed, once the building is complete.

All of that takes time – a lot of time. Each individual log had to be measured, cut, and then drilled. Then, the next log had to be drilled exactly the way the first log was drilled, and that's a time consuming process, too.

Plus, I had a fireplace put in, and that took an unbelievable amount of time. I chose river rock as the siding inside the house and brick on the outside. There were days when the men installing the chimney took a full day to put up ten pieces of rock. I was astounded, but they did good work and it looked fantastic when they were finished.

About six months later, I had a magnificent two-story log home, up on stilts, with a spectacular fireplace and a beautiful front porch. People driving by would stop and stare. Some people drove up to the cabin and just asked if they could look around. The man who installed the washer and dryer called his wife from my house and said, "You'll never guess where I'm working today." Everybody loved it, but no one more than I did. I was quite pleased with what I had accomplished.

As fate would have it, the cabin was fully constructed and ready for me to move in at exactly the same time that Caitlin finished the Spring semester with me, and at exactly the same time when my time as an in-house defense lawyer came to an end. When Caitlin moved home, and I quit that job, I took Bailey and we moved to Cedar Key.

I say that I "quit" my job. In fact, it was a mutual decision. They didn't care for me and I disliked them intensely. However, I didn't have an "off-ramp" when it happened.

As I look back on my life, I have trouble explaining that time of my life. What was I thinking? I knew that it was always a wise thing to keep a job until you had another one. I knew that, yet I left the job with the insurance company and had no other job lined up.

I had debts, I had three children in college at about that time. I had no income, yet I was confident it would all work out. I don't know what I was thinking, but I wasn't thinking clearly. I was thinking with my heart, not my head.

I wasn't drinking to excess (I rarely have more than three beers), I wasn't doing any drugs (and hadn't since I first began practicing law in 1976), I wasn't gambling (although I loved going to Jai-Alai, the horse track and the dog track when in Miami, before children), and I wasn't spending money foolishly, but I had no income, so how was I going to pay my living expenses? I didn't know.

Furthermore, I had job offers from other insurance defense firms. I was still in the prime of my days as a lawyer, but as you know, having read what I've written so far, I was miserable. I didn't want to continue to live the life I had been living.

That was the period in my life when I was under the most stress, I believe. I remember going back to my apartment and lying down, in the middle of the afternoon, sometimes, and just wondering what the heck I was going to do. I had gotten myself into a mess and I didn't know how to get myself out of it.

Furthermore, I knew that stress can kill you. Christine's brother, Kenny, who was a year older than me, had a heart attack while at work at about that time and he died, suddenly. He didn't have any health problems to cause anyone to suspect that might happen. It was a shock to everyone. I honestly felt that could happen to me, although I was in otherwise excellent health, or so I thought.

I had the cabin in Cedar Key and, when the job officially ended, and Caitlin was out of school and out of the apartment, I went to Cedar Key. I had nowhere else to go. I was excited about my prospects in many ways, unrealistic though that was.

Because I wasn't fired, I was eligible for unemployment, and I applied for it. Imagine that, a lawyer, who had been making in excess of six figures, drawing unemployment? Sad, but true, and it wasn't very much, like $375 per week, as I recall, but that's all I had and I had a mortgage to pay and other expenses.

After a very short time, maybe a couple of months, I began looking for work, but I had no interest in returning to the Tampa/St. Petersburg area, although there were job opportunities there. Again, I wasn't thinking clearly. I was thinking with my heart and not my head.

I wanted to pursue my writing, and I was still pitching "A Very Fine Line," writing short stories, and I was just starting to write a book about Cedar Key. I was making some money from my tennis book and the legal text, but not much, definitely not nearly enough to support me.

Also, that was when I stopped playing tennis. Vision in my left eye had worsened and I now needed cataract surgery on it. My whole life was being turned upside down.

So I had the cataract surgery done at some point during that period of time, while I still had good health insurance. That was another thing, I had insurance through COBRA, which required that I was allowed to continue with health insurance after leaving employment for a period of a year or so, as I recall, but I had to pay for it once I was no longer an employee. Cataract surgery was, once again, performed by Dr. James Gill, a friend, who did an excellent job and it was, quite miraculously, successful, again.

Fortunately, a friend from tennis, Dick Woltmann, who was the director of the legal services program in Tampa, and on my Youth Tennis Foundation Board of Directors, helped me to find a job with the Three Rivers Legal Services program in Gainesville. Dick and I played every Friday for those years when I lived in Tampa. We had met in Maine, of all places, back when I was a teenager, up visiting my uncle who lived in Massachusetts.

We remembered each other and reconnected. He had played at Rollins College and was an excellent player. We'd play for a couple of hours, then go have dinner at the club he belonged to, drink some beer and talk about tennis and a whole bunch of other things. I wrote a short story about his days in Africa with the Peace Corps.

That was an amazing story. There he was, in the middle of the Congo, as I recall, being a Peace Corps volunteer, where there were NO other white people in the area, until one day a beautiful, blonde-haired caucasian woman walked into his village, by herself. That, truly, was a match made in heaven. They were married when he completed his tour of duty with the Peace Corps.

I was to be the Litigation Director of the program. I had more litigation experience than all of the other lawyers in the office combined, and none of the other attorneys had any trial experience, except for one, and she'd had just a couple of trials, all of which she had lost. The director felt as if the staff attorneys were just giving advice and counsel and not filing enough law suits, or appeals, or doing any truly meaningful and substantive legal work.

My job was to review the files of each and every attorney in the program, including the paralegals, and do my best to make them better. Some of the staff didn't appreciate that. No one likes to be told that they're not doing a good enough job, but that was my job – to tell them that they needed to do better, and to tell them that they weren't doing as well as they could be doing.

I was to be working out of the Gainesville office. There were offices in Lake City and Jacksonville, too, and I was responsible for those offices, too. The office covered seventeen counties, as I recall. It was a big job, but I was perfect for it.

At first, I commuted an hour back and forth, each way, from Cedar Key every day, but after a while, I tired of that, so I found an apartment in Gainesville where I stayed from Monday night to Thursday night. The hours at the office were long and the drive from Cedar Key to Gainesville on State Road 24 – a straight shot, literally, was tiresome. There were very few turns in the road, and not much between U.S. 19 and the city limits of Cedar Key. Furthermore, at night, I could hit deer, hog or the occasional alligator, as I once did.

Parenthetically, I should add that up to this point in time, I'd attend mass on either Saturday afternoons or Sunday mornings in either Tarpon Springs or Tampa. I also did my best to make sure that my children went to church, too. All of my children had gone to public schools since we moved out of Miami, but all had received First Communion and then Confirmation through the Catholic Church in Tarpon Springs. Christine was either an atheist or an agnostic, she wasn't sure which, and she didn't participate with their religious education.

I took them to and from church on Sundays until I moved to Cedar Key, and then I think all of that pretty much ended, but they all received a religious education. After that, it was up to them. I don't think any of them go to church anymore, which saddens me.

While living in Cedar Key, the closest Catholic church was in Chiefland, half an hour away. The priest there was from India and I think I understood about every third word. It was a complete waste of time, but I went, religiously, despite that.

As best I recall, I worked at Three Rivers Legal Services from about September of 2003 until July of 2005, a little less than two full years. Then I resigned, somewhat suddenly, and moved to Fort Myers, Florida to work with Paul Sullivan, the friend I had met in Cumberland, Maryland, back in 1979, soon after I moved to West Virginia.

I had done a good job during my years at TRLS, and I had cleaned up all of the files, brought down the number of cases each lawyer and paralegal was responsible for to a workable level, so all could be more productive. Having too many cases, which is usually the case in a legal services office, can absolutely overwhelm a person and make them both ineffective and seriously depressed.

Also, we began to be more aggressive in the areas of consumer protection and in landlord-tenant matters. Everyone wants a free lawyer and it's sometimes extremely hard to say no. The result is that you end up with more cases than you can handle, and the problem continues to grow, never resolving itself.

While I was there, during that two year time period, we became involved in a major landlord-tenant case involving the largest landlord in the country. It had over a million tenants in 47 states throughout the country, including a complex called Kennedy Homes, which was the biggest housing complex in the city of Gainesville. Several hundred people lived there, most of whom were African-American.

After a fire devastated several of the buildings, instead of repairing the damage and bringing the buildings up to code, they closed the entire complex down. Our argument was that the landlord had received moneys from the Federal government for years and that the landlord had a duty to keep the premises in good order, but had failed to do so. The fire was the result of neglect on the part of the landlord.

I over-saw the progress of that case, but I was not counsel of record at that time. It was, by far, the biggest case in the program. It was to re-enter my life not too long thereafter, though.

As far as tennis was concerned, I wasn't playing anymore, as I mentioned previously, and the Youth Tennis Foundation was basically dormant during the years after 1987. We didn't have any money, once the Florida Tennis Association decided to de-fund us. However, I kept it alive by continuing to pay the moneys due the State of Florida and the United States government to keep our not-for-profit corporation and 501(c)(3) status alive and well, sometimes out of my own pocket.

I had a Board of Directors that included my two brothers, Christopher and Allan, Bob and Ed Jagger, Tug Miller, Dick Woltmann and a few others. We met once a year, usually by phone, and did what we had to do to comply with the rules and regulations regarding non-profit corporations. We had no money to do anything else.

I don't know what made me keep it alive. We were about down to zero dollars in our bank account, and I had no idea how we would ever get any money, but I kept it alive, with help from my brothers and some of my best friends, as I mentioned.

So I was sitting at my desk at the TRLS office in Gainesville one afternoon and I received a call from an attorney in West Palm Beach, who asked if I was Pierce Kelley. When I told him that I was, he asked, are you the president of the Youth Tennis Foundation of Florida, Inc. When I told him that I was, he said, "A man named John van Ryn has recently died, and in his Last Will and Testament he has left $500,000 to your organization and one other."

Needless to say, that was a pleasant surprise. Then he went on to add that we wouldn't be receiving any money yet, because his wife was still alive and the trust that he had created provided that she was to be taken care of until her death, and at that time we would receive whatever amount of money was left in the trust. She was well up into her eighties, and might have been in her 90s, so she didn't have too much time to live, he confided.

For the next several years, Ed Jagger, who handled probate cases, would write a letter to that West Palm Beach probate attorney and ask, as delicately as possible, how the widow was doing. He was really just asking if she was still alive. It was kind of a morbid thing for us to do, but that's what we had to do and that's what we did.

Sometime in 2006, the widow passed and we received $250,000. Half of the money went to some Catholic Nuns. The money revitalized the Youth Tennis Foundation, and that revitalized my involvement with the game of tennis, even though my playing days were over. We had no idea what to do with the money at that point, and we scheduled a meeting for later that year.

Shortly after receiving that phone call, I received another meaningful, and unexpected, call. That's when Paul Sullivan called and asked if I would be willing to come down to Ft. Myers to work with him. He had joined a personal injury firm that handled only plaintiffs cases and they needed some trial attorneys. They were advertizing on television and had more cases than they could handle. He assured me that I was going to make a whole lot of money if I would join him.

Legal Services lawyers don't make a whole lot of money. In fact, they don't make much money at all. Most of them are good-hearted people who truly believe that what they are doing is God's work, and that they were part of the "War on Poverty" that had begun back in the late '60s, just as I did, way back when. They work hard at what is, basically, a thank-less job, but they feel good about doing so. They are altruistic.

By that time, I had worn out my welcome at TRLS. There were some who no longer appreciated me or what I was doing. After all, my job was, basically, to find fault with everything that was going on, or, stated differently, figure out what was going wrong in the office and fix it.

Some people appreciated me for what I was doing, but some didn't, and they resented me for what I had done, and that was never going to change. I needed the money, my work there was done, so I accepted his offer and left TRLS sometime in early 2006. I was headed for a new destination, Fort Myers, Florida, where I would now be doing something different – plaintiffs' personal injury work.

Chapter Eighteen
Fort Myers, Florida

Fort Myers is about a five hour drive from Cedar Key. To get there, I would drive back to Tampa, along the same, familiar route, and then catch I-75 south and go almost to the end, just short of Naples, where the road turns east and goes towards Fort Lauderdale and the Miami area. Paul had a beautiful condominium in a gated community, where there were many vehicles which were much more valuable than me and all of my assets put together. It is one of the wealthiest communities in the country.

I stayed with Paul for a few days, and then found a place to rent, which was located right in downtown Ft. Myers, alongside the Caloosahatchee River. It was ideal. The place was to be torn down within the next year, so I was allowed to keep Bailey with me in the apartment, which was, quite literally, within 20 feet of the river. A pool was less than 50 feet away. The office was less than a quarter of a mile away. It was perfect.

I was to be paid every two weeks and I was to receive about twice as much as I had been earning at TRLS. The first sign of trouble came when I was to receive my first paycheck. The owner of the firm was in Europe for three weeks and I would have to wait until he returned in order to get paid. When he returned to the United States, two weeks later, I was paid. I wasn't happy about that.

The second sign of trouble came when I was to be paid a month later. This time, the owner was in Hawaii and I would again have to wait for him to return before getting paid. When he returned, two weeks later, I was again paid, but those were warning signs and they caused me some problems. I was spending money I didn't have, using credit cards to pay my bills most of the time.

Other than Paul, I had one friend in Ft. Myers, and he was a lawyer I had met in Clearwater when I was with Robert E. Jagger as an assistant Public Defender. That was Jeff Myers and we had played softball, basketball, tennis and golf together. Also, we had both gone to Tulane at about the same time, but we didn't know each other back then. He and his wife, Linda, were good friends.

I brought my canoe down with me from Cedar Key, and Bailey and I would canoe over to an island in the middle of the river when I got off work. I'd take her on walks across that huge bridge over the river which connected Fort Myers to Cape Coral. There were restaurants and bars within a short distance from my apartment.

Also, in the southwest part of Florida there are a number of beautiful beaches, but the pearl of that part of the state is Sanibel Island, which is famous for its pearly white sand and the shells tourists search for on a daily basis. It is a barrier island and, as such, gets a fresh supply of shells on a regular basis. Bailey and I visited those beaches after work, some days, but I drove back to Cedar Key every weekend.

It was a busy office, and I couldn't leave too early on a Friday afternoon, so I'd get back to Cedar Key, at the earliest, around 10:00 at night. Then I'd have to head back to Fort Myers late Sunday afternoons to arrive at a decent hour. That was tiresome. That was another difficult stretch for me.

Although I'd been a personal injury lawyer for many years by that point, I'd never worked in an office that did only plaintiffs work. I'd come to dislike representing insurance companies, because they began each case thinking that the plaintiffs weren't being truthful or they were exaggerating their claims. I discovered that there's a "dirty" side of being a plaintiff's lawyer, too. Some of the cases I was given to work on were truly hard to imagine.

For example, one case involved a man walking out of a restaurant and tripping over the back of a chair that was pushed in to one of the tables, where it belonged. The claim was that the chair constituted a hazard and the restaurant was liable for the injuries. I found that hard to believe, and said so.

Another, one of my favorites, actually, involved a group of guys who were at a restaurant and they had too much to drink and spilled beer on the floor. After the restaurant cleaned up the mess the men caused, one of the men slipped and fell in the spots that had been cleaned up, but were still a little damp. He sued, claiming the restaurant was responsible for causing him to slip and fall.

Yet another case involved a lawsuit against a man, who was not related to this other person, who told a friend not to drive home from a restaurant, because that person had been drinking too much. He offered to drive him home. Unfortunately, the man didn't take his offer or his advice and was involved in a car accident on the way home and died. The lawsuit claimed that the friend had a "duty" not to let the man drive home. I didn't agree.

Maybe I had been a defense lawyer too long, but I had trouble handling some of the cases assigned to me. As a defense lawyer, if it was a bad case, the insurance company was going to have to pay some money, it was just a matter of how much. In a plaintiff's personal injury law firm, it seemed as if every case, no matter how bad the facts were, was worth some money, and they'd file suit.

To be honest, now that I'm out of the game, it's a dirty business no matter what side of the fence you're on. Without any question, there are valid cases and people must sue in order to be compensated for wrongs done unto them. However, there are many cases that truly shouldn't be in court, but they are.

So it's not as if one side is right and the other side is wrong, it's just that it's all about money and both sides will do the best they can either to get the most they can or pay the least they can, and there is nothing wrong with that, but there isn't any real "cause" involved. It's just an ongoing game to see who can get the best of the other, and truth is oftentimes nowhere to be found in the process. My heart wasn't in it.

The best thing that I can say about my time with the firm in Fort Myers is that they paid me to take a trip to Glacier, Montana, to attend a Writer's conference. They did so because I won an internal contest to see who was able to make the most money for the firm over a certain period of time. I was teamed with another lawyer who made a whole lot of money, a whole lot more than I did, and, because of him, I was able to go, and I took Caitlin with me.

She was attending St. Petersburg College and living at home, working at a low-paying job at a dry-cleaning establishment. I bought a used car from one of the lawyers in the program for her and the first thing she did was spend a lot of money to put a huge sound system in it, the kind that makes a lot of noise going down the road. That made her happy, and I was happy to make her happy.

We left for Montana on the first of October, planning to stay for a week. I didn't realize how cold it gets up there by then, but it does. The "Road to the Sun," which is the main path through the park from one side to the other was closed. It closes in mid September every year, apparently, but I didn't know that.

However, we were able to get part way into the park, up to the Avalanche Trail, where we were able to walk for several hours to a magnificent spot where you come out of the trees and are surrounded on three sides by a horseshoe shaped mountain that goes straight up at a ninety degree angle several hundred feet. There's a large lake there, called Avalanche Lake. It was a beautiful spot and I got someone to take a picture of the two of us, which I cherish. In fact, it's on the back of one of my books.

The best part, though, other than the Writer's conference, where I learned more things about becoming an author, getting an agent, a publisher, and how to market books, was going rafting down the Middle Fork of the Flathead River with a man named Reno Baldwin, the owner of the Great Northern Rafting Company. Whenever I went anyplace with any of my children, I would always find a place to go down a river or go for a trail ride. Montana was no exception.

However, by October 1, all of the rafting companies had closed down for the winter. Just by chance, my first call was to Reno. He told me that he was closed, and gave me suggestions for people to call. I called him back, told him that no one would help, and he gave me more suggestions. Finally, after all else failed, he said, "Alright, I'll take you and your daughter down the river," and he did. I was delighted.

Unfortunately, the day we went was a cold, blustery day, with temperatures hovering just above freezing. In fact, I think we had snow flurries while on the river. My daughter was not happy. I loved it.

Reno had found two other people to go with us, so the five of us went down the river in a raft that could probably hold ten. Along the way, Reno told us stories about the various spots on the river and all about his thirty-some years of experiences. I was enraptured. My daughter could have cared less. She just wanted to get off the river as fast as possible. She was born in 1987, so she would have been nineteen at the time, I think – still a teenager.

He explained that in all those years, no one had ever died or been seriously injured except for one time, when a large tree fell on a raft as it was going by. There was no way to anticipate that, and there was nothing that could have been done to avoid that or prevent that from happening. He said that the state and federal authorities fully investigated the matter and he and his company were praised, not criticized, for how they handled the situation.

A few years later, when I wrote a book about my friend, Matthew Chatowsky, who had been seriously injured in a horse-back riding incident, the very first chapter begins with a rafting trip down the Middle Fork of the Flathead River. I remembered everything Reno had told me and I recounted all of that in there. For me, as I said, that was the highlight of the trip, except for the quality time spent with my daughter, of course. We also went on a couple of trail rides and I think she enjoyed herself and being with me, just a little.

I handled a number of interesting cases while with that firm in Fort Myers, including a number of cases involving defective tires, auto accidents, slips/trips and falls, motorcycle cases and even a medical malpractice case, but the biggest case that was assigned to me involved GAP insurance, that is routinely sold to people who purchase cars. My employers thought that case was worth a billion dollars – yes, a billion dollars. They were quite adept at bringing class action lawsuits and that case was one of them. I helped move that case along quite a bit while there.

After several months, I tired of the five hours of driving back and forth to Cedar Key, each way, so I sold my cabin. It didn't take long for that to sell and I made a tidy sum in the process. It really was a beautiful place and everyone who ever saw it, especially from the inside, absolutely loved it.

However, after about nine months, when I hadn't realized the enormous increase in money that I was assured would be forthcoming, I tired of the work and told Paul that I was thinking of leaving. This time, I didn't do it without first finding a job. The owners were really good at making money, but even better at spending it, and it didn't trickle down.

I went back to Legal Services work. Three Rivers Legal Services had an opening for a staff attorney in its Lake City office and I applied for the job. Since I had done such a good job while there before, I was welcomed back by the Director of the program, but not by some of the staff attorneys. Better still, I was only going to have to work part-time, so I could spend more time with my writing, which is what I wanted to do in the first place, ever since leaving the Tampa area.

I found a place to live, right on a lake, ten minutes from the office, and I began working there in mid 2006. I was basically floundering. I still considered myself to be a competent attorney, with excellent trial skills, definitely so when compared to all of the other attorneys in the office, but I certainly wasn't going down a successful legal path. I was just going down.

Ever since I left Kevin's office, my legal trajectory was headed in the wrong direction. I realized that. I knew that better than anyone. It wasn't because of lack of ability, or lack of opportunity, I just didn't want to be a lawyer. That was basically it. I remained hopeful that I would achieve success as a writer. I just needed to keep a "day job," which is what even the most successful authors of the twentieth century said, even Hemingway.

In late 2006, my first novel, A Very Fine Line, was officially published. It had been a six year effort. I hadn't been able to find a traditional publisher to work with, nor had I been able to find an agent, so I decided to self-publish. I went with a company called iUniverse, which had its main office in Kansas City.

The advantages of self-publishing were that the company would handle all aspects of the publication and distribution of the book. Also, books would be printed "on-demand," meaning that I wouldn't have to buy two thousand of them and carry them around in boxes for years, as I'd done with my tennis book. I was very tired of "schlepping" to and from the Post Office to mail books off to Amazon and other places. They would take care of all of that.

Plus, they gave assurances that my book would be available for purchase on Amazon and through Barnes & Noble, plus other such markets, and they did so for what I considered to be a very reasonable price of about a thousand dollars. The primary reason I did so was because I had tried hard to find an agent and a traditional publisher, but I'd had no success. It was nothing like what I had experienced with my tennis book or the legal text book. Novels were different and I was ready to move on to my next book. I guess I just gave up on going the "traditional" way. I just couldn't wait any longer.

There were downsides to doing so. Perhaps most importantly, there was probably no way that I would ever rid myself of the stigma in the industry for self-published authors. I was and would always be, by definition, an author who had not come up through the proper ranks. Anyone could self-publish. All you had to do was pay money. There was no "vetting" of a book. It was all about money ... unless one of my books could somehow hit the jackpot and be discovered.

Being fully cognizant of the downsides, I chose to self-publish. I had books to write and I was not going to just let my book languish, hoping and waiting for a traditional publisher to pick it up. Besides, with self-publishing, I could have a book in hand within four to six months, not twelve to eighteen months, as is the case with traditional publishing houses.

Looking back, I don't regret my decision in that respect. However, I sure do wish an agent had agreed to represent me, or a traditional publisher had agreed to publish my book, but that didn't happen. I wish one of my books has been made into a movie, but that hasn't happened, either. Becoming a successful author is a long shot.

I've read where less than 1 percent of authors get their books published, let alone make money. I did get published and paid money for a few of my books, but I haven't made much money with any of my novels. Maybe I just wasn't good enough. Then again, maybe I just wasn't lucky enough.

I think that there's a lot of luck involved with becoming successful at anything, actually. Regardless, and for whatever reason, I was not enjoying any financial success from my writing. I wasn't doing it for the money, though I certainly wanted to achieve success. It was a passion. Though I was disappointed, I wasn't discouraged or deterred. I would continue to write.

I was going back to Gainesville to be a staff attorney with Three Rivers Legal Services. I was to work part-time, or thirty hours, not the forty hours that others were required to work. I had a place to live but I didn't know anyone in Lake City, other than the four or five people who worked in the TRLS office. I was beginning a new chapter of life, and it seemed as if I was starting all over again in many ways.

Chapter Nineteen

Three Rivers Legal
Services, Partie Deux

The people in the Lake City office welcomed me back, even the attorneys. The lawyers in the Gainesville office were the ones who didn't like me too much. It was a relatively new office, having been opened maybe five years earlier, so everything had a fresh feeling about it, like the furniture, the carpet and everything else.

The work was rather plebian, though, given what I had been doing in Fort Myers, and what I had done while working as the Director of Litigation for TRLS during the years of 2003 to mid-2005, and all the years before. I was a staff attorney assigned to divorce cases, landlord-tenant cases and the like. I had no title and no additional responsibilities. I was a "staff attorney."

Not knowing anyone in Lake City, I had no social life, and I hadn't had an intimate relationship of any length in years, ever since the divorce, really, although there were some short encounters with people of the opposite sex that didn't last too long and never led to anything. I was definitely missing that and I wanted to find someone. I was tired of being alone, and that was one of the reasons I left Cedar Key. There were no eligible women there for me.

One of the first things I did, after finding a place to live, and beginning work, was to join a dating site. I chose e-harmony, which was said to be the best of the many available sites. Unlike any of the others, it required a detailed psychological profile, seemingly prepared by a team of psychologists, and it refused to post any pictures until people exchanged messages, also unlike any of the others. Not knowing any better, I paid my money and went along with the program.

As fate would have it, I connected with the very first person I met on-line. Her name was Susan and she lived outside of Gainesville, not too far away, but not all that close, either. We agreed to meet at a restaurant in Gainesville late one weekday afternoon, but when we arrived at the agreed upon location, the restaurant was closed.

She was a tall, attractive, lithesome, woman with long brown hair, who had a bicycle on the back of her SUV. I was immediately attracted by her looks. We talked for a few minutes and decided upon plan B.

So we drove to a nearby park and just sat on a park bench and talked. Bailey was with me and I threw balls to her while we talked. After a while, we went looking for another restaurant. We drove in her car and I left Bailey in my car.

We found a seafood restaurant not too far away and things went well there, too. We both wanted to see each other again, and soon. We got together the next day for a walk in the Itchetucknee Springs State Park, which was about half way between us.

The relationship developed quickly and we began seeing each other regularly, even after work during the week. Most often, we would meet in High Springs, at Oleno State Park, to ride bicycles. She was an avid cyclist, much more so than I was. I had what I thought was a decent road bike, with three gears in front and eight in the back, but she was much better than I was. Afterwards, we would go have dinner at a nearby restaurant where they had live music several days a week.

Also, she was an excellent guitarist. I had been trying to learn to play the guitar for decades, without success, but I had purchased a bass guitar in Fort Myers and was trying to learn how to play it. I had even taken some lessons down there. We began playing together. I began to learn how to play the bass, one note at a time, one finger at a time.

Plus, she liked to hike and she was a camper. We were a great match, and the sparks that were flying between us had become a fire that was burning brightly. We became inseparable rather quickly.

However, before meeting her, I had made all of the necessary arrangements for me to go to Ireland and take my four children with me. They were as excited about that as I was. I had purchased the tickets, rented a vehicle and made arrangements for us to rent a cottage in County Kerry, overlooking the Atlantic Ocean, just south of the Cliffs of Moher and the city of Galway months earlier.

We met on April 10, and I was flying to Shannon airport on the first Saturday in May, so that interrupted our courtship a bit. I had only been to Ireland twice before, one to run the Dublin Marathon with Patrick Doherty and then, again, in 2001 with Bob Jagger to play the Irish Open Tennis Championships. I was really looking forward to the trip for a number of reasons, not the least of which was to spend time with my children.

The five of us flew from Tampa to New York, with a lay-over of several hours there, and then on to Shannon, arriving in Ireland early the next morning. We went down to Manhattan and walked around Time Square. We watched the Kentucky Derby from an ESPN Sports Zone bar there, after visiting the Twin Towers site, the Statue of Liberty and the Empire State Building. In fact, we had trouble finding our way back to the airport and almost missed our flight, which was boarding when we finally got there.

Once we arrived in Shannon, we quickly found out that the car I had rented wasn't large enough to hold the five of us and all of our luggage, so I had to rent a second car. Patrick and Brendan loved that. They got a much smaller vehicle that went much faster.

Before going to our cottage, we stopped at Bunratty Castle, which was on the way. It was a fully restored village, with all of the businesses that would have been there during the 14th and 15th centuries, like the Catholic church, a blacksmith, a bakery and more. The castle was decorated appropriately, as well.

Plus, there was an Irish bar, called Dirty Nelly's, next door, where we ate and drank a beer none had ever had before, called Bulmer's. It has an apple cider kind of taste, and everyone loved it, especially Patrick. From there, we went on to our cottage.

The idea of renting a cottage had seemed so logical when I did it, after going from Bed and Breakfast places on my two prior visits to Ireland as I had, but I didn't take into consideration the roads in Ireland – they're small, narrow things, with rock walls on both sides, that wind around and around, with "round-abouts" scattered here and there throughout. It's a nightmare to drive, and that's without taking into consideration the fact that they drive on the left side of the road and the steering wheel is on the right (wrong) side of the car. Patrick didn't seem to have a problem with it, however, but I certainly did, plus the car I had rented filled up the entire lane, with no room to spare.

It was late afternoon by the time we arrived at our cottage, and we were able to witness a magnificent sight – the sun setting over the Atlantic Ocean, with the Cliffs of Moher to our right and the Aran Islands off in the distance. I don't know how that affected the four of them, but I was impressed. It was a sight to behold. We all slept well that night.

On our first full day in Ireland, we drove to visit the Blarney Castle and kissed the stone, a ridiculous, but obligatory, custom. You lie flat on your back and are lowered down a couple of feet, with someone you don't know holding your knees, and kiss this one particular stone among the tens of thousands of stones that look just like it, while someone is taking a picture of you. We all did it. For me, it was the third time I'd done it. You'd think I'd have learned my lesson, but I hadn't, and still haven't.

The next day we took a ferry to the Aran Islands, which sit about 11 miles off the coast. We left from Galway. Once there, we rented bicycles and rode out to Dun Angus, an ancient castle which is famous as being a "ringed fort."

There are three long rows of stones that appear to be lines of defense. The castle backed up to the ocean, which was hundreds of feet below. There was no way out, either the defenders were successful defending the castle or they died. It was quite a day and we dined at a traditional Irish bar that night on our way back "home."

The next day we went to Killarney, my favorite city in all of Ireland, and the ancestral home of our Sullivan family. My mother was a Sullivan. There is a National Forest there and we rode horses on a trail ride.

However, this was unlike any trail ride I'd ever been on. They required us to gallop the horses. In the U.S., they never allow you to let them gallop, for insurance reasons. We also hiked around the park and ate dinner at one of the many Irish bars in Killarney, and there are many. Of course, all the bars in Ireland are Irish, right? So that's what's called "redundant."

Over the remainder of our days we visited castles, more Irish bars, a beautiful golf course where we dined by ourselves in luxury, more

Irish bars and more castles, AND we saw the "original" boat sailed by a man named Tim Severin a few years earlier from Ireland to the United States, duplicating what St. Brendan the Navigator did in the 5th century. I was impressed. I hope that Brendan was, too. That's where he got his name.

We did some other things, too, and on our very last day in Ireland, before heading back to Shannon and flying out, we visited the city of Galway. It was a memorable event for several reasons. First, as we were walking around the city, not knowing where we were going, but trying to follow directions, we weren't seeing much of anything. The "natives" were restless. "Dad! What are we doing here! This is boring!" I had no adequate response.

Then, we turned a corner and all of a sudden it was like a switch was turned on. We came upon thousands of people on the streets, with musicians, jugglers, mimes, street people and, most importantly, young people their age. Their attitudes changed instantly. We found a bar, that was jam-packed, drank some beer, made some friends (they did) and had a great time.

In fact, they all stayed out into the wee hours of the morning while I went back to the hotel room I rented for us, anticipating that such a thing might happen. It was one of the only nights that they got to mingle without their father being around, and they appreciated it.

The trip back to the U.S. was uneventful, except for the fact that I had backed up and hit a rock when leaving the cottage, which cost me $1,500.00, about as much as the plane tickets. I hadn't paid for the excess insurance and it came out of my credit card. I had no recourse. There was no way the damage was that excessive, but there was nothing I could do. I was stuck. I always got excess insurance when traveling from then on, especially in Ireland, where driving is no pleasure.

However, that unfortunate circumstance didn't diminish my enjoyment of the trip. It was, and it will always be, the best trip I ever took with my children, and I am so glad that I did it. It was, as they say, "priceless."

Upon returning home to the Gainesville/Lake City area, the romance with Susan was quickly re-kindled. The fires hadn't burned out. In fact, absence made the heart grow fonder, it seemed, and we picked up right where we left off.

The distance between Lake City and Gainesville is about 30 some miles, but we were about an hour apart. That didn't stop us, but we didn't see each other every night. We were together every weekend, though, either at her place or mine. She really enjoyed canoeing and kayaking as much as I did, and she had a 12 foot boat which she liked to ski behind, and we did that, too, as well as bicycle frequently.

I was plugging away at the office, but I was being given cases that were in litigation and were the most difficult to handle. Some of them were actually quite interesting and controversial. I was the one who wanted those cases, no one else did.

For example, I settled a major housing discrimination case for a couple trying to buy a house in Lake City, which involved a legal issue of "racial steering." That occurred when a real estate salesperson told an African-American couple that they should look in a particular area of town to buy, which was the "black" section of town. That was a classic case of "steering" a prospective buyer to a location for a racially motivated reason.

That case caused quite a stir in the real estate community and they held conferences to educate the sales people not to do things like that. The legal community was not happy with me because of it. TRLS, however, was quite pleased with the result.

I also created a program that was quite novel for the legal services community, which was also very much appreciated, and that was when I started a radio show. Another attorney and I found a radio station in Perry, Florida, which is in Taylor County, and within our service area, that was willing to give us a half hour per week to put on a show we called "Law Matters." Rocky Cabagnot and I talked about issues affecting the poor in our service area. We took phone calls and spread the gospel, so to speak. We enjoyed doing it and I'm proud of it. It was fun, actually.

However, I got a big break when I was assigned to become involved with the Kennedy Homes case that had been in litigation long before the time I became the Director of Litigation back in 2003. I was now going to be lead counsel on the case for TRLS. It was, as I explained earlier, a major case against the largest landlord in the entire country.

One of the first things I did was to associate with Southern Legal Counsel, another entity much like Three Rivers Legal Services, which provides free legal assistance to the poor. The difference is that they specialize more with cases involving civil rights, education and disabilities. They didn't handle divorces, landlord-tenant, social security or other issues, which constitute the majority of cases handled by TRLS.

Also, they had recently hired a lawyer from Miami, who was retired from a successful practice involving plaintiffs personal injury and workers compensation matters. He had more experience than I did and, most importantly, SLC had a whole lot more money to fund a successful prosecution of the case than TRLS did. I needed his help and their help, and they gladly came on board.

It was an awful case, actually. Kennedy Homes was built in the late 1960s and it was named after John F. Kennedy. It was part of the "War on Poverty," and there were hundreds of such complexes built to house poor people all over the country. The problem was that the houses were now almost 50 years old and most were badly in need of renovation.

The biggest problem was that the mood of the country had changed dramatically since the optimism of the '60s. George W. Bush was now the president, and he was not a democrat. There was absolutely no movement afoot anywhere in the country, at any level of government, to spend the money necessary to do the needed repairs to Kennedy Homes or any of the other dilapidated housing complexes around the country.

A fire had occurred in one of the buildings within the Kennedy Homes complex and it affected dozens of apartments. About a hundred and fifty families living within the complex at the time. The landlord, which had been paid millions by the Federal government to provide the housing to those poor people over the years, through their Section 8 program, decided not to make any repairs and just shut the complex down, causing a crisis to all who lived there.

The case was now set for trial and discovery was ongoing. Once I got involved, it got a whole lot more intense. Depositions were to be taken of people all over the country, and I was the only one in TRLS who had any experience with complex litigation like this case involved. I don't think the attorneys at TRLS had ever taken too many depositions at all. I'd taken thousands of them.

Fortunately for me, I was transferred down to the Gainesville office, because that's where all the files were located. An entire room was filled with boxes which contained all of the legal work that had been done on the case. An attorney had stamped and numbered each and every piece of paper to help us keep track of it all. There were about a hundred thousand pieces of paper. It was a nightmare.

When that happened, I moved in with Susan and gave up my place in Lake City. That deepened our relationship considerably. It saved me a whole lot of driving time to and from work, too, like an hour or two per day.

Also, although I had no idea this would happen, it gave me more time to work on my books. I began writing at night, in the wee hours of the morning, from 2:00 to 4:00, or maybe 3:00 to 5:00. I'd wake up in the middle of the night, not knowing what time it was, and start writing. I'd go back to sleep for an hour or two, and then go to work.

I wrote several books during that stretch. A Very Fine Line had come out by then, and it was followed by Fistfight at the L & M Saloon that same year, that being 2006. After struggling for so many years to get my first novel into print, the second one was much, much easier, and the third was even easier than that.

For a book to be considered a novel, it should contain at least 60,000 words and as many as 90,000, according to the books I'd read and the conferences I'd attended. More pages than that was frowned upon by publishers because the cost of production goes up and the ability to make a profit goes down, unless the book was a big seller. I always made sure that my books reached at least the 75,000 word mark, and they all did. In fact, all but a few are over 90,000 and many are well over 100,000 words.

I found that I could write, on average, about 2,000 words per night for a two or three hour session. Stephen King averages 3,000 words per day, but I'm not Stephen King. At 2,000 words per day, or night, I'd have 100,000 words in 50 days. So I could write a book in less than two months, and then it would take me another two or three months to edit it. At that pace, I would be able to average about two books a year.

Fistfight at the L & M Saloon was a story about Cedar Key. The L & M was a bar in Cedar Key that had been the scene of many a bar fight over the years it was in existence. It closed not longer after I moved there. It was actually a story about the crime of being an accessory after the fact to a crime. It gave me the opportunity to tell readers all about the little town of Cedar Key that I had adopted.

One of my favorite stories about the L & M came from a local fisherman. When I told him that I had written the book he said, "Yeah! That was a tough place! They'd search you for knives and guns before letting you in." When I commented that I could understand why, he added, "and if you didn't have one, they gave you one, 'cause you were gonna need it!"

In 2007, my book of short stories, entitled <u>Pieces to the Puzzle</u>, went into print, as did two other novels, <u>A Plenary Indulgence</u> and <u>Bocas del Toro.</u> By that point, I had just about given up on the idea of finding an agent and getting published by a traditional publisher. I hadn't given up entirely, but I wasn't trying as hard as I once did. Plus, I wasn't doing a very good job of promoting my books. They were coming out as fast as I could write them.

<u>A Plenary Indulgence</u> was a story about a Korean-American man I had met in Tampa who owned and operated a Thai food restaurant. We had become friendly because I ate at his place at least once a week for over a year. He had been robbed at gunpoint one night and the story was front page news in the Tampa papers.

When I saw that on the news, I wrote the book to explain to him exactly what was going to happen to him at trial. I told him that he had to read it before trial began. He did and thanked me for what I'd done for him. In fact, he called me from the courtroom once the verdict was announced.

In <u>Bocas del Toro</u>, I tell a story of drug-smuggling in Cedar Key. In it, at the end, the protagonist sails off to Bocas del Toro, which is an archipilago of islands between Costa Rica and Panama in the Caribbean Sea. It gained fame when one of the survivor programs was filmed there. Because of that, it became a major destination for tourists after that occurred. Many of my friends told me that it hit a little too close to home for some of the residents of Cedar Key, where most of the action takes place.

In 2008, I wrote <u>A Tinker's Damn!</u>, which is a story about Red, the Irishman I'd met back in 1972 while working at the Harbor Island Spa. That was, quite loosely, a story of his life. After meeting him, as you may recall, I had to get out of Miami and Dade County. He was too dangerous for me to be around. It's about Ireland, the IRA, drug smuggling, informants and other criminal matters.

In 2009, the Kennedy Homes case settled, and I wrote a book about it. A poker-playing friend of mine who was an advocate for a large Housing program told me that the book is quite famous in that community. The fact that the conditions were awful didn't outweigh the fact that those units were "home" for those who lived there. That was the most interesting part of the book to those housing advocates. The tenants would have preferred to stay at Kennedy Homes, despite the defective conditions.

That year, 2009, was a busy one for me what with all the responsibilities I had as a lawyer, handling the Kennedy Homes lawsuit, and everything else that was going on in my life, so that was the only book I wrote that year. Still, I had become somewhat prolific during the years 2006 to 2009, having written as much as I did. Though I was not enjoying any financial success as an author despite my best efforts, I was "compelled" to do what I did, and I wasn't done yet.

Looking back, I really don't know how, or why, I did that, but I did. I had a passion for writing, that was obvious, but I didn't realize it ran that deep, but it did. I had stories inside of me that had to come out and I was willing to get up at all hours of the morning, something I've never done before or since, to write those stories. It amazes me. It really does.

I was extremely busy traveling for work during that time, too. I had to fly to New York on a few occasions for depositions in the case, plus there were depositions in Colorado and elsewhere throughout other parts of the country. Also, there were many hearings, like in Colorado and New York where the company tried to prevent us from taking the depositions of some of the corporate higher-ups.

A Federal Judge in New York held a half hour hearing on whether or not I could depose the head of the entire corporation. She ruled in our favor and I deposed the man in one of the floors of the Empire State Building. They were not happy about that.

He testified that he had no knowledge of who made the decision to close the complex. I never did find out who the person was, but it was probative that no one could satisfactorily explain why the complex was closed or who made the decision.

We mediated the case a couple of times, which required the hundred and fifty plaintiffs, plus about six insurance companies, with their team of lawyers, to meet in a main ballroom of one of the larger hotels. It was a complicated case and, since Kennedy Homes had been completely leveled by the time the case neared trial, all of our clients, or most of them, were without a suitable place to live.

Many were being housed on a "temporary" basis in a motel that was to be demolished. Most still wanted to go back to their apartments in Kennedy Homes, despite all of the problems that needed to be fixed, but that was no longer a possibility. The case was all about money at that point.

We also had a team of law students from the University of Florida working with us on the case, perhaps as many as a dozen, doing legal research on various aspects of the case. There were many issues involving discovery. The landlord, and his team of lawyers, fought us on producing documents and on just about every legal issue they could think of. For many months, it was the only case I was working on.

Susan was a physical therapist by day, and on days when she didn't have to work too late, we would ride bikes or go for long walks with Bailey after work. On weekends, we would usually go for a ride in her boat on the Suwannee River, or out on Lake Santa Fe, or elsewhere, or we'd canoe the Itchetucknee River, or the Santa Fe, Silver or other rivers.

We were always doing something of a physical nature, which we both loved doing. We were a really good match, and there was a strong emotional component, too. Although it was an extremely busy time of life, I was enjoying it fully – burning the candle at both ends, as they say.

After a while, we began to play music at open-mics, where musicians, who aren't professionals, get on stage and play between four and six songs in front of other musicians doing the same thing. There were several places around Gainesville, High Springs and Cedar Key where we did that. She would sing and play her guitar, and I'd accompany her on the bass.

When we had the time, we went camping in places like the Nantahala National Forest, which we did several times. We also flew to Spokane and drove out to Glacier and camped there for a week one year. We camped in Georgia and visited Cumberland Island a few times. We camped at St. George's State Park a couple of times, and at St. Vincent Island, both of which are in the panhandle area of Florida.

We also camped at Amicalola State Park in Georgia, where the Appalachian Trail begins, and at Fort Clinch in Fernandina Beach.

Anastasia State Park in St. Augustine was one of our favorite places, but there were others. She wasn't afraid of "roughing it." She enjoyed it.

However, after a few years of sleeping in tents on sleeping bags, I bought a twenty-four foot travel trailer which we pulled around for years after that. We were a great match and we were happy. We were in love with one another.

I must admit that I was disappointed when the Kennedy Homes case eventually settled. Those poor people who had been out of their homes for so long, just decided to cave in and take the best offer we could wrangle out of the landlord and their insurance companies. I wanted to take the case to trial, but the clients were the ones who had to decide whether to settle the case or go in front of a jury in Federal Court and risk losing everything.

I couldn't blame them. There was no guarantee that we would win, and they couldn't afford to lose, although they weren't paying any of the costs. They all decided to accept the money that was offered to them and move on.

In that respect, it was a victory, since they all "won" some money, but there was no legal precedent to come out of it, and the settlement was, by agreement, kept private, so I can't reveal how much it was. As I said, it was disappointing to me, as their lawyer, but they were the ones who made the decision to settle. It isn't easy being poor, and being poor definitely affected their judgment.

When the Kennedy Homes case ended, I was sent back to the Lake City office to be a staff attorney again. That was in late 2008 and it was George W. Bush's last year in office. As everyone remembers, the economy had taken a huge tumble due to a crisis with sub-prime mortgage loans.

Banks were going under, the Stock Exchange dropped to 800 points, and the government bailed out the automobile companies, except for Ford. People were losing their houses, land values plummeted, and the country was in what was called "The Great Recession." Those were the worst economic days our country had seen since the Great Depression which began in 1929 and lasted for nearly a decade.

The bad economic times meant less money for programs like legal services. Since I was a part-time attorney making more money than many full-time staff attorneys with less experience, I was one who was let go. My last day of work at TRLS was on December 31, 2008.

I decided to go into private practice out in Cedar Key. I loved it out there and I still wanted to spend more time writing books. I didn't want to get back into the full-time practice of law. I certainly wasn't about to go back to doing insurance defense work, plaintiff's personal injury work, commercial litigation, criminal or anything else I'd done in my life. I was still living with Susan, though, and the commute was going to be difficult as Cedar Key was about 45 minutes away from where she lived.

Chapter Twenty

Cedar Key Part deux

On January 1, 2009, I opened the Law Office of R. Pierce Kelley, Jr. in the tiny town of Cedar Key, population 850 people. Hundreds more lived outside of the city limits, but an even larger number of people came to visit every weekend of the year, especially from the end of November to the middle of April, right after the Easter weekend.

Cedar Key was not, by any stretch of the imagination, a good place to open a law office. There was one other attorney already there, Terry Tataru, a very nice man, who specialized in real estate matters, though he also handled DUIs, and there were many of those citations handed out on a regular basis. Cedar Key has a healthy population of bars, which are usually fully occupied on Friday and Saturday nights, and the police had become quite aggressive in making arrests in recent years.

The only place I could find to rent was a small, wooden building, that had been a fish and bait shop a few months earlier. It sat right on the channel leading out from the Marina to the Gulf on the back side, and it fronted State Road 24. Everyone coming into or out of Cedar Key passed right by my office. However, there weren't all that many people actually in need of legal assistance out there, and those that did, didn't have much money.

My main source of income during the early days came from the Florida Bar Referral Service, which charged a 12% referral fee. Also, I was required, by written agreement, to give free consultations to seniors and low-income individuals, as determined by them. I joined two pre-paid legal companies, which is to say that employees would pay a monthly fee for legal assistance, if and when they needed it.

Mostly, I represented people in family law matters, not criminal. I had the right to refuse or accept cases with all three programs. None paid too much or too well.

The rent was really cheap and I had all of the furniture and equipment I needed, so I didn't have to make too much money to pay my bills. One of my biggest expenses was my gas bill. It was an 80 mile round-trip drive from her house to my office and back.

By that time, I was really "cooking" as far as my writing was concerned, since I wasn't nearly as active with my legal work as I had been. I wrote two more books that year: <u>A Foreseeable Risk</u>; and <u>Asleep at the Wheel</u>. I was doing my best to promote my books, which I did by getting all of the local newspapers to publish press releases about my book, speaking at as many of the local libraries as possible, and attending book fairs and author events everywhere I could, within the north Florida area.

I began doing Public Service Announcements for as many of the local papers as would allow me to do so, including a few in Levy County, and also in Gilchrist, Taylor, LaFayette, Suwannee, Columbia, Alachua, Union, Dixie and Madison counties. Many of the editors of those newspapers would review my books, which helped, too. Some of the reviews I put on the covers of books.

I had learned that there were, basically, four steps to writing a book. The first was the actual writing of the book – getting it out of your head and onto paper, or in the computer, to be more accurate. That step included the research necessary to write the book. My first few books were all about legal issues and I didn't have to do too much research to write those, but that changed after a while. I tired of writing books about legal issues, and there were plenty of lawyers writing such books. It was a crowded field.

Actually, I had learned that legal fiction, like what John Grisham, Scott Turow and others write, is a very small piece of the literary pie, and there are many others who have been successful in that small circle, just not as successful as those two. Children's books, from the very young, to the intermediate age level, up through high school were, by far, the biggest category. Over half of the books purchased in the United States are for young readers up to the YA, or young adult, readers. So legal fiction was a very small part of the pie.

Then there were the books most usually read by adults, such as romance novels, the science fiction books, horror, mystery, thriller, historical fiction, fantasy, humor, literary fiction, and others, and that didn't include the works of non-fiction, like biographies, auto-biographies, history, spirituality, true crime and others, and then, on top of that, there is what J. K. Rowling did with the Harry Potter books about wizardry, which is a genre unto itself, which was astonishing. Plus, the publishing world was changing. E-books were now becoming the rage, and there is precious little money in those E-books for authors.

Despite that, I was determined to be a writer, and I continued to try to be successful at it. Fortunately, or unfortunately, depending upon your perspective, I didn't read the statistics which indicated how many authors actually made money from writing books. It's an extremely low number, and nearly a million new books are put into circulation every year. Like the starving artists, street musicians and most creative types, I was undaunted.

If that wasn't enough to discourage would-be authors, like me, I don't know what would be. I was undeterred. I was on a "Mission from God," as John Belushi and Dan Aykroyd proclaimed in the movie Blues Brothers.

Actually, I have read that people like me have something inside them that compels them to get it out, like a disease. I liken it to having a baby – you write and write and then edit and edit, and, finally, mercifully, you have a baby.

Kennedy Homes: An American Tragedy, was a non-fiction book about the lawsuit I had been involved in for years. I felt as though the legal services community should have the benefit of knowing exactly what took place in that case, so that they could learn from it. I didn't want to see all of that legal knowledge go to waste.

As I mentioned, I have been told that my book was and still is extremely well-thought of in a certain, quite limited, circle of our society, mostly the sociologists, not the lawyers, though. It is what it is, and I haven't made a dime from it. It cost me money to publish it, money that I never recovered. I don't regret writing it one little bit, though I do wish that it had made money, obviously.

A Foreseeable Risk, is a novel about my friend, Matthew Chatowsky, from Cedar Key, who was injured in the horse-back riding incident. I've received many favorable comments about the book, as has Matt, but other friends have said that they didn't want to read about something like that. It just didn't interest them. It's a difficult topic to discuss, or even think about, going from a virile, adventurous man to being a paraplegic, as he did.

It hurts Matt to think about those things, but I believe that he's glad we did it. He doesn't like to talk about it, but the book tells his story, and it's a compelling one. He was broken, but he's not broke. He is alive and well and thriving as a musician as I write. Plus, he's a great fisherman and he loves to go scalloping. We're still the best of friends.

The next book written in 2010, was Asleep at the Wheel. It is a totally fabricated story that begins with two men fishing in Cedar Key, having a wonderful day on the water, as many fishermen do there. After having some beers, cleaning the fish, they head home, but the driver falls asleep at the wheel of his truck on the way.

In doing my research, it surprised me to learn that nearly half of the people in the country admit to falling asleep while driving at least once in their lives. Most wake up before something terrible happens, but some don't. The passenger, his best friend, died in the accident.

That book really tells a story of what a personal injury lawsuit is all about, from the perspective of all concerned parties: the driver, the family of the deceased person, the lawyers and the insurance companies for both. Of all of the books I have written, this one was more about me just wanting to explain, in some detail, what I truly disliked about being a lawyer involved with personal injury lawsuits. It's probably my least favorite book, but I'm glad I wrote it. I was expurgating some demons from my brain.

Sue and I were still going strong. We were playing more music than ever and I was getting better. She was one who didn't like to be on stage, bringing attention to herself, although she was, and still is, very talented. I, being the trial lawyer and professional athlete, enjoy the spotlight. I don't shy away from being on a stage, even though I wasn't all that talented at playing the bass. We both improved, and it was fun to practice together, getting ready for an event of some kind, and then performing. We did dozens of those things.

In late 2010, the two of us took a trip to Ireland together. We rented a cottage in a little village called Columbkille, in Donegal County. While there, we explored the northwest part of Ireland and visited the many sites there. We hiked, swam in the Atlantic, and visited Glenveigh National Park, Slieve League and a place called the "Golden Strand," among other things.

Slieve League is the second-highest sea cliffs in Ireland, some two thousand feet above the ocean. It was spectacular to walk along the mountain tops and look down below, where sheep were grazing, perilously close to the edge. We had to be careful. I slipped and fell on the wet grass several times.

In fact, as we were walking up the mountain one day, a man who was walking right in front of us, stopped suddenly, removed a rifle from his coat, that was hidden from sight, and began firing shots at the sheep. We stopped, because he was right in our way, and I asked him what he was doing. I was, understandably, somewhat alarmed by it. Susan was in shock.

He told me that those were his sheep and he was trying to scare them, to make them move away from the edge. He said he had lost dozens of sheep who simply fell off into the ocean to die. Unbelievable, but true.

The "Golden Strand" is actually a name given to many sites throughout Ireland. The word "strand" means beach, and there are many places along the coast of Ireland where a beach has been formed in the shape of a horseshoe, with high cliffs surrounding it, which seems to be golden when the sun hits it just right.

It truly was a magnificent place to swim. You had to walk down hundreds of feet to get there, and then walk back up when you were finished. The water was cold, but it was a memorable place to be.

Glenveigh National Park was and is the most well-known destinations in County Donegal and it is magnificent. It is a restored mansion from the days when wealthy Scots were given large grants of land by the English monarchs to simply move to Ireland and do whatever they wished, without regard for the Irish Catholics who lived there. Irish Catholics weren't allowed to own land at that time.

On our way there, we stopped at Gweedore, a small town where the Irish band, Clannad, was from, as well as their more famous sister, Enya. The family owns and operates a restaurant there, where we decided to eat, in hopes of seeing one of them. Unfortunately, and not surprisingly, none of the children were there.

We had a fabulous trip, and did our best not to be too touristy. We wanted to experience as much of the "real" Ireland as possible, and we did. We spent months learning how to speak Gaelic before we left. In Donegal, the street and road signs are in Gaelic. Donegal sits astride northern Ireland and there have been many, many problems all along that border for centuries, but not while we were there, fortunately.

My office, being a former "bait shop," was really not a very professional place, so I changed locations after a year was up, as I had signed a year's lease. I moved just a few hundred yards towards the main part of town into a building where there was a canvas shop and a coffee shop. At least I could get really good coffee and something to eat anytime I wanted. It was a move "up," and I was beginning to get business from the locals. I was making more money, but I was working harder, too.

I only wrote one book in 2011, and that was another tough one, about my friend, George, who I'd met in Fort Myers. He was suffering from the effects of PTSD from his days in Viet Nam. He was, and still is, as nice a man as you could ever hope to meet, but he has had demons.

That book is called A Thousand Yard Stare. The title comes from a play written by Sophocles telling of how Ajax the Great, one of the Greek heroes from the Trojan War, suffered mental problems as a result of the many battles he fought. It is said to be the first mention of an illness in literature now known as Post Traumatic Stress Disorder, or PTSD.

George allowed me to tell his story, and I'm pleased to report that he is proud of the fact that I have told his story. Some fifty years after the War ended, George and others like him finally received some benefits from the Veteran's Administration as a result of his service and the illness he suffered from. PTSD was not recognized as a "legitimate" illness for years. I am told that his picture and the book I wrote about him are in the Soldiers and Sailors Museum in Chicago. He has become somewhat of a celebrity.

As far as my law practice was concerned, I was really just trying to make enough money to pay my bills and allow me to continue writing books. I guess I still believed that something I would write would catch the attention of someone and, somehow, take off. I still had a passion for it, and I was still waking up at all hours of the morning to write.

Susan and I were going still going strong, and we were as active as ever. We were playing more and more and we were getting better. Sue was becoming more at ease with performing. I was still plucking away, one note at a time, one finger at a time, using two fingers. We actually received some money for playing music at a restaurant/bar in Cedar Key. That didn't happen too often.

In the Fall of that year, we flew to Spokane, just as Caitlin and I had done years earlier, rented a car and drove to Montana. We stayed at a cabin on the Northern Railway Rafting Company site, still owned by Reno Baldwin, and hiked with him and his wife several times through the mountains. We rafted, played music, and I even had a book-signing event at a local coffee shop.

However, a few months later, Susan sustained an injury at work to her cervical spine which changed everything quite a bit. She wasn't able to work, nor could she play her guitar, and was, basically, rendered immobile for a long while. With my help, she filed a worker's compensation claim, which lasted for nearly two years and ultimately led to surgery.

She wasn't able to do too much during those days, but we were able to go canoeing, with me doing all of the paddling, which was fine. We swam more in the rivers and springs, and we went camping fairly often, too. I did all the driving and everything else, but it still affected our relationship in many ways.

In fact, sometime after she began to recover from that whole ordeal I moved out of her house and rented a house in Cedar Key where I had my office and I could live there during the week. I went back on weekends, but things were different. She needed her "space," and so did I.

In 2012, I wrote a non-fiction book about the immigration problem in America. Through my friend, Matt Chatowsky, I met Jorge Frias, a Mexican man who had been living in the United States for over twenty years as an illegal immigrant. I didn't know any illegal immigrants before meeting him.

I wondered how he did it. How did he stay in the United States for so long without being detected? I had no idea, so I asked him if he'd let me write a book about his journey and he agreed to allow me to do so. At the time I met him, he had been captured and was awaiting deportation, so he wasn't in any danger and he was actually "free" to roam the country, which was strange.

He was a very nice man, who has recently left us, unfortunately, but we became friends. In fact, after he was deported, I flew down to Cancun, a major tourist attraction in the Yucatan Peninsula and drove over to Progreso, where he lived.

It is a port city on the Gulf of Mexico, with an incredibly long pier where huge cruise ships make stops on a daily basis. I wanted to investigate the area and learn the details necessary to paint the picture of Jorge, his family and his life. I needed to do that to tell his story.

When I arrived, he was working for one of the tour groups as a guide, taking visitors to the many Mayan temples in the area, such as Chichen-Itza, Tulum, Kukulcan and others. He took me to all of those places and we swam in several cenotes, ran the beaches and had a great time. His father is a well-known and well-respected journalist and he comes from a distinguished family.

I called the book Father, I Must Go. He left his family, his city, his country for twenty years to live as an illegal alien in the United States. Why? He had everything a man could want in Progreso, but he wanted to come to the U.S. and live in our country. Matt says that he was "como el viento," or "like the wind." He wrote poetry and was a beautiful soul.

In the book, I detailed the history of immigration in the United States, after the point in time when we, quite famously, said to the world:

"Give me your tired, your poor, your huddled masses, yearning to breathe free, the wretched refuse of your teeming shores. Send these, the homeless, tempest-tost to me, I lift my lamp beside the golden door."

The woman on the statue has been called many names over the years, but the one I like the best is "Lady of the Harbor."

It is now 2022 as I write and I am absolutely amazed that there has been precious little done in the ensuing ten years since I wrote that book about the immigration problem. I truly thought that maybe, just maybe, I had written a book that would catch the pulse of the country. I was wrong, it didn't, but I sure did learn a lot in the process of writing that book. Meeting "Georgie" was the best part.

Immigration was then, and it is even more so now, a serious problem that our country must address. Trump tried to build a wall to keep people from sneaking into our country across our southern border, but that hasn't worked. It is, truly, a national emergency, yet nothing has been done about it. My book hasn't received the recognition it truly deserves – yet. It is as worthy, and as relevant, now as it was then.

I went back to Mexico a year later to promote the book. In fact, Susan was supposed to come with me on that trip, but she couldn't travel. Her neck was still causing her too much pain and she feared that she couldn't sit in a plane that long, so I went by myself.

Jorge always told me that he had Mayan blood in him, and he looked very much like the mayans that are pictured in the history books. No one knows what happened to that ancient civilization that thrived for over twenty-five hundred years before suddenly disappearing in about A.D. 1000. It truly remains a puzzle, which no one has provided a satisfactory answer to yet.

During that time, while Susan was injured, I started running more. As part of her rehabilitation, even before the surgery, swimming was recommended, and we started swimming a lot. Although she wasn't able to ride for a long while, I was still riding some, and I entered some of the mini-triathlons, just for fun. However, there weren't many men in my age-group, so I'd win.

In 2012, I wrote Roxy Blues, a book about the opiate crisis in America. I had a client who was a clammer in Cedar Key who became addicted to Oxycontin after sustaining an injury out on the water. He explained that the pills were called "roxies" on the street. That was at the time the drug was causing enormous problems throughout the country.

Again, I hoped that maybe, just maybe, I had written a book that caught the "pulse" of our nation, but it didn't happen with that book, either. It was and it is a good book but, like the others, it didn't enjoy financial success. In many ways, I was hiding under a rock, out in the "boonies," but I was enjoying the process. That's what it means to be passionate about something. You do it because you love it.

By that time, I had learned that what I really needed to do was hire a publicist. However, they are extremely expensive, and I didn't have the money to do that. Clearly, I was doing everything wrong. It was going to take a miracle for my books to be "discovered."

In 2013, I was seeing Susan only on weekends, and our relationship was floundering. I had tired of the daily drive years ago, but there was no solution to that problem. She was, by that time, back to work on a very limited basis, and my office was in Cedar Key. I had a clientele and had built a very modest following.

We enjoyed our weekends together and, in the late summer of 2013, we took another great trip together. We went out to hike the Presidential Peaks in Colorado, a couple of hours southwest of Denver. I drove out, taking Bailey with me, and I met her at the airport in Denver. She had found us a beautiful cottage alongside the Arkansas River in Salida and Buena Vista.

We had a great trip together, doing some amazing hikes up Mount Princeton, Mount Yale, Mount Harvard and Mount Columbia, four of the 14,000 foot peaks in Colorado. The views from those mountain tops were unforgettable. We were snowed upon a few times, and could have been lost a time or two, but we always seemed to find one of the many hot springs nearby.

Salida and Buena Vista are two very cool little mountain towns. They are called "down-valley," situated along Highway 24, which is somewhat famous for passing by and between over a dozen "fourteeners." Those are mountains which are over 14,000 feet in elevation.

One of the many highlights of the trip was hearing Grace Pettis play at one of the local bars. She's the daughter of Pierce Pettis, who I'd met in Gainesville years before, and befriended, because of our names, primarily. He didn't know anyone else named Pierce, nor did I. He has played all over the country for over four decades now.

However, before picking Susan up at the airport, I drove to Pawhuska, Oklahoma, the ancestral home of the Osage tribe. That's where Mose Tallchief, and his son, lived. I pitched a tent on his 80 acre farm just outside of town and spent a week with the two of them, traveling around that part of the country with them to write the book they said that I could write about them and their heritage years before. I was now ready to write that book.

I had read many books about the Osage, and many books about Native American Indians, prior to driving out there, but I hadn't quite figured out what my book was going to be. I had to be there, to see it with my own eyes, and through their eyes, to figure that out. After being there with them, as I was, the book came into vision and I wrote it with no difficulty whatsoever.

As with so many of my books, I learned so much about the people and things I write about that it's amazing to me. I'm writing books while learning about things that I chose to learn about. I was especially delighted to learn of the experience of the Osage through the eyes of two Osage Indians.

I truly knew nothing about the Osage before embarking on that project. I am incredibly grateful to Mose and his son for allowing me into their lives as they did. I spoke to Mose just a few weeks ago.

Like most Americans, I'd read Bury my Heart at Wounded Knee, and seen the movie of the same name, starring Dustin Hoffman, as well as Dances with Wolves, starring Kevin Costner, and everything else everyone else has seen, going back to Gene Autrey, Roy Rogers, the Lone Ranger, Gunsmoke, Maverick and all the rest, but this was real. To be honest, I really didn't know all that much about the Native American experience, for that matter, before beginning that project.

It's an unbelievable story, really, and, as we all know, not a very good one from the perspective of Native American Indians. I don't think the hundreds of tribes, who continue to do their best to maintain their cultural identities to this very day, have assimilated into traditional American life, and I don't think that they want to. They remain proud of their history and their culture and they want to keep it, apparently. Who can blame them?

Everyone knows about all of the treaties broken by the United States government with virtually all of the tribes, but I didn't know that it was Teddy Roosevelt who actually hurt them the most, in my opinion, although Andrew Jackson is certainly in the running for that award. Many presidents bought into the idea of "Manifest Destiny" as a justification for the United States to simply conquer all tribes in what is now the continental United States. England, and then Canada, did the same thing to them.

Teddy broke up the tribes and their system of governance, but he didn't kill any of them. Andrew did that, and he forcibly moved tribes out of their ancestral lands. Teddy did what he did by telling all tribes to count their members and, once they did, he then divided up the land that each tribe held as its "reservation land," by the number of tribal members, reserving only a very small part for the tribe itself. Each member was given a "headright" and a deed to land, so that each individual Indian owned land, just like other Americans did.

Mose's grandfather received 320 acres, but it was given to him in four 80 acre plots. Mose never could understand why it was done that way, but that's the way it was done. Also, it was done that way with all tribes, not just the Osage. Mose had, by the time I met him, several headrights, acquired from other family members, and he had deeds to several parcels of land. I stayed in my tent, with Bailey sleeping outside to protect me, on one of those 80 acre parcels.

Mose was not at all like what I thought a Native American Indian would be like - nothing. He was not the least bit angry or remorseful about anything that had happened to him or his tribe, really. He considered himself as American as any other citizen of our country, and he loved this country, despite the many things done to him and his ancestors in the past and to this very date.

While I was there, which was quite a coincidence and helped me figure out the story to tell, President Obama approved a settlement of a lawsuit involving all tribes in the country regarding how the tribes were mistreated going back nearly a hundred years. Every other president had "kicked the can" down the road, but the buck stopped with Obama. Mose, as well as all other Indians with "headrights," received some money. Mose received a lot of money because the Osage had so much more wealth than any of the other tribes in the country.

From all accounts, it was nowhere near what they were entitled to, though. The controversy had gone on for decades and had to be ended. The Indians, like the African-Americans at Kennedy Homes, took what they could get. That settlement was, in large part, the basis for the book.

I called it <u>A Deadly Legacy</u>. The reason I did so was because the moneys they had received a hundred years before, from oil profits, had proven to be a deathly experience for the Osage back then. When the Osage transferred the bottom half of Kansas to the Cherokee Indians, in exchange for a much smaller parcel in the northeast corner of Oklahoma, the chief said, "This land isn't good for anything. Maybe the white man will leave us alone if we stay here and mind our own business."

Unfortunately, or fortunately, if you will, oil was discovered on that

Osage reservation land – the mother lode. The Osage nation became immensely wealthy. At a time when one in eleven Americans owned a car, an Osage might own eleven cars. They had mansions and lived in their tepees.

So the United States government determined that Indians didn't know how to manage their money, and they appointed men, white men, to act as "guardians" of that money. Needless to say, that didn't go well for the Indians. Essentially, that was the basis of the lawsuits.

However, other crimes were committed against Indians back then, too. The Osage, because they were so wealthy, were prime targets. There was a killing spree in the 1920s, which were called the "Osage Indian Murders," by which white men married Osage Indian women to get their headrights, and then killed them. It was the first big case that the FBI first became involved with. That was the backstory to my book. It's true. You can look it up.

Again, it's a great book, in my opinion, which tells so much about Native Americans and their experience, but it, like the others, hasn't done well from a financial point of view. Mose was happy with it, although it's not entirely complimentary. It is a novel, but it's based upon fact and it is what is called historical fiction. I'm proud of it.

Meanwhile, during all of those years, those being from 2006 until 2014, my relationship with my children wasn't getting any better. Meagan got married in 2012, to a man whose family has a whole lot of money. They arranged for a wedding and reception that cost tens of thousands of dollars. I wasn't consulted, and I wasn't asked to contribute. I would not have recommended anything of that magnitude for any of my children, but Meagan didn't ask for my advice.

Caitlin was happily married and now had two children. She and her husband were living in Norfolk, Virginia, where he was stationed. They were doing well and I visited them a few times.

Brendan was in Hawaii. He was learning how to surf and waiting tables, making a lot of money, after a patchy start. Patrick was just starting to work at Prudential as a Financial Advisor. He was passing all of the tests and making his way up the ladder, slowly.

None of my children ever came to see me in Gainesville or Cedar Key. They were all on their own, now, and no longer sought any advice from me.

That wasn't the way I had planned things when I decided to get married and have children. Needless to say, I'm not proud of that.

At the end of that year, 2013, Susan and I took a trip to North Carolina, in the Smokies, not far from Cherokee, and spent a week in a cabin in the woods. It was intended to be a romantic time for the two of us to rekindle our love for each other. Unfortunately, it didn't work out that way.

When we returned to Florida, she went home to her house and I began to finish working on a log cabin I was building on the property the two of us had bought in Three Rivers Estates six years earlier. Our relationship had come to an end. The next chapter to my life was about to begin.

Chapter Twenty-One
A Cabin in the Woods

Beginning back when I first moved out of Susan's house in 2011, I realized that I had no place to live, other than at her place, as I had been doing for the last four years. So I began making plans to build a cabin, much like the one I'd built in Cedar Key in 2003, at the property we had bought together in Three Rivers Estates, not long after we met. I'd bought her out long before that. She had no interest in building a second home and the property was all mine now.

So I began the process of finding building plans, with the goal of getting a loan and starting to build. It wasn't as easy as I'd hoped it would be. I found plans easy enough. That wasn't the problem.

All I wanted was a two bedroom, two bath house in the woods, and I didn't want a full log cabin. I had learned a lesson from my Cedar Key home and I now wanted a place that looked like a log cabin, but wasn't. I wanted a "stick-built" home with traditional two by four studs and logs, split in half, on the outside.

I found a supplier of the log package easily enough. He would supply all of the materials to get me under roof, and he recommended a builder. He was located in Williston, Florida, not too far away, and the builder was from Lake City, very close to where I was to build.

I didn't have too much trouble getting pre-approved for a mortgage loan, but it takes a lot of time to go through the entire process as they require a whole lot of financial information and they go through the documents meticulously. After several more months, I was approved from a financial perspective, which was good. A problem arose, however, when the bank did a title search.

The original developer had reserved mineral rights to the property. The bank wouldn't loan me any money to build until those rights were extinguished. I had to find the original developer, which I was able to do, but it took time, a long time, and he had to file a formal release of mineral rights with the County to satisfy the bank. That caused a delay of several more months.

Then, when going through Columbia County Building and Zoning officials, a problem developed with the septic tank I needed for the cabin. Since I was so close to the Santa Fe River, they wouldn't allow me to have a regular septic tank installed, so I had to get a much more expensive one. A team of specialists came out and did tests and, finally, after several more months, I was approved for a much more expensive unit, that was much like having my own water treatment facility. It requires annual inspections, too.

Then, a survey had to be performed, which took more time to get a surveyor out there, and he found that my proposed cabin was about five feet below the 100 year flood level, meaning I would have to build up at least five feet. I decided to just go ahead and build up eight feet, and that way I could park a car under the cabin, but that required further engineering and a re-drafting of the building plans – more time and more money.

Finally, after almost a year and a half of wrangling, I was all set, ready to go, but then, on the very day when the contractor was ready to put a shovel in the ground, the county said I had to be thirty feet off of Santa Fe Drive, not the ten feet I'd planned on. Another delay occurred. It was, quite literally, one thing after another.

First, footers had to be dug and a concrete slab had to be poured. Plus, I wanted underground electrical service, so that had to be arranged. I ended up digging the thirty foot long and three foot deep trench required, just to save some money and get it done as quickly as possible. I did that myself. No one helped me with that. It wasn't easy.

Once the general contractor actually began work, things started to go fairly quickly, until yet another delay occurred – my general contractor and his son, were arrested for some criminal activity unrelated to my job.

I had to pay his foreman to finish the job and find various contractors, like someone to do the tile; sheetrock; insulation; plumbing; and electrical work necessary to finish things up.

In April of 2013, after over two years of effort, I was finally given a "Certificate of Occupancy," and I could move into my cabin. It was an ordeal, but the finished product was well worth the effort. Everyone who saw it, loved it, and so did I.

That was just about the time when Susan and I officially stopped seeing each other, so the timing was good in that respect. Fort White is a very small community, and I lived about 15 minutes outside of town. It has one red light, three gas stations, a Subway, a Hungry-Howie's pizza place, a post office, a True-Value Hardware store, a branch library, an elementary and junior high school, a Dollar General and a Family Dollar, located right next to one another, which made no sense whatsoever, and a population of just over five hundred people, as of the last census. I was living in the "boonies."

The best part of living where I did, of course, was the Itchetucknee Springs State Park, the Itchetucknee River itself, and the Santa Fe River. I was about a hundred yards from the Santa Fe, with a Three Rivers Estates' park, called the "Fishing Park," where I could swim, about two hundred yards away. Deer surrounded me and I began feeding them.

I also saw raccoons, foxes, about a hundred squirrels, possum, snakes, birds of many feathers, and three Bard owls who had nests either on or very close to my cabin. It really was a spectacular place to live, with few neighbors too close. The owls were a particularly significant benefit for me. I developed a close relationship with one of them, who I named "Ollie," or "Oliver."

There were many encounters with Ollie over the years, but my favorite is the one involving a squirrel that was bound and determined to build a nest underneath my home. He would crawl into the joists and I would force him out by covering up his points of entry. He would then create another way to get in what was the floor space under my house, which was eight feet off the ground.

I was battling that damn squirrel for weeks, buying steel mesh and doing everything I could to convince that squirrel that he should find another place to live. I own a .22 calibre shotgun and I was just about ready to get it out. Then, Ollie came to the rescue.

I was walking around the deck, and I had a full walk-around deck to the cabin, and I saw the squirrel. Just as I was about to go back in the house to get my shotgun, I saw Ollie in one of the limbs of a nearby tree. I had trees a hundred feet high surrounding my place. I watched as he swooped down, picked up that squirrel in his talons, and took that squirrel way up to the top of the tree, never to be seen again. Thank you, Ollie!

Because I spent as much time as possible around the jobsite during the building phase, I didn't write a book during that year. I was just too busy doing all things necessary to get that house built. Though I was no carpenter, I knew enough to be dangerous, and I was always a good laborer. I enjoyed all of the physical challenges of building that cabin and, when it was complete, I went back to writing.

My next book was To Valhalla, and it was about a client of mine who had recently returned from Afghanistan. He'd been in the Army for nearly ten years and had, allegedly, fathered a child during that time. He had been paying child support for years. He received word from friends that it was possible that he wasn't the father, after all, and he wanted me to help him with that issue.

Fortunately, for him, DNA tests confirmed that he wasn't the father and he was delighted with the outcome. The mother had been hateful towards him and never gave him an opportunity to "bond" with the child. He'd met the woman on-line and she had traveled to see him for a weekend of sex.

He never saw her again or heard from her again after that one fateful weekend, until he received papers from the state of Florida requiring him to pay money to support the child, since the woman was receiving public benefits. The father had been, reportedly, an illegal alien who couldn't support her, so she set out to find a "soldier-boy" who could support her child, and she did. Thank goodness for DNA tests, right?

After the case was concluded, I asked him if he would allow me to write a book about his days in Afghanistan. This was at a time when, as we all recall, the United States military was still in Afghanistan, keeping the Taliban at bay and trying to keep Al-Qaeda and other terrorist groups out of Afghanistan. Osama bin Laden was killed on May 2, 2011, and that's when the U.S. began to dramatically reduce its military presence in the country. He was in Afghanistan during the days when the fighting was the worst and he was in the worst part of the country for that.

The war in Afghanistan is now referred to as our longest war. After Osama bin Laden was killed, many questioned why we stayed there any longer. U.S. soldiers were still being killed and injured as a result of the ongoing conflict, many dying because of road-side bombs or suicide bombers. There were no direct military conflicts involving soldiers in uniforms squaring off against each other, as is going on in Ukraine as I write.

Rather, men wearing turbans and goat-skinned clothing, were carrying rifles and other military weapons they'd obtained from the United States, for the most part. We had helped them rid their country of the Russians during the late 1980s when they were the enemy. Now, we were the enemy, and they were using our guns against us.

Initially, we were there to find and kill Osama bin Laden. Secondarily, we wanted to rid the country of al-Qaeda and all other terrorists groups which had training camps there. However, job number one was to defeat the Taliban and prevent them from re-taking the country. We did not want them to continue to impose "Sharia law," which the entire civilized world abhors.

However, the military said it had learned lessons from the Vietnam days and it was now trying to "win the minds and hearts of the people," instead of just defeating them militarily. It was an ill-fated quest. That was never going to happen. Afghanistan is, and will be for the foreseeable future, a third-world country. To think that we could transform them into something that they are not was foolhardy, at best.

I chose the title because of my familiarity with the Vikings. Valhalla was a place for Norsemen who died in battle to go. It was a place of honor. Even though the Vikings slaughtered the harmless, innocent priests and other Christians in Ireland and across the British Isles for several hundred years a thousand years earlier, people like me continue to romanticize those marauders. There wasn't much honor in any of what they did to my ancestors in Ireland.

My point in choosing the title was to focus on the soldiers who didn't die in battle - the ones who were injured, some catastrophically, who return home, and don't go to Valhalla. My client was one of those. He sustained physical injuries, and he suffered from PTSD as a result of his days in Afghanistan. He didn't go to Valhalla, though many other U.S. soldiers did.

I understood our reasons for going to Afghanistan, and I fully supported them. We needed to find and either capture or kill bin Laden for what he did to us on September 11, 2001. How he continued to avoid us for almost ten years is truly inexplicable. I have no doubt that we would not have found him if we weren't there, on the ground, looking for him. Still, why did it take us so long?

My book tells the story of being in Afghanistan from a soldier's point of view. It was, much like our war in Vietnam, a stupid military exercise, in my view, and anyone who reads it now will fully understand why the Taliban is, once again, fully in control of the country. I could have told you that ten years ago, and I did so in that book.

Again, like all of the others, my book failed to get any traction, although I had tried, once again, to find the "pulse" of the country. My topic was relevant and germane to a major issue in the country, but my book wasn't promoted, or publicized, the way it could have been and should have been. That was my fault, and it was all because I didn't have the money to do so.

I'm very pleased to report that my client liked the book that I wrote about him, and that's extremely important to me. We talked for hours and hours to enable me to write it. We remain friends.

I fictionalized his story quite a bit, however, by adding large sections of the book to the time after he left Afghanistan. I kept him in the military and had him become a drone operator, stationed in Arizona, hunting for the leader of the Taliban, Mullah Omar. Incredibly, we had a hard time finding him, too, and we never did. He died of tuberculosis on April 13, 2013.

I was still practicing law, but I was now living in my cabin. The drive from Fort White to Cedar Key is over an hour long, and I was making that drive back and forth every day. I soon tired of it.

I had purchased a shed, which I modified into my office, and placed it on my property about 200 feet away from my cabin. I fixed it up beautifully, with tongue-in-groove pine on the floors, walls and ceiling, a huge plate-glass window, a nice veranda, air-conditioned, a ceiling fan, nice furniture and, before too long, I closed my office in Cedar Key.

Meagan had had her first child, Madison, in 2013, and Caitlin now had a third child on the way, but neither Patrick nor Brendan had found a partner, though both were looking to get married and have children. I still wasn't seeing them at all, which continued to disappoint me. They came to visit me once on Father's Day one year, but that was about it. None of them cared much about my lifestyle and the things I liked to do, or me.

However, I had Bailey, and she loved that place. She and I would walk just about every night in the Itchetucknee River State Park. I became a volunteer Park Ranger and had a uniform and hat to prove it. Mostly, I helped with canoe trips down the river. I'd throw balls in the river for Bailey to retrieve until my arm felt like it was about to fall off, and then we'd swim in the river.

We were always the last ones to leave the park at night. There were many times when a ranger would be standing at the gate, ready to close it behind me. After a while, they just told me to lock the gate when I left. I was, after all, a ranger. Those were peaceful, quiet and wonderful days, which I enjoyed immensely.

After Susan and I split up, I had no one to play music with, and it's hard to play the bass by yourself. Think about it, no one plays a solo bass concert, or sings a song playing the bass all by himself. I took lessons for a year or so, trying to get better at the bass, but it really was a futile effort. I needed to have someone who played the guitar for me to accompany.

So, one New Year's Eve, I made a resolution to learn to play the guitar. I bought a Michael J. Kelley guitar for several hundred dollars and vowed to practice every night for at least fifteen minutes to half an hour and get better. I chose that guitar because my great-grandfather's name was Michael J. Kelley. The "J" was for Joseph. My grandfather was Joseph Michael Kelley.

Gradually, I began to improve at the guitar. It took me well over a year, or two before I got to the point where I could do an open-mic by myself with my guitar, but I did it. Also, I learned to play the ukelele. I did that because Brendan said that he was now learning how to play the ukelele. In Hawaii, where he was living, the uke is a very popular instrument.

Also, the Youth Tennis Foundation was going strong. It was still a small group of some of my best friends and two of my brothers, though I'd added a nephew, Allan's son, Michael, to the mix. We were all getting older and we needed some new, young, blood.

We were doing some things that were innovative and exciting, at least for me. We started some college tournaments for the Division II, NAIA and Junior College programs in the state of Florida. Many colleges and universities across the country had abandoned their tennis programs, citing cost concerns, since tennis isn't a sport that generates any revenue. We wanted to support the college game, and we did.

We had other worthwhile programs going on, and basically, we give away money to deserving kids. We also helped local community organizations to develop tennis programs for kids. We are a state-wide organization and we support programs from Pensacola, to Jacksonville, Lake City to Orlando and points in between and all the way down to Miami, covering north, south, east and west.

We send kids to the Evert Tennis Academy for week-long summer camps, and to a tennis program which prepares advanced players to play tennis in college. We help the beginners and the advanced junior players in Florida as much as we can, and I'm proud of what we do. We can't compete with the United States Tennis Association, and we don't try to, but we find gaps and do the best we can with what we've got.

I hadn't found anyone to replace Susan, though, just yet, and I've been trying. I went back on-line, using a dating site, to find women, and I met many. I had relationships of varying lengths with many women during those years, but it was difficult, since they all lived so far away from me. There was no one of interest within at least twenty-five miles or so from where I was living. Again, I was in the "boonies."

Still, I wasn't terribly dis-satisfied with my life. I was living where I had chosen to live, in a house that I had built, doing activities that I loved to do, writing books, playing music and actively trying to find a mate. Unfortunately, things just didn't work out on a long-term basis with any of them. I'm still good friends with many of those women, who were and are nice people, just not the "perfect" partner I was looking for.

I was still practicing law, doing mostly domestic relations kind of cases, meaning divorces, child custody and other such family law matters, which was painful, but necessary. I was making enough money to pay my bills and still have some left over for travel. I wasn't working too hard, but I was doing what I wanted to do, for the most part, though there were definitely some voids in there.

One of the women I met was particularly unusual. She was what I call a "conduit." She claimed to have the ability to connect with "higher powers" and I came to believe that she had some "special" talents and insights. I still do.

Talking to her helped me get a different perspective of just who I was, what I was doing and where I was going. She told me things about myself that hit home. I truly didn't, and don't, understand exactly how she was able to do those things, but she got my attention.

In fact, I stopped dating her because she was too powerful. I didn't want her to be my enemy, and I didn't want her to control me. She scared me, to be honest. She still does, but we're friends, and I truly believe that she has extraordinary powers. Maybe she is just extremely intuitive, but I thought, and I continue to think, that she was and is something quite unusual. I have never met anyone quite like her, though she had some friends who, like her, also had "special talents."

I was going through a period of introspection and she helped me with that. I was born into a Catholic family and, primarily because of my mother, I was raised Catholic. I continue to identify myself as a Catholic and a follower of Jesus, but I, like most everyone else, I expect, have had questions about various aspects of religious dogma, which I think is normal. I don't talk about such things with many people, but I was going through a period of time when I was giving the issue of religion a great deal of thought.

As I have told people for years, when asked, I believe that there is absolutely no question that there is a God. For me, the only question is how you define the term. After all, what is "God"? I don't believe that "God" is a person, place or thing. I don't believe that "God" is a man or a woman, or that "it" has any sexual identity. And I don't believe that the "God" depicted in the Bible has been in existence for over 13 billion years.

However, I also don't believe that all that exists can be explained by the current "scientific" model. I don't believe that the "Big Bang" theory answers all the questions about how the world as we know it, let alone the universe, came into existence. There are things in the universe that we cannot see and cannot comprehend, yet I, and we, try to comprehend such things.

For me, this woman I had met, and two other women who she introduced me to, were "conduits" between that outside world and tbe world that those of us who are mere mortals live in. There are things that we cannot see, hear or touch that is out there, and it is "real." I truly have no idea what that other world, or "outer world," consists of.

I admit to being fascinated by what can only be described as the "occult." A definition of that word is that it is the study of "mystical, magical and supernatural powers or phenomena." I liken it to palm-reading, tarot cards, seances, those who read crystal balls, and other such things. I think that there is an element of truth to all of those things, though they are, as a general rule, discredited by scientists and most rational people.

During those years, I was talking to three such people, one of whom was that woman who I dated for several months. The other two I never met and spoke to by phone. I don't regret doing so, and I continue to believe that all three had great insight into the unseen world. Again, I don't understand it, and have no idea what is "out there," but I believe that there is "something" out there.

One of the things all three had to say was that my "soul," and all of our "souls," have reincarnated. I think it's fair to say that most people on earth believe that we all have a soul and, when we die, our soul goes somewhere, somehow. That is what "heaven" is all about, right? That is the concept of an "after-life."

As best as I understood things, at that time, Buddhists, Hindus, Sikhs and others, like Christians, Jews and Muslims, believed in reincarnation, but in a slightly different way. They believed that our souls evolve, some reaching "nirvana," before ceasing to reincarnate. Christians, Muslims and Jews believe in an after-life, but maybe not reincarnation. It seems as if "Heaven" was and is the final destination for them, but most, if not all "religions" believe in an after-life of some sort.

To state the obvious, atheists believe that when you die that is the end – there is nothing more. Agnostics aren't so sure. They "doubt" everything.

I didn't have the answers, but I was searching for answers. Beginning in early 2015, I was reading books by Einstein, who believed in Cosmic religion, meaning that he believed in whoever or whatever created the universe. I was also reading books authored by Stephen Hawking, who died a few years ago, and what he thought of religion, as we know it. He didn't really help move the discussion along too much. Rather, he asked what came before the "Big Bang" and said that there may have been several such events.

The debate was, and still is, to my knowledge, the idea of creationism and/or the science of evolution. Pope Francis suggests that both are inextricably intertwined, thereby implicitly acknowledging the "science" of evolution, to some appreciable degree. No one had answers, nor could they, but I wanted to find answers for me, knowing that I never could. I just had to find an answer that I could live with, or, more importantly, answers before I die, even if they're not the correct answers. I knew that they wouldn't be, but they would be my answers.

I was thinking of writing a science fiction book about some aspect of that, and how anything can come into existence from nothing. Who created the thing that went "BANG!" I was interested in the "God project," still going on in Switzerland some two miles underground at this very moment. Scientists are trying to find a particle in nature that explains how humans came into existence, independent from a creator. They call it the "God" particle. They have had limited success, but they persevere.

I wasn't tormented by the obvious conundrum I was confronting. I was simply exploring it. In my younger years, I didn't have the time or the inclination to do so. I had a wife, children, a career and I didn't have the luxury to delve into such metaphysical areas. I told myself that I was reaching a different stage of life, that this was normal.

So it was, on February 15, 2015, as I was watching the nightly news on one of the networks, that I saw something that changed my life in a meaningful way. I was about to go on a "quest" which would educate me in a meaningful way, and it involved the issue of religion.

Chapter Twenty-Two
ISIS

On that fateful day, February 15, 2015, I watched 21 men, dressed in orange jumpsuits, with collars around their necks, being led by armed men, who were holding them by a chain attached to those iron collars. The men were taken down a path which led to a body of water, which appeared to be a lake. Those men were then forced to kneel down, and they were beheaded. All of that was graphically detailed in a video for the world to see.

I was absolutely stunned by what I saw. I could not believe it. Beheaded! It is such a gruesome and barbaric act as to defy imagination. Who would do such a thing? And there it was, on television, for all humans on our planet to see.

It was ISIS, of course - the Islamic State of Iraq and Syria, sometimes called the Levant, which refers to the region along the eastern Mediterranean shores, now including modern-day Israel, Lebanon, Jordan and Syria. Its origins date to the days after the United States invaded Iraq and toppled Saddam Hussein, but it was in June of 2014, when it captured the city of Mosul, one of Iraq's biggest cities, that the entire world took notice of them.

ISIS was proud of what it did. It wanted the world to take notice. It wanted a global "jihad" wherein Muslim extremists, like them, would bring about a Sunni Islamic caliphate to rule Iraq, Syria, and beyond. The video of the event was played on networks all across the globe, just as they planned.

And they were proud of it! ... and they continued to show many other horrific acts in the ensuing months and years, like putting a captured

Jordanian pilot in a cage and burning him to death, and other beheadings. There was an English-speaking "Jihadi-John," who said awful things on camera prior to cutting off someone's head.

ISIS still exist today, although they were militarily defeated in March of 2019 in Syria, but then they went underground. They are believed to be actively engaged in insurrectionist activities in Afghanistan as of the time I write, but there are, undoubtedly, groups of followers elsewhere in the region and the world. Interestingly, even the Taliban doesn't accept their radical ideology and the two groups fight with each other in Afghanistan at the moment.

As ghastly as the event was to watch, the main takeaway, for me, was how the men who were about to die accepted what was about to happen to them. Those men were unafraid to die. There was no crying or begging for mercy that I saw. I saw looks of defiance. I saw men who were willing to die for their faith – they were all Christians.

My immediate reaction, beyond the horror of it all, was to wonder who those Christians were? Were they Catholics? Methodists? What? What brand of Christians were they?

When I learned that they were Coptic Christians, that didn't help. I wasn't familiar with the Copt religion. I just didn't know. I had never heard of them before.

I don't mind admitting that to you, although you might expect that I should have heard of them before. After all, as I soon discovered, the religion has been in existence for almost two thousand years, but I had just never heard of it before. I was totally unfamiliar with it. Even now, when I ask people if they have ever heard of Copts, few respond affirmatively. I began to do research on the subject.

I can't say that the idea of writing a book about what I'd just seen came to mind at that time. It didn't. I just wanted to find out more about what I'd just seen, not only about the Copts, but also about ISIS. They were still a relatively unknown group at the time.

I did google searches and I learned that the Coptic religion came into existence shortly after Christ died. Its first pope was none other than Mark, one of the four authors of the New Testament gospels. No one, apparently, knows who, exactly, Mark was, but it appeared to be undisputed among religious scholars that Mark accompanied Peter to

Rome and spent approximately seven years with Peter before leaving Rome and going to Alexandria, Egypt, where he created the Copt religion. He was its first pope and it has had its own pope ever since. It was, and still is, primarily located in Egypt. I had no idea of any of that.

I dug deeper. I wondered if their were any Copts in the United States. To my surprise, there were, and are, Coptic churches all over the United States, including in several of the main cities in Florida. I saw where there was a Coptic church in Jacksonville, not far from where I was living. I reached out to the pastor and he responded.

He agreed to meet with me in the small town of Baldwin, which is halfway between us. We met at a barbeque place, which was a bad choice by me, but that was the only place I could think to meet. It's a very small town, and the only reason I knew of it was because there was a 14 mile long "Rails to Trails" bike path in it that I had ridden on many times.

He explained a good deal about his religion, and the religious beliefs of the early "Christians" as well. He told me how the 21 men were poor, uneducated laborers who had left their homes in a small village in Egypt to go make some money in Syria. Looking back, that was an incredibly nice gesture on his part, and I very much appreciate what he did for me.

By that point, I was committed to writing a book about the Copts who had died and those who had killed them, ISIS. I bought books on the topics, including one on Constantine the Great, who was the Roman emperor who proclaimed in 324 A.D., or thereabouts, that Christians would no longer be persecuted.

He did so after seeing a cross in the sky shortly before his forces fought the Battle of the Milvian Bridge in A.D. 312. After he was victorious, he reportedly determined that the cross in the sky was, indeed, a sign from a "Christian" god. He then proclaimed that Christians would no longer be persecuted by Romans.

The expression "In hoc signo vinco" came into existence, which means, loosely, "in this sign I will conquer." It is the motto of the Sigma Chi fraternity to this day. I was a member of Sigma Chi at Tulane, although that had nothing to do with anything, other than it was a coincidence.

I was amazed to learn that Constantine assembled the first council at Nicaea in 325 A.D. at which time hundreds of the leaders of the Christian community from all across the area were asked to explain to him exactly what Christians believed. There was much debate about that issue. The Christian leaders couldn't agree on everything, but they did, ultimately, agree on what is now the Nicene Creed.

I learned that the main centers of Christian followers in the years following the death of Christ were in Rome, Alexandria, what is now Istanbul, Damascus and Jerusalem. There were others, but those five were considered the five largest Christian communities. It was a disparate group, since most Christians had to hide in order to avoid persecution. There was little communication between the various groups.

The Roman Catholic church, the Greek Orthodox church, the Syrian Orthodox church and the Coptic church were four of the larger sects. Although I was raised a Catholic, attended Catholic schools in my early years, and attended church regularly for decades, I wasn't aware of much of what I was learning. I thought all Christians back then were Catholics, until the rape of Constantinople in 1204 during the Fourth Crusade, when the Greeks split off from Rome, but I was wrong.

All of that was somewhat unrelated to the issue of the 21 Copts who had been killed by ISIS, but it fascinated me. I was researching the modern-day Coptic church and what had happened to those 21 men in Sirte, Libya. The Coptic priest, who didn't want me to use his name, or give him any credit whatsoever, continued to help me.

After several weeks of research, I finally began the task of writing a book. I called it <u>Massacre at Sirte</u>. With the assistance of the Coptic priest, I was able to obtain a "digital chronography" created by a Copt named Tony Rezk, who lives in the Washington, D.C. area which depicts the 21 men killed by ISIS as martyrs on their way to heaven.

It is called "Windows to Heaven," and is an iconic depiction of the tragedy, much revered by the Coptic community. It is on the front cover of my book. I am honored to have been allowed to use it as I did.

In it, I begin with the capture of the 21 men as they were working that fateful day in 2015, except I added a 22nd person, a sixteen year-old boy, who I name Mekhaeil. The first half of the book relates the conversations which the men have on the night before they are executed. The younger men wonder why they are being killed. What had they ever done in their lives to deserve such treatment? Why were they hated the way they were?

The older men explain the origins of the three religions – Judaism, Christianity and Islam – and how and when the hostilities began, and why they continue to exist. It gave me an opportunity to learn all of those things for myself, as well as share all of that information with readers. Mostly, I learned about Mohammad and the history of Judaism. I learned about Abraham, Ishmael and Joseph and all of that, much of which I had only a minimal degree of knowledge. We weren't taught any of that at Catholic schools or from the pulpits on Sundays.

In my book, when the 21 Copts are led away to be beheaded, ISIS releases Mekhaeil and tells him to tell the world what he has seen and what happened to his two brothers and his fellow Egyptians. They wanted the world to fear them. They wanted the world to know what they had done.

In the last half of the book, Mekhaeil deals with the shame he feels about him being released while the others died. He wishes he had been killed, too. He stumbles into a Coptic church in Alexandria and meets a priest who consoles him.

Mekhaeil finally accepts the fact that he has become a hero to his fellow Copts. The Coptic community, and all of Egypt, are so happy that someone survived who can tell them what happened. The book ends with a celebration of the lives of the 21 martyrs, involving the entire Coptic church, and even the president of Egypt, who decries the merciless actions of ISIS.

That book was published in 2016. Again, I thought that I might, just maybe, catch the pulse of the country, and the world, with that book. I really believed that it explained the historical basis for the differences which exist in the Middle East and why such hatred remains to this day. Moreover, I thought it would be informative regarding the Copts and their religion. Unfortunately, for me, that didn't happen, but I learned so very much from the process that I was, without any doubt whatsoever, much the better person for having written the book.

I tried, unsuccessfully, to promote the book. I did all of the same things that had failed so miserably in the past, like press releases, speaking engagements, and everything else I could think of. I even spent $500 to promote it on a radio station out of Atlanta that guaranteed millions of people would hear all about it. I should say I wasted $500. Nothing came of it – nothing, not one dime. I spent money on other things to promote it, too, like putting an advertizement in a Christian Christmas catalogue.

Still, I tried and I don't regret what I did or the time spent working on the book, though others were certainly questioning my sanity. If I am anything, I am persistent, to a fault, many would say. Truthfully, I was discouraged. I was not getting anywhere with my writing. I knew that I was doing things wrong, but I didn't know how to change anything because it was really all about money. I needed to hire a publicist and spend the money to properly publicize my book. I didn't do that. I didn't have the money to do that.

One good thing did occur during that time involving my book, and that was that it received an award! I entered it into a contest and it won third place in two categories – one for theology and one for contemporary fiction, as I recall. I could honestly say that it was, therefore, "award-winning," although it didn't take first place. It was a minor victory, but a victory nonetheless, and I was happy about that.

Otherwise, that was a bit of a low point for me, to be honest. I was hoping for more. That was a relevant, contemporary issue which the entire world should have had some interest in. ISIS was like a cancer, or a plague, affecting everyone, even though it was located only in the Middle East at that time. My book deserved a better fate.

Life was still going on, however, and I was practicing law, working on mundane cases that were uninteresting to everyone except for the people I was representing. To them, it was the most important thing in their lives, and I understood that. I was still a lawyer, and I took that very seriously. It is a profession that requires one to do so. You can't be cavalier with the lives of others.

I did the best I could for all of my clients and I still considered myself to be a competent attorney who had done a whole lot more in law than most of the lawyers I was dealing with, but my heart wasn't in it. I wanted to be an author – a successful author, and I wasn't.

I was still playing music every night, walking in the park with Bailey most every night, searching for the elusive female partner, working on Youth Tennis Foundation matters, riding my bicycle on a daily basis and kayaking at least once a week. Plus, I was living in a beautiful place, surrounded by trees that were a hundred feet high, across from the Santa Fe River, in a peaceful, quiet, rural neighborhood, with owls as my spirit guides, but I had my demons.

It saddened me to think of my relationship with my children, and I really did want to be in a healthy relationship with a person of the opposite sex. I would be seventy years old before too long, and I didn't want to keep working as I was as a lawyer, but I had to. I needed the money.

I was still talking to my three "conduits" during that period of time. I was speaking with one of them once a month, and the other two only every now and then, when I felt that I needed some advice. I continued to find all of those conversations meaningful.

It was during one of those conversations with one of those conduits that I received a message that would change my life in a dramatic way, once again. I say that it was a "message from God" and that message was going to cause me to journey thousands of miles, across different continents, in search of the answers to questions I was asking myself.

Chapter Twenty-Three

A Message from God

Before receiving the message from God, after finishing <u>Massacre at Sirte</u>, I decided to ask two friends of mine who were from India if they would allow me to write a book about them. I did that because I wanted to learn more about the Hindu religion, and I figured that they would surely know. Their names are Vettereeth and Annamma. I had known them for years as he did my taxes.

He was a certified public accountant. She was a retired nurse. They were, and they are, very nice people, and I had dined with them on several occasions, but I didn't really know too much about them, other than that they were from India. I wanted to learn more about them and about India – that was about it.

So I asked them if they would allow me to do so, and they agreed. He knew that I was an author, and he had read at least one of my books before. I was thinking that it would be a biography of the two of them. How did they get to the United States and why? I assumed, mistakenly, that they were Hindus, since over 80 percent of the country are. About 15 percent are Muslim. About 2 percent are Sikhs.

I didn't think that there were many Christians in India, and I had no idea that either of them was, but I was wrong. Both of them were! It shocked me! They were Marthoma Christians.

I had no idea what a Marthoma Christian was and told them so. They explained that after Christ was crucified, most of the apostles went to Damascus, and then on to Antioch, where they lived in hiding for about a year, before venturing out to spread the news about Christ across much of the known world. Thomas, most frequently referred to as "doubting Thomas," traveled to the southernmost part of India and established a group of seven or more churches in Kerala, one of twenty-eight states in the country. It is surrounded on three sides by water, namely the Arabian Sea to the south and west and the Western Ghats to the east.

The term "mar" translates as "water," and "thoma" refers to Thomas, hence the name Marthoma. I was absolutely flabbergasted to think that St. Thomas had walked, or ridden a camel, that far, since that is a distance of over three thousand miles, and that's as a crow flies, not by land. I was even more surprised to learn that the church still existed AND that Vettereeth and Annamma were two of the first Marthoma Christians to spread the faith to the United States.

I asked myself why would anyone travel that far to tell people, who undoubtedly didn't speak the same language that he did, about Jesus Christ, if not as a result of an incredibly deep and abiding faith in his beliefs? For that matter, why did all of the apostles do what they did, if not for a deep and abiding faith in Jesus? It wasn't for fame or fortune. Most died horrible deaths, and many were crucified, as Christ was, some upside down.

I had many dinners at their house over the next couple of months as I researched the history of India and learned more about their lives. Annamma, having been a nurse, was allowed into the country in the late 1960s because of that skill. Vettereeth was allowed entry into the U.S. afterwards, not at the same time, because they were married. They moved to Brooklyn and lived there for many years before moving to Gainesville.

They had led extremely interesting lives and I thoroughly enjoyed learning all about their lives in India and how they managed to find their way to this country. For example, both came from large families and both had over a dozen siblings, but the two of them were the only ones from either family who chose their spouses. The others had arranged marriages. I found that startling in this day and age.

They also told me all about the Maramon convention held annually along the banks of the Pampa River, not far from where they lived. It is the largest convention of Christians in the world and has been held annually for over a hundred years. They explained the "caste system" to me and how they had experienced it, though they, themselves, were not "out-castes," or the "undesirables."

I wrote over fifteen thousand words and was well on my way to doing much more when they decided, one day, that they did not want me to write their stories. They were convinced that no one would be interested in reading about their lives. They knew of several friends of theirs who were much more important and well-known than they were who'd written books, or had books written about them, which no one read. I disagreed, but there was no changing their minds, so that project ended, or so I thought.

Later that year, that being the summer of 2016, I did something that I'd never done before. I took off from work and all of my responsibilities for a month and a half! I'd never had the luxury of doing that since the days before I first began practicing law, back in my tennis-playing days. Like most people, I had a week or two of vacation time every year and that was it. After a while, I was allowed three weeks of vacation.

In July of that year I turned 69. Up to that point in my life, the longest I'd ever been away from the legal profession and all of my responsibilities had been three weeks, and that was never one continuous stretch. I wasn't ready to retire, because I still needed the income, but I was ready to travel.

The truth is that I was losing sight in my right eye, the one that was injured when hit by a tennis ball way back in 1965. I was afraid that I might lose my license to drive if I was blind in one eye. I didn't know, for sure, and I wasn't going to ask. I could still see well enough to drive – that wasn't the issue - but I just didn't know what the State of Florida would do with me.

So I decided to drive to Alaska while I still had a license to drive! When I made that decision, I didn't fully realize just how long of a drive that was. I made all of the necessary plans through AAA, and had maps, tour books, trip-tickets and the rest, but I really didn't fully understand what I was getting myself into until I was actually doing it, and barely making it across western Canada from one gas station to the next. It's a long way – almost 5,000 miles. I won't do it again.

My youngest son, Brendan, flew from Kauai, Hawaii to Anchorage, Alaska, to meet me. From there, we drove to Homer, Alaska, and camped out on what is called a "spit," which is a strip of beach on the shores of Kachemak Bay, in the Kenai Peninsula. It is a 4 ½ mile long road, which is said to be the longest road into ocean waters in the entire world. We camped on a beach and could watch whales go by and eagles fly overhead.

Since it was summertime, the days were long and the nights extremely short. I went to bed one night, or I should say "day," since it was still sunlight, and woke up to more sunlight. I became extremely agitated because Brendan wasn't in his tent. I was in my trailer. I was sure he'd been arrested or somehow got himself in trouble. Where was he?

Not long after, he came home. He'd been at the Salty Dog Tavern, making friends and having a great time. I hadn't taken into consideration the fact that Alaska is called the "land of the midnight sun." We laughed about it, but the joke was on me.

He fished for salmon in the Fox River, after getting all of the gear, without any success. I kayaked instead, having learned my lesson in Nova Scotia years before about catching salmon that were there to spawn. He enjoyed himself, and that was the most important thing. At least he tried.

After leaving Homer, we drove to Denali and hiked for days while there. On the way, we stopped in Talkeetna, where planes fly out of the airport there to take hikers up the mountain. The planes take them half way up the mountain where there's a landing spot, shortening the trek considerably. It was formerly called Mount McKinley, named after our president, but its Indian name of Denali, which means "the High One," was restored in 1980.

We camped out for ten days at various sites, but there were no vacancies within the Denali National Park itself. Those spots were all taken a year beforehand. It's a lot like that at Yosemite, Glacier, Yellowstone and other national parks.

One of the campground hosts told us that grizzlies had been visiting at night and handed me a black garbage bag. When I asked what to do with it, in the event I came across one, she told me to spread it out as far as I could and hold it as high above my head as possible, and shake it back and forth. I thought she was kidding, but she wasn't. We didn't stray far from our tent/trailer that night.

We did, however come upon some grizzlies while hiking one day. We went with two park rangers on a hike through the tundra, on a path that was not marked, up to a hill, not far off the 92 mile long road through the park. Unauthorized cars are only allowed to go 15 miles into the park.

We rode a bus with the rangers to a point where they told the driver to stop. When he did, the driver suggested that we not get out there as a mama grizzly and two cubs were a few hundred feet away. We all agreed.

We went about half a mile further down the road and got out, but we could see the three grizzlies the entire time we hiked. That was interesting. Everyone who goes to Denali hopes to see the grizzlies, but no one wants to see them up close and personal. They're not friendly farm animals.

Brendan and I played golf on his last day in Alaska, at a course not far from the airport, at midnight! When we finished, I drove him to the airport, and he flew home. That was interesting, and we didn't lose any balls! He won.

I then started the long trek home. It took me ten days to get there and ten days to drive back, with ten days in Alaska with Brendan. I stopped and saw friends coming and going, but it was a tortuously long trip. I won't do it again, but I'm glad I did it. Priceless.

Shortly after returning home to Florida, I was having a conversation with one of my "conduits," the one who lives in Idaho, when she told me that I would be writing a series of five books, and she explained that the cover of the books would be red. She didn't know what the books would be about, but she told me to ask one of the other "conduits," the woman in Gainesville who I'd dated, and said she could provide other details.

When I asked the other conduit, at first she said that she had no idea what the other woman was talking about, and then she began to see things and provided some more details. As soon as she began to talk, the nucleus of the five book series immediately came into focus for me. Anyone who knows me, or has read what I have written thus far, may find that hard to believe, but it's true.

I knew, right then and there, that the first book in the five book series I was to write had already been written, and it was <u>Massacre at Sirte</u>. The second book would be about Vettereeth and Annamma's life in India, and the third book would be about their lives in America. I can't honestly recall if I knew what books four and five would be about, but that was enough to get me started, and so I did. Vettereeth and Annamma were okay with that.

I had ended <u>Massacre</u> with Mekhaeil giving a heart-felt speech to a gathering of mourners at the church in his home town. In it, he is seen as a hero to his fellow Copts and even to President al-Sisi, who condemned violence against Christians and anyone else based on religious differences.

President al-Sisi is a Muslim and he rose to power when he, while a military officer, led a revolt against the Muslim Brotherhood in 2014. At the time, the Copts, Jews and others, were being discriminated against by the newly-elected Muslim Brotherhood regime and there were many acts of violence throughout the country including against Shiites. They were Sunni Muslims. It remains a problem to this day in Egypt.

I decided to pick up the story from there and have President al-Sisi tell those close to Mehkaeil that ISIS now planned to kill him. ISIS wanted the world to fear them more after what they did in Sirte, not less. They were not pleased to see Mehkaeil become a hero.

When Mehkaeil is summoned by President al-Sisi to come to Cairo to attend an event, he is whisked away by government officials so that he won't be killed. I have him taken to Kuriannoor, India, which was the hometown of Vettereeth and Annamma. In fact, I have him taken in by a Christian family living in Vettereeth's home, the one he had told me all about.

I then proceeded to tell all of the various stories that Vettereeth and Annamma had told me about what it was like living in Kuriannoor. The picture on the cover of the book is taken of Vettereeth's farm. A picture of an elephant is on the back cover and it is one he gave me. The elephant was kept not far from his farm.

Vettereeth and his family were serious farmers and they raised several different kinds of crops, had milk cows and other animals, and they lived not far from the Pampa River where the Maramon convention was held. I related stories about wild monkeys, tigers, the "untouchables," and other such things, just as Vettereeth and Annamma had told me.

However, when Mehkaeil attends the Maramon convention with his surrogate family, he is recognized by a man in the crowd and his "cover" was blown. Hiram, the Egyptian security official who had taken Mehkaeil to India, returns in order to move him again. He had learned, through his sources, that ISIS was on its way to find and kill him.

The name of that book is <u>Hunted</u>. ISIS had "hunted" for Mehkaeil and they had found him. The book ends with Mehkaeil being taken away, not knowing where he was being taken next. That book went into print in 2017. I published it with Xulon Press, which calls itself the "largest Christian book publisher in North America. I was hoping that it would attract some Christian readers. It didn't attract too many.

The third book in the series is called <u>Hiding in America</u>. It relates much of what Vettereeth and Annamma experienced when they came to the United States. I relate many of the stories they told me about their experiences when they first came to the U.S. I include the same neighborhoods and addresses where they lived and where Vettereeth worked.

In it, Mehkaeil gets a job, with Hiram's help, and he falls in love, for the first time in his life, with a Muslim girl, no less. He visits all of the traditional tourist spots in Manhattan, like the Empire State Building, the Statue of Liberty and other places, with his girlfriend, who is from Syria. She is a refugee from violence, just as he was.

Mekhaeil is totally taken by all that the "Big Apple" has to offer, and by his first love. He loses sight of who he is and why he's there. His faith, his family and his homeland are no longer the most important things in his life. He is lost.

However, Mekhaeil discovers that there were several Coptic churches in New York City - and in real life, there are – and Mehkaeil happens to walk by one. When he wanders in, he is recognized by the priest, although the priest didn't reveal that he knew who Mekhaeil was. Unbeknownst to Mehkaeil, the priest then relays back the sighting to Father Bishoy in Alexandria. No one in Egypt knew where he was, not even his family, after he was taken from Cairo by Hiram, in secrecy, many months before.

Father Bishoy flies to New York and surprises Mehkaeil, but he's not pleased when he sees what has become of him. He tells him that he shouldn't return to Egypt until he sorts things out. Has he lost his faith? Has he totally forgotten about his religion? Does he not realize how important he is to his fellow Copts and to those who love him back home? What is he doing with his life?

Mehkaeil is extremely remorseful. He realizes how far he has strayed and wishes to repent. Father Bishoy suggests that he needs to do some serious soul-searching. Mehkaeil makes mention of doing a pilgrimage to sort things out, having seen something about it on television one night. He mentions el Camino de Santiago, the largest, longest Christian pilgrimage in the world. The book ends with Mehkaeil contemplating doing el Camino.

That book, <u>Hiding in America</u>, was written in 2017, but it was published in 2018. This time I used AuthorHouse as my publisher. It, too, is a print-on-demand publisher, not much different from iUniverse, but I'd had no luck with either iUniverse or Xulon, so I wanted to try something different. Unfortunately, it was more of the same, and it didn't do well, either.

The thing about self-publishing is that it means self-promoting, too. The companies that do print-on-demand publishing get their money up front and they spend absolutely no time marketing your book. They will do marketing, but for a much higher price tag, which mostly involves social media. They'll send out thousands and thousands of emails, blurbs and whatever. Authors are still the ones who have to do the work to make the books sell.

However, I was now heavily invested in this story, and the next book suddenly appeared. I had received "instructions" from the universe. I was on my way to Spain to walk el Camino de Santiago, just as Mehkaeil was about to do. I couldn't write that book without walking the walk, right?

Needless to say, that was to be a significant event in my life, perhaps the most significant thing I'd ever done in my life. I fully realized just how difficult it would be. I began making all of the necessary arrangements to walk 500 miles in Northern Spain, as I now told myself that I was going to do. I was in good shape and had no doubt about my ability to do so.

The bigger question was why. Why was I doing it? It wasn't just to write a book, was it? It was more about me and my journey on this planet, but that's what I told others – I told them that I was going to Spain to write the fourth book in this five book series, but I was now Mehkaeil, or Mehkaeil was now me, one or the other.

Chapter Twenty-Four

El Camino de Santiago

I am not, by any stretch of the imagination, an ardent Catholic. As a priest once told me, in a confessional, I am a "cafeteria Catholic." When I asked, he told me that was like someone who goes through a cafeteria line and picks and chooses what he wants to eat. He said you can't do that as a Catholic – either you take everything on the plate or nothing at all.

There are some things in the Catholic church and its dogma that trouble me, like all of the pedophile priests that have been allowed to continue to be priests, even after being discovered, or all of the Magdalene laundries that were allowed to flourish in Ireland for decades, before being outlawed, or why women can't be priests, and a whole bunch of other things, like virgin birth and the transformation of the host and the wine into the body and blood of Jesus at Mass. The main tenet of the Catholic religion and all Christian religions is that Jesus of Nazareth is the son of God and he was crucified, died and was buried, only to rise from the dead and now sits at the right hand of God. I am not so sure about all of that, either, but I say prayers and talk to Jesus on a daily basis.

I struggle with all of that, even with the most basic concept of all, that being the existence of God as God is explained to us in the Bible. Adam and Eve? Even from Genesis it's apparent that there were others living in and around the Garden of Eden. How did Cain and Abel have children? Who did they marry? Who were their wives?

The story of Abraham baffles me, not to mention that Moses is said to have written the first five books of the Bible a thousand years after Abraham died. How did Moses know those things? And God, or Yahweh, tells Abraham to kill his beloved son as a test? What God would do that, yet Abraham willingly proceeds to do so, until stopped? And then Jacob "argues" with God and God listens? Joseph is sold as a slave by his brothers? Needless to say, there is much to question about the "Old Testament."

As I have said before, there is no doubt in my mind that there is a God, the only question is how to define the term. I consider the five book series I have written to be more of a comparative examination of the five major religions in the world, those being Christian, Muslim, Hindu, Buddhist and Judaism, than a declaration that Christians are right and everyone else in the world is wrong. I think that I'm looking over and beyond the religions of the world toward what Native American Indians call the "Great Spirit," or George Lucas calls "The Force." That was my thinking <u>before</u> I decided to do el Camino.

I say all of that to let readers know that for me to make the decision to go on a pilgrimage to northern Spain and walk 500 miles was beyond imagination at any time in my life. The thought never entered my mind – never – until I decided to write this five book series. Again, I say that I, like the Blues Brothers, received a "message from God." The message came from the two "conduits," but they received the message from who knows where. I choose to call that "God," or the Universe.

I mean that sincerely. I was struggling with questions for which there are no answers, and I knew it, yet this was the path I chose to take to continue searching for those answers. Writing the books was the justification for doing the thing I was about to do.

I had watched the movie "The Way," starring Martin Sheen. It was produced and directed by his son, Emilio Estevez, who also wrote the screenplay. It was all about walking el Camino de Santiago. I had never heard of it before and I have no idea how I happened upon it in the first place. When I learned of it, that's about the same time as I figured out the five book series and that I was to walk el Camino. That was how book four came to be, and it's somewhat serendipitous, if not something else.

It's important to note that I did not know what book five was to be at that point. As you will soon discover, that, too, was, perhaps, not an accident. The entire project was shrouded in mystery, and that includes the story of me and my life. It has, indeed, been a "long, strange trip," as Jerry Garcia famously sang.

Having been an athlete all of my life, I really didn't have any question at all about my ability to walk 500 hundred miles, but there's a lot more to it than just the walking. I read books and watched other movies about it and I began to train, and I began to pack. I'd never walked more than ten or fifteen miles at a time, to my knowledge, though I'd walked portions of the Appalachian Trail many times, and I'd run a couple of marathons, as I mentioned before.

The physical part was never an issue. I could do it, I knew I could, but why was still the question. What was I going to write? What was the story? What was that going to be like. I did not know.

Making the journey represented a monumental challenge on several levels, and it would be an adventure, for sure, but there was more to it than that. Clearly, writing the book was the main purpose, but that wasn't the only thing. I, too, like Mekhaeil, was questioning my faith. Although I hid behind Mekhaeil, that was really me doing the walking, searching for answers.

I did all of the things anyone should do before embarking on a trip as I was about to do, including making a list of everything I would need to take with me. After all, I'd be carrying it on my back. I watched the movie a dozen times and knew all about the alburgues and how the pilgrims, or peregrinos, as they're called in Spain, were supposed to travel.

I bought two guide books which told all there is to know about el Camino, including where to stay, all the sites along the way, the history of it and a detailed, mile-by-mile description of the route. I did everything I could think of to prepare. When the time came, I was as ready as I could be, and I was confidant I could do it.

So, on September 3, 2017, I flew from Jacksonville to Barcelona, Spain, thinking that I was completely prepared for the journey. I spent a night in Barcelona, just a week or so after several hundred thousand people marched in the streets, seeking to secede from Spain and become a separate country. That was interesting. The first clue regarding what I was in for was that there weren't many people speaking English anywhere I went.

I then traveled by train to Pamplona, a four hour trip, before boarding a bus to take me to St. Jean Pied de Port, France, which wound through the Pyrenees mountains for a couple of hours, before arriving in St. Jean. That is the starting place for what is called the Camino Frances, the traditional path for pilgrims, although there are many others paths to get to Santiago de Compostela, the destination for all pilgrims. I was following the script.

The first thing I did was go to the office where peregrinos check in and receive their passport for the Camino. Pilgrims have to get at least two stamps on it every day of their journey to prove that they did, indeed, walk the 500 miles, or 800 kilometers, in order to receive a document at the end, written in Latin, which confirms that you actually did what you set out to do. That was absolutely mandatory.

At this point, I will interject and tell readers exactly what the cathedral at Santiago, the final destination for pilgrims, represents. It is said to be the final resting point for the bones of St. James, the apostle. After Christ was crucified, he, like St. Thomas, hid with the others in Damascus. He then walked to Hispania, or the Iberian Peninsula, as it was known then, to spread the word, while Thomas walked to the southernmost part of India.

However, James didn't do too well and, apparently, didn't convert many people or start any churches, as Thomas did. Instead, he returned to Jerusalem and became quite active in that community. He was still a Jew trying to convince other Jews that they had strayed from the path established by Abraham, Moses and the others before him, just as Jesus had preached.

Historians say that James, canonized a millenia later, died in 44 A.D. in Jerusalem, and that he was killed by order King Herod. He was beheaded. His bones, presumably, would have been buried somewhere in Jerusalem, one would think, yes?

However, sometime during the ninth century, a shepherd in Galicia saw a star that shown a light on a certain spot in a field where he was tending to his sheep. The shepherd explored the area where the light from the star was shining and found the bones of a human. The local priest declared that the bones the shepherd found were those of St. James, though it is unclear how he was able to make that determination.

When the king of Spain, Alonso II, heard about it, he went to inspect for himself. He, too, concluded that the bones found by the shepherd were those of St. James. At his direction, a church was erected on that spot, and it was called the church of the "compostella," or "field of stars." Santiago is the spanish word for James, or Santiago de Compostella. That church was destroyed by the Moors years later, but a magnificent cathedral was constructed in its place in the eleventh century.

There is a legend that the bones were miraculously transported by angels from Jerusalem to Spain. There is also a theory that his bones were taken there by others who attempted to convert the people of Galicia to Christianity after his death, as St. James had tried to do. There is little proof of either theory, but there is an abiding faith amongst the believers that the bones in the crypt at the cathedral in Santiago de Compostela are the bones of St. James.

In any event, and despite any questions or concerns any skeptics might have, no one can deny that for over a thousand years Christians have made a pilgrimage to northern Spain to honor St. James at that cathedral named in his honor. He was one of the first Christians martyred because of his belief that Jesus was the messiah. He was one of the original four apostles who were there that day when Jesus came upon four men fishing in the Sea of Galilee almost two thousand years ago. Peter and his brother, Andrew, and James and his brother, John, were the four fisherman. I was one of who knows how many millions upon millions of people to make that journey in honor of St. James.

There were dozens of people there in St. Jean with me at that Pilgrims office and many languages were spoken, mostly French and Spanish. I read where less than 5% of the peregrinos were from the United States. There were half a dozen women sitting behind desks, helping people like me, and I wasn't hearing anyone speak English.

Most were from Spain where, as I had learned, it is somewhat obligatory for every Catholic Spaniard to walk el Camino at least once in their life. In fact, the manager of the hotel where I stayed in Barcelona had taken a month off to do the very same thing I was doing. I met a woman in Pamplona who was married with older children who was walking yet another leg of el Camino. She was doing it in stages.

For me, the language barrier was a bit unexpected. I had studied Spanish in school and knew enough to get by, barely, but in most of my travels to Mexico and other places where Spanish was the predominant language, people had been able to speak English, too. That wasn't the case here, and it wasn't the case for most of my journey.

For the next thirty-one days I walked an average of about seventeen miles a day before reaching Santiago. I won't say too much more about the book, because there is so much to be said and it's in the book. I don't want to repeat myself. Those who are interested can read the book, should they care to do so.

For purposes of this book, I would say that it was not what I expected it to be - it was much more than I expected. My friends, Patrick and Marlene Doherty, had no interest in going, for fear that it would be too religious in nature for them. I realized that could be a problem, but I was unphazed. That was not, however, what I experienced, though there were many devout Christians who made the pilgrimage for entirely religious reasons.

People were there for a variety of reasons totally unrelated to the religious experience. Historically, the sole reason why the original pilgrims made the trek was for a deeply religious purpose. That was no longer the case in today's world, or at least that was not what I experienced.

I met people from countries all over the world, and I estimate that those people came from over thirty-five countries, if not more. Conversations with most people, regardless of what language they spoke, was, with rare exception, the traditional greeting of "Buen Camino!" Almost everyone greeted each other in that fashion, and they had a smile on their face when they said it. They meant it!

Some people were there for the exercise, others were there for adventure, and still others were there to meet people from all over the world in a friendly, non-threatening manner. I never heard a discouraging word or witnessed an unfriendly encounter. I think anyone and everyone who commits to walking el Camino de Santiago is an interesting person and all have their own tales to tell, though many don't care to share their reasons for making the trek. It's certainly not something anyone does lightly.

The language barrier was a real problem, though, as far as I was concerned. It made it virtually impossible to have a meaningful conversation with fellow pilgrims about deeper topics if we couldn't understand each other. When I met people who spoke English, and if conversations lasted more than a few minutes, I told them that I was writing a book and that they were talking to a sixteen year old Egyptian boy. If they were so inclined, and not put-off by that, the conversation continued.

Fortunately, I talked to just enough people to be able to fully tell Mekhaeil's story in the book I wrote, which is entitled "Pilgrimage." That, too, was somewhat magical. I think that I, quite literally, met exactly the right number of people I needed to meet in order to adequately tell the story I wanted to write.

For me, personally, looking back at what I did five years ago, I must say that the experience was truly remarkable. I can't say that it changed me in any appreciable way, but I can say that I am a much "richer" person for having done what I did. The people I met and the experiences I had, good and bad, were simply exceptional – probably the best thing I've ever done in my life, on a personal level, to date. I am a "better" person as a result, whatever that means.

I'm proud of myself for completing the journey. It was extremely challenging and I was, quite literally, dead-tired at the end of each and every day. Taking off those boots was such an enormous relief after walking anywhere between eight and twelve hours per day. My toes were blistered and became infected very early on. I began to apply medicine and bandages to them every day. My feet felt like they were cast in concrete, but my body held up.

My focus was on writing the book at all times, though. That was paramount in my mind. However, I would have had to have been totally blind not to appreciate the beauty of the countryside and the historical significance of el Camino. It was spectacular.

Ever since the late ninth century, people have made a pilgrimage to the cathedral at Santiago de Compostela in Galicia, even during the days when Moors controlled much of the area. That was why el Camino de Santiago, or the "road to Santiago," came into existence and continues to exist. The history of el Camino is inextricably tied to the religion of Spain. There is absolutely no doubt about that and visitors should never question that, in my opinion. To the Christians of Spain, and many other peregrinos, that is sacred ground.

Those early pilgrims were praying for miracles or repenting, paying a price, for past sins, or for some other reason not involving making money or realizing a treasure of some kind. Many were sick, deathly ill, and there were plenty of old hospitales along the way. Most were poor peasants, although King Ferdinand and Queen Isabella made the journey, or at least a portion of it, while on the throne, after 1492.

In fact, I read where many of the churches I passed along the way were built by Ferdinand and Isabella, or those who followed, with the gold they had received after the discovery of the new world. Every town or village had a church – every one, no matter how small.

Some of the cathedrals were simply astounding to view, like those in Burgos, Pamplona, Leon, Sarria or in Santiago. They are architectural marvels, but the churches in every little hamlet, village, town or city along the way were something to admire, too. Pilgrim masses were said every day in every church along the way, sometimes broadcast over microphones to pilgrims, like me, who walked by, not stopping to pray. There were masses in the morning and at night in many places.

El Camino de Santiago was and is, more than anything else, intended to be a deeply religious experience for those who make the extreme effort to make a "pilgrimage." That cannot be under-stated, even though that wasn't the expressed intent of the majority of the people I spoke to. I confess, it was not my primary intent.

A definition of the word "pilgrimage" is a "journey, especially a long one, to a sacred place as an act of religious devotion." For Mekhaeil, he was trying to reconcile how monstrously cruel men, like ISIS, could kill innocent Christians, like his brothers and friends, who had done nothing wrong, in the name of their "god," and how or why Jesus Christ and the God of Christians could allow that to happen. Acts such as that had happened for thousands of years between varying religious groups, but ever since the days of Mohammad, who died in AD 632, Muslims have ruled the area, and Christians and Jews have been discriminated against.

For me, there was, and there is, no denying that Jesus Christ is the single most significant person to ever walk the face of the earth. I think that is undeniable, although the roots of Christianity are being shaken nowadays. There was a time in the not too distant past when 90% of Americans identified themselves as Christians. Even now, one-third of the people on earth are said to be Christians. That number is diminishing here in the United States and, maybe, in other countries, but it seems to remain strong in both Central and South America, and in most of Europe, though I could be wrong about that.

I have read where the word "faith" means believing in something for which there is no objective proof. I believe that is a fair characterization of the word. The problem that I see is that so many people who have "faith" in the teachings of their respective religions, do so with a passion that allows them to kill in the name of that religion, and they do so even though there is no objective proof that they are "right" and all others are "wrong."

Moreover, who is to say that Christians are "right" and Jesus is the "only" path to "heaven," making everyone else wrong? What about Siddhartha Gautama, the Buddha? Or Mohammad, said to be the last and the greatest prophet, or Abraham, the patriarch of Hebrews and the biblical foundation for Christians and Muslims as well, or Lord Krishna, the founder of Hinduism?, Is there just one person who deserves such recognition? What of the remainder of the world's population who are not followers of Jesus of Nazareth? Jews, Hindus, Muslims, Buddhists, Sikhs and others constitute two-thirds of the people on earth.

Mekhaeil met many people of different political and religious orientations on his journey, as did I. Mekhaeil asks himself, after meeting so many other people who are different from those in his homeland of Egypt, if Jesus is the only path to God. I ask the same question.

Furthermore, if everyone continues to say that "we are right and you are wrong," how will the world ever end the conflicts that have existed for millenia because of differences of opinions over religious beliefs, especially when there is no objective "proof" that one is right and the others are wrong? Mekhaeil continues to ask questions as he continues his walk. There is, of course, no good answer to that question. How it will end remains to be seen but wars stemming from religious differences continue to be fought, as the situation involving Iran and Israel continues to demonstrate.

Mehkaeil ends his journey at the cathedral in Santiago de Compostela, but he is still not sure of just what he believes. He's not ready to go back to Egypt and face Father Bishoy, his family, his countrymen or his fellow Copts, and he knows it. So what is he to do?

Instead, almost as an afterthought, once the journey is over and he has completed his "pilgrimage," he decides to go to Israel and follow in the footsteps of Jesus. He hopes to get more insight into who and what Jesus was. Needless to say, I, too, decided to go to Israel, to get more insight into Jesus.

Like Mekhaeil, I hadn't answered the questions in the book, nor had I satisfactorily answered the questions in my head. Who was this Jesus of Nazareth? I didn't know all that much about him, either.

I had read the Bible, and listened to countless sermons, watched movies, read books about the five greatest religions in the world, taken classes in college on comparative religions, and otherwise given much thought to things I had been taught by my parents and others, but I had unanswered questions. It seemed like a good way to end the book and it seemed like a good way to complete the "mission" assigned to me. I was going to Israel.

That was to be book five. It's hard to believe, even now, but I didn't realize that a trip to Israel was to be book 5 until I finished walking el Camino. I still had to write the book about my trip to Spain, but I began making plans to go to Israel shortly after returning home.

Chapter Twenty-Five
The Jesus Trail

In early April of 2018 I flew from Miami International Airport to the Ben Gurian airport in Tel Aviv, Israel. Unlike what I did in Spain, when I basically just walked on an unguided trip, with no reservations made in advance, this time I booked a trip with a company called, appropriately enough, The Jesus Trail. They provided me with lodging along the way, and they transported my bags from one location to the next, but I was responsible for getting to the starting point, which was in Nazareth.

I had made reservations through a company called Abraham Hostels to stay in Jerusalem prior to beginning the hike, and I took a taxi from the airport to Jerusalem upon my arrival in Israel. It was about an hour and a half drive. Tel Aviv is on about the same latitude as Miami Beach and the weather is about the same, and it has an impressive beach, much like Miami Beach does, except it is on the Mediterranean Sea and Miami Beach is on the Atlantic Ocean.

It was warm, but not hot yet. Early spring is a good time to make the journey. It gets extremely hot in Israel during the summer months, just as it does in Miami Beach.

The Jesus Trail itself is a seven day and six night trip, consisting of about a fifty mile walk from Nazareth to the Sea of Galilee. The last stop on the hike was at a kibbutz in Ginnossar, not far from Taghba and Capernaum. It figured to be a much easier trek than el Camino, not nearly as far and there were no mountains to climb as there were in Spain.

Again, I have written a book about that trip, entitled <u>The Jesus Trail</u>, so I won't go into the details of that trip in this book. Any readers who are interested are invited to read that book. I learned a great deal about the history of the Hebrews, from the days of Abraham to the present, including the current political turmoil. While I was in the country, dozens of people were killed in the Gaza Strip by Israeli soldiers.

I hasten to add that I never felt the least bit threatened while in Israel, although civil war was being waged in Syria, just across the other side of the Sea of Galilee, or Lake Tiberias, as it is also called, among other names, and there were problems in Lebanon, on the northern border, too. I didn't go to the West Bank, but that was a major topic of conversation, and there was much strife in that area, while I was there.

The Gaza Strip is at the bottom of the country and I was at the top. Israel is 290 miles long from top to bottom and 85 miles wide from east to west. I was as far away from Gaza as I could possibly have been and still been in the country.

The purpose of this book is to address the reasons why I took the trip in the first place and to try and figure out why I did it and what I learned from doing it. First of all, I would tell you, as I told you about my trip to Spain to walk el Camino de Santiago, that I had absolutely no interest whatsoever in visiting Israel prior to going there - none. I went there to write book five of this series. I went because that was where Mekhaeil Zacharias went. That said, I am so glad that I went on many levels.

However, I could have died on the trip. I fell coming down Mt. Arbel at the very end of the hike and severely injured my right ankle. I was barely able to hobble out of an extremely remote area, where I wasn't supposed to be, which was full of about a billion "Devil's Walking Sticks," which are, technically, a shrub, called "Aralia spinosa," and it is covered with "viciously sharp, spiny stems" that stick to your clothes and cause you to bleed.

These particular plants were about four feet tall and they were everyplace, as far as I could see. There was a cowpath leading through them and I was on it, mistakenly thinking that I was on the path I was supposed to be on. I had to crawl under an electric fence that was no more than an inch from my face to get out of that hell-hole, but I did.

Truly, I could have died that day, because no one would have come looking for me and no one was within shouting distance of where I was. Fortunately, though I was injured, I didn't die and I wasn't hurt too seriously, just a badly sprained ankle that I was afraid might have been broken. I could barely walk through that field, however.

What was most unusual about this hike was that I saw virtually no one else on it. I did come across a father and son who were walking the Israel National Trail, which goes from one end of the country to the other, from south to north, during a small section of the Jesus Trail where they coincide, but there was no one else on the Jesus Trail besides me, coming or going. That was extremely unusual, and completely unexpected. However, this "trail" has only been in existence for about fifteen years as a commercial operation, and that might explain why.

In fact, one of the first persons to walk the "trail" was none other than Tony Blair, shortly after he stepped down as the Prime Minister of Great Britain, which I found interesting. He converted to Catholicism at about the same time. He was married to a Catholic woman for years before that, but he probably didn't dare to make that announcement while he was the leader of Great Britain.

The most exciting, and truly remarkable part of the hike was to find the ancient synagogue in Magdala where the Magdala stone was discovered in 2009, nine years before I arrived. It dates back to the time of Christ and coins were found there with Tiberias' name and likeness on them. It truly was, without any doubt whatsoever, absolutely the most astounding part of the journey.

It's what I usually begin with when I tell people about that trip. How could that place have remained undiscovered for nearly two thousand years? It is extremely significant to Israel because it is said to be the oldest synagogue ever found in the country and it is significant to Roman Catholics, too, because of the stone and Mary Magdalene. A replica of the stone is in the Vatican. Israel has the original.

For whatever reason, and no one can satisfactorily explain it, to my knowledge, and I asked and I have looked, the synagogue was covered up for nearly two thousand years by either dirt or water. How did it get covered up? Did the waters of the Sea of Galilee rise dramatically from the time of Christ to do that? Did some sort of geologic event, like an earthquake, occur? Did the Romans do it after the revolt of AD 66? No one seems to know.

However, the story of how it came to be discovered is truly an unbelievable story, too, so I'll tell you about that, because it does pertain to my personal quest. A priest from Mexico decided that his purpose in life was to start a Catholic parish in Israel, somewhere along the coastline of the Sea of Galilee. He didn't have any particular place in mind, but he somehow found a small parcel of land for sale not far from Migdal, a small town of less than a thousand people that was founded in 1910.

Even that is a story. Migdal did exist back in Jesus' day, but it was founded in 1910? Where was it? In 2009, there wasn't much there, but that's where this Mexican priest went looking to find a spot to build a church. Migdal is probably less than 20 or 30 kilometers from many famous sites in the area, like Taghba and Copernaum.

So this priest bought this small parcel of land with the idea of building a small church and, gradually, establishing a parish. He didn't have much money, but that was his plan. To build the church, he needed to get approval from the local building department, since all land in that area is deemed sensitive, for obvious reasons.

It was during the inspection period that Israeli authorities discovered an ancient treasure or two, and then they began to discover many more. Once something was discovered, a team of archeologists and other scientists were on the scene doing an excavation. The discoveries were extraordinary, but none more so than the Magdala Stone.

The Magdala Stone is a carved, stone block with symbols of ancient Jewish life all over. It stands one foot high, and about two feet wide by two feet long. It is thought to have held some of the ancient scrolls and other religious objects, and it clearly dates back to about 31 A.D., which is when Tiberias Claudius Nero was the emperor of Rome. He ruled from about 14 A.D. to 37 A.D. The nearby city of Tiberius is named after him and it was the biggest city on the Lake, which was also named after him, Lake Tiberius, at the time of Christ.

The "Sea" of Galilee is not a "sea" at all. A sea is defined to mean a part of an ocean, containing salt water. The "Sea of Galilee" is a freshwater lake. It was called Lake Kinneret, before the Romans renamed it. The word "kinneret" means violin, and the Sea of Galilee is shaped like a violin, to some ancient observers.

The authenticity of the Magdala Stone has been confirmed and the original is now held by the Israeli Department of Antiquities. Replicas are on display in Magdala and at the Vatican. I was dumbfounded when I stumbled upon this small area where digs were still being conducted. It is an active place of scientific research, and it is just now being discovered by tourists to the area.

When I was there, there weren't too many people. I had a one-on-one guided trip from a young man from Mexico who was there as a volunteer. He was a true believer and he was absolutely joyful about sharing all of the information that he could with me.

However, there is a modern church right behind the remains of the ancient synagogue, and that is a story, too. This Catholic priest from Mexico still had no permission to build a church, and the land he had purchased was now an archeological site of great significance. He feared that his dreams of building a church and a parish might be dashed.

When news of his discovery spread, the owners of Corona beer donated enough money for the priest to buy adjacent land and build a simple, but beautiful church. He did so, and it is called "Duc in altam." The name translates to mean "put out in deep water," which is a reference to the biblical passage when Jesus is said to have calmed the seas.

There's more to the story, but that was, and it remains, the most amazing part of my journey. I don't think that anyone denies that a man named Jesus walked the earth some 2000 years ago. Who and what he was is debatable. Without much doubt, it would seem fairly obvious that Jesus would have preached at that synagogue if you believe even a particle of the story of Jesus' life and times.

Mary Magdalene, as she is now known, was, technically, Mary of Magdala, or Mary the Magdalene. That Mary and Jesus were intertwined with one another seems to be an accepted fact as well. I found the whole experience that day to be revelatory and extraordinary.

Did that discovery tend to support the teachings of the four gospels? Yes. There can be little doubt about that. No one, not atheists, agnostics or anyone else can deny that the life of Jesus has changed the world more than any other human being who ever lived, can they, even if they don't believe he was the Messiah or that he is the son of God, as Christians do?

At this very date and time, two thousand years later, more people on earth worship in his name. No other person in the history of the world has done anything to rival that – none. However, it must be kept in mind that one in four people on earth follow the teachings of Mohammad. Regardless, I believe the evidence supports the conclusion that Jesus was there in Magdala with Mary the Magdalene, preaching in that synagogue.

Did that cause me to believe that Jesus is the only begotten son of God, born of the virgin Mary? I can't say that it did, but any reasonable person would have to admit that the actions of his disciples after his death certainly must be taken into consideration when evaluating the question of who and what was Jesus. Why would those men have done what they did if Jesus was an ordinary person, even a well-spoken rabbi?

Was it because of his oratory skills that those men walked all over the known world to spread the news of his life? Unlikely. They risked death on a daily basis, with no apparent reward for doing so. It would seem to be a fair conclusion to draw that they did so because of the effect his life had on them, though others will or may dispute that.

It must be mentioned and acknowledged that the only recorded information we have about the life and times of Jesus comes from the four gospels and the writings of Paul, who never met Jesus. Only Matthew and John actually knew Jesus, to our collective knowledge. Matthew was the tax collector who abandoned his profession to become a follower, and John was, by his account, the first of the apostles to meet him, and that was when Jesus was baptized by John the Baptist in the river Jordan.

Luke was a companion of Paul who met the others in Damascus, and no one seems to know when Mark first appears, but it is believed that it was after the time when Jesus was crucified, and it would have been in Damascus, as well. We are told that Mark accompanied Peter to Rome and spent nine years with him there, before going to Alexandria. Most scholars think that Mark's gospel contains things that Peter would have told him and that it really should be called the gospel of Peter.

I have read the Gnostic Gospels which claim to contain the "gospels" of other disciples, like Mary and Thomas. I don't know that they have been authenticated, but from what I read they certainly indicate that Jesus and Mary had an intimate relationship, among other things. If he was fully human, and fully divine, why would that surprise anyone?

I read all four gospels several times while in Israel as I wanted to make sure that I visited all of the places where Jesus walked while there. I wasn't able to find all of the places, but I did the best I could. Some just hadn't been developed or restored.

Did that change the way I feel about Jesus or the teachings of the Catholic Church? No, it didn't, at least not to any appreciable degree. I certainly learned more about Jesus, his life and times, and more about both the New and the Old Testament.

Still, only a third of the people on earth are Christians. Muslims, who are "people of the book," recognize Jesus as a prophet. Jews recognize Jesus as a rabbi who strayed too far from orthodoxy. They recognize that Jesus walked the earth, but they deny his divinity.

I still think that all religions are paths to the concept we call "God," or Yahweh, the Great Spirit, the Creator, or any other name given to whatever created the universe and all contained within it. I should say "universes," as there are millions more that cannot be seen. Scientists tell us that they are out there.

That's another thing, not touched upon in this book, or in any discussion of science, and that is the distance between these millions of universes. It is unfathomable! And we are told that the collective universes continue to expand at a rate that is unimaginable!

As far as Mekhaeil's journey is concerned, it ends in Jerusalem when Miriam, the sister of his boyhood best friend, gets him thinking clearly enough so that he can return home to Egypt and reunite with his family and all of his Coptic friends, including Father Bishoy. Although he has unanswered questions, he realizes that they can never be answered, and he is content to accept those things that he cannot change and ascribe to those things that he "believes" to be true.

Like Mekhaeil, I, too, have lingering questions about things that I know cannot be answered. I did, however, complete the journey, along with Mehkaeil, and that story is concluded, for now. I have no place else to go, at least not at this time, to continue that search for answers.

Ever since I can remember, whenever I thought of things imponderable, I always came to a stopping point when I asked myself how anything came into being in the first place. How is there any matter at all? Any atoms? Any chemicals? Gases? I could not and cannot get past that question.

Having completed the journey(s) that I truly felt I was instructed to go upon, I have waited to see what would become of it all. Nothing came immediately, and nothing has happened of any great import since 2019 when the last book went into print. Maybe what I did was all for my own personal elucidation, but maybe it will be of benefit to some. Who knows?

After completing The Jesus Trail, the book, I had no topics in mind to write about. I didn't know if I would write any more books. I was entering my 73rd year on this planet on July 14, 2019, and I was weary of being a lawyer.

I was still looking for a partner, a "soul-mate," if you will, without success, although there were plenty of suitors. I was tired of going so deep into religious theory and I wanted to lighten up, but I didn't know just where to go or what to do. I really wasn't giving it a lot of thought. I'd been deeply immersed in religious thought for several years, and I was at a dead-end on that topic.

Out of curiosity, since six of my eight great-grandparents are from Ireland, and two are not, I paid for an Ancestry.com analysis of my hereditary roots, and was told that I am 97% Irish, which pleased me. That was all of the impetus I needed. I decided that my next adventure was going to involve going back to Ireland, again, and this time, it would be to write another book, though I hadn't figured out exactly what I would write about. I thought it might be fun to walk the Ring of Kerry, since my mother was a Sullivan, and that was the ancestral home of the Sullivan clan.

I still had an urge to write another book, and I chose to do another hike, this time in Ireland, to do so – maybe the "auld sod" would provide some inspiration and guidance, or maybe it would just be an enjoyable trek. I didn't know, but it wasn't going to be about a religious topic, or so I thought.

Chapter Twenty-Six

Ireland, again

I began to do my research, as I always do, once I've selected a topic to write about, and I found an outfitter who would arrange an eleven night, ten day walk around the Ring of Kerry for us. My friends, Patrick and Marlene Doherty, were excited to join me. The Ireland Walk/Hike/Bike agency would find the places for us to stay, and move our luggage from place to place, for a reasonable amount of money. We signed up to go in the Fall of 2019.

I found a small village on the "Ring" called Sneem, that looked like a charming, little place to center the story around. The journey is about 100 miles, so we'd be walking ten miles per day, and it would be across hills and valleys, not mountains, or so we thought. I settled upon an idea to write a story about an aging professor from Trinity College Dublin who is diagnosed with Alzheimer's and how he deals with it.

My father, who was a Harvard graduate and a lawyer, died of complications related to Alzheimer's in 1991, at the age of seventy-four. It was a horrid experience, as anyone who has any familiarity with the disease will tell you. I have told my family that I won't go down that path, and I firmly intend to stick to that plan, should I be confronted with that situation.

However, as I say in the book that I wrote after completing the trek, it is not as easy to avoid the years of degradation and ultimate demise as one might think. There are laws against suicide in all states and most civilized countries, and then there is the church to consider, which forbids it and says that doing so subverts God's will.

In Florida, as in all but six states in the country, if a person attempts to commit suicide, that person is likely to be "Baker-acted," meaning he or she would be placed in a mental institution as being "likely to do harm to himself or herself." There is no criminal penalty for attempting to do so. California, Oregon, Washington, Colorado, Vermont and Montana are the states that allow "assisted suicide," but only under certain prescribed circumstances.

Thanks to my sister, our family was able to provide for our father as well as could possibly be hoped for, but it was an awful experience, even under the best of circumstances for him and all of us. We were able to keep him in his home right up to the bitter end, and he had 24 hour, round-the-clock care, once that became necessary. It's not just the patient who suffers. The experience is gruesome for the family and all who provide palliative care to the patient.

The book, entitled <u>Elysium</u>, is not morbid. It is a serious look at a deadly disease, but it is seen through the eyes of a young man studying to become a clinical psychologist. I consider it to be light-hearted and entertaining, despite the subject matter and the ending. There is a "love story" between the narrator and a fellow class-mate and there is humor throughout.

The word "Elysium" comes from the ancient Greeks and Romans. It was considered to be a place where heroic figures who died in battle went. Later, those who had led distinguished lives were said to be welcomed there.

Again, those who are interested in the book, and all of the anecdotes about Ireland and the Ring of Kerry contained therein, are welcome to read it. I won't recite any more details about it. I trust that it will make you laugh, cry, reflect and think about how your life will end. Mine will not end the way my father's did if I have anything to say about it.

However, saying that raises the specter of what will happen to us after we die, as all of us will do. Do we "dare" to defy the teachings of our church or the laws of our state and country? Do we "dare" to do whatever mechanism we choose to bring about the desired result? It's not something to be taken lightly. And how will that affect our transition to the after-life, if there is one? Do we "dare" to disobey the laws of our religion?

Furthermore, this discussion isn't limited to those who suffer from Alzheimer's. Obviously, there are those with cancer and a myriad of other diseases and medical problems that are painful to endure, for which there is no cure. Hospice care is an industry that is exploding around the country as doctors and others in the field of medicine seek to preserve and prolong life.

I have a friend, who is one of the most intelligent, ethical, moral and honorable people I know, who told me how his father berated him unmercifully for refusing to assist him in ending his life. He was suffering, with no hope of ever regaining his health, and wanted his life to come to an end, but my friend wouldn't participate.

It takes courage to address the problem, no matter which side of the debate you stand on, which brings me to the last chapter of this book, in which I address the multitude of issues surrounding our sojourn on this planet and what it all means.

The title of this book, Anima, involves a search for "soul." I haven't addressed that issue yet, but lurking in the background, somewhere between conscious thought, the brain, or our minds, and our physical body, is this amorphous entity we euphemistically call our "soul." That analysis is still to come.

Not long after returning from Ireland, the Covid pandemic hit the country and the world. Everyone was on lockdown, including me. All in-person hearings in court were suspended and the legal profession, as well as the business world, learned about zoom meetings. It effectively eliminated a large portion of my legal practice.

During that period of time, I worked on my house and built, with the help of some clients/friends who were skilled carpenters, an addition, including a large room to play music, with a bar, two bedrooms and a bathroom. It dramatically increased the value of my property.

Also, I researched Newfoundland, thinking that I would like to visit that part of the world and see for myself what climate change is doing to the northern part of our planet. I was most interested to read of an "iceburg highway" passing by Newfoundland. Iceburgs that stand ten stories high float by during May and June up there.

I read books about the Acadians, thinking that might be a good story to tell, as I have friends who are from Canada and are Acadians by heritage.

However, I learned that the Acadians came from western Nova Scotia, and had nothing to do with Newfoundland, as far as I could see. I abandoned that idea because I wasn't able to get into Canada, due to the pandemic. I haven't traveled anyplace since Ireland, but hoped to get to Newfoundland this summer, that being 2022, but then another strain of Covid hit, Russia invaded Ukraine, gas prices doubled and my plans were altered.

Also, late in 2021, I sold my cabin at a greatly inflated price and bought a condominium in Horseshoe Beach, a small, fishing community on the Gulf Coast of Florida, about an hour away from Fort White. It was and is a great place to write, as there are few distractions, and that is where this book was written. Only 150 people live there and I met some very nice people and made some good friends. Also, I kayaked, ran, rode my bicycle and played some music.

In June, I sold that condominium and bought a condo in Vero Beach, closer to family. I tell people that I, like Jeremiah Johnson, am coming in out of the cold, returning to civilization. Vero Beach, like much of the east coast of Florida, has some gorgeous beaches that are protected and will remain protected. It's a beautiful place, but it is expanding rapidly. I don't know how long I'll be here, but it's time to bring this book to a conclusion, and this is where I will end this book, but not before resolving some of the questions raised in it.

Chapter Twenty-Seven

Denouement

The word, denouement is defined to mean the final outcome of the main dramatic complication in a literary work. From my years of writing, I have learned that a novel is, generally speaking, divided into three basic components: a beginning, a middle and an end. In the beginning, an author sets the stage, so to speak, by presenting a conflict of some sort, and identifies the main characters.

In the middle, the plot thickens and the author weaves a tale of some sort of intrigue and the various issues involved, whether it's a romantic novel, a mystery, horror, or whatever the topic. In the end, the author brings the story to a close, resolving the problems. In this book, I've told anyone and everyone who has read this far all about the life I have led, thinking that it would be necessary, or at least helpful, for readers to know those things in order to better understand who I am and why I think the way I do. Our experiences in life are, quite obviously, very important in that regard. We are who we are.

I have written over two dozen books about a wide variety of topics that I think have great merit and could be of interest to those who like to read books. I sincerely doubt that there are many people who are particularly interested in this one, my autobiography. I don't even expect my family to read this book, except for one brother, Allan, who is an accomplished lawyer, a devoted husband for over forty years and the father of six gifted and successful children. I think he's read most of my books, and I thank him for that.

Despite that, I will see this project to the end, primarily so that I answer the questions which all human beings have asked since the beginning of time. I think that we all need to do that before our journey ends. It's one thing to think about the various topics, it's quite another to say them out loud, to another person, and then something entirely different to actually reduce to writing exactly what you think. Though I have more years to live, hopefully, and more stories to write, this is where I am "at" at this point in life.

Let's start with the single most important question all of us ask ourselves – is there a God?

As I have said several times herein, my answer is that there is absolutely no doubt in my mind whatsoever that there is a God. The only question is how to define the term.

Synonyms for the word, God, include Allah, Jehovah, Yahweh, Brahman, the Creator, the Almighty, universal life force, infinite spirit, devas, and, more colloquially, the "Force," as in "May the Force be with you," among many others. There are some major theological groups, such as Daoists and Shintoists, who don't profess to believe in a God, per se, but they believe in the power of nature, although that does not encapsulate their traditions, by any means. By any name, the word "God" is universally accepted to mean who or what created all that is, at least that is how I define the term. That still doesn't answer the question, though, does it?

Scientists tell us that, approximately 13.8 billion years ago, a tiny, incredibly dense fireball exploded and that is how the universe came into existence. They have yet to be able to explain how that tiny, dense fireball came into existence, or what caused it to explode. They now tell us that through the ongoing explorations of space we will learn more about the beginning of time as we know it. The late Stephen Hawking opined that there must have been some "time" before the "big bang" occurred, too.

Planet Earth is said to have come into existence approximately 4.5 billion years, when swirling gases and dust coalesced, due to gravity caused by our sun. The earliest signs of life are said to have first appeared on Earth approximately 3.7 billion years ago, and those were microscopic organisms. By any metric, those are extremely large numbers.

When one considers that ape-like creatures first appeared on earth 5 to 7 million years ago, those numbers grow even larger. Homo sapiens, or human beings, as we now call ourselves, first appeared on earth, according to some, about 300,000 years ago – I repeat, for emphasis, 300,000 years ago!

In 1974, an "ancestor" of human beings, called "Lucy," was discovered in Africa, in Ethiopia, to be exact. It is estimated that she lived 3.18 million years ago. The main characteristic that causes us to believe that she is an ancestor of ours is that she is said to have walked on two legs. Most humans don't like to think that we evolved from apes, but that remains a distinct possibility.

Regardless, in the great scheme of things, that is a minute fraction of those larger numbers, especially when one considers that dinosaurs ruled the planed for over 165 million years and didn't disappear until about 66 million years ago. Stop to think about that … we have been on earth for 300,000 years and dinosaurs roamed the earth for 165 million years … have you allowed those numbers to sink in?

Furthermore, dinosaurs were a form of "life." They were creatures. Where did they come from? Human beings are focused on human beings. We still think of ourselves as being the "center" of the universe, don't we? We think that God made us in his image AND that we are all GOD-like. We have a healthy opinion of ourselves, don't we?

Our planet revolves around a solitary sun and we are a small part of a galaxy called "The Milky Way." Scientists now tell us that there are at least 100 billion galaxies in the "universe," and it could be as many as 200 billion galaxies. Those numbers are beyond staggering when one thinks that we are barely able to see even the tiniest glimpse of any other galaxy with the naked eye.

For me, it is hard to believe that anyone could think that we are are the only species in existence within the entire universe of galaxies. It's hard to believe that anyone could think that in the 13.7 billion years since the "big bang" that there haven't been other signs of life, similar to human beings. Apparently, some people do.

Further still, it's hard for me to believe that the explosion of a tiny, incredibly dense fireball could cause all of those galaxies to come into existence, yet some do, and those are the best and the brightest of our scientific minds. Those are the people who we call astrophysicists. We accept that theory as if it came down from the heavens on granite slabs, much like the Ten Commandments. I don't. They may be correct, but I choose to believe that they don't know … that is just their theory.

Albert Einstein, still regarded as the brightest of modern-era scientists, though he's been dead for nearly seventy years, believed that the universe was so perfectly arranged that it could not have been the random act of nature. He believed in what he called "Cosmic Religion," which is to say that he believed in whatever created what exists. He had no explanation other than that for what that might be. He mentioned a theory that something like "black holes" might exist, and now "black holes" is the rage, though no one knows exactly what they are or what they do, except that without them the universe couldn't exist.

Many people in the United States, and across the world, believe in the theory of "evolution" - that we "evolved" through the forces of nature, called "survival of the fittest," and that is how we came to be as we are. We are said to come from a small, water-born, single-celled amoeba like creature, after those microscopic life forms developed. They don't know, do they? That is their theory, and that theory has only come into being in the last hundred years or so.

Others, called "creationists," believe that we were "created" by an entity we call "God." They rely on the Bible for authentification. Some of those people will kill you if you don't agree with them.

Those two factions, creationism versus evolution, represent an overwhelmingly large majority of people on earth, and they are bitterly divided, as we all know. Each certain that the other is wrong.

Those two concepts are not necessarily in conflict according to Pope Frances. He recently stated that the two are not mutually exclusive. God, as he knows that term, through Jesus Christ, could have brought about evolution of life in exactly the way it has developed. That is seen to be a major concession by some.

Please note that the question of religious belief has nothing to do with most of what I have stated above, and I have tried to be as factual as possible, though many of the "facts" upon which we base our beliefs, are not "facts" at all. They are beliefs. Please remember that the definition of faith is believing in something for which there is no objective proof, but I am getting ahead of myself, to some extent.

At this point, I'm going to state a conclusion that I have reached with regard to religion, and by that I mean all religions, and that is that they are all paths to explain how everything that exists came to be. They don't know. None of them do, yet, as I have said repeatedly, people will kill those who don't believe as they do in the name of their religion. That is what disturbs me most. Why? Why? When no one knows who is right and who is wrong?

The bigger question, and the one that perplexes me the most, is who or what could possibly be "God"? Does anyone think that a "person" existed 13.8 billion years ago? Or an entity we call "God" was present 13.8 billion years ago and continues to exist to this day? It is beyond our collective imagination that such could be the case, isn't it?

It seems to me that the collective wisdom of our period of time in the history of the world as we know it is that "energy" is God, or God is energy. There are wave lengths of energy which power our computers and our satellites and send signals through the air which are received by other computers and turned into pictures, videos, words, images and the rest, like magic, or quite magically, to be more accurate.

So how is it possible that some "thing" with intellectual capabilities could possibly create all that exists with the mathematical and scientific precision that Einstein and all other scientists are in awe of? Conversely, how could fields of "energy," without any intellectual thought, possibly "create" all that exists? And that begs the question as to how energy came into existence in the first place, or how the entity with intellectual thought came into existence?

After all, $E=mc$ squared – energy equals matter times the speed of light squared, right? Don't even try to figure out how Einstein came up with that theory, which the world dismissed as folly, at first, and now embraces as if it, too, came down on tablets of stone from God.

I think that's enough for me to justify what I am about to say, and that is: there is a "God" and that "God" is what created all that is on planet earth. That is not any different from what Einstein had to say. It doesn't answer the question adequately, but it is an answer.

I am not going to attempt to explain who created the small, dense fireball that went "bang" 13.8 billion years ago, nor could Albert, but here's what I think about how human beings came to be on planet earth: a higher form of life, from a different galaxy, planted seeds on this blue planet, and is, or may be, watching it grow, continuing to experiment.

That higher form of life may have just planted the seeds and then gone away, never to return. Or, more likely, that higher form of life is tinkering with us – still experimenting. That is not such a novel idea, and I know that others have said the same thing.

It's not all that far-fetched, either. As we all know and must acknowledge, every now and then a new "being," with superhuman powers, or powers far beyond his peers, is placed upon this earth and that human moves the human race forward to some appreciable degree. That is consistent with the idea that our "God" is actually a higher form of life from a different galaxy.

Obviously, I don't know that to be true, but I don't have a better explanation, and that's my answer, for now. To be clear, my explanation is that the entity we call "God" is actually a higher form of life, from a different planet, in a different solar system, in a different universe, and it has created life on planet earth as we know it, through scientific experiments that are ongoing.

Please note that my answer to that initial question does not rule out the existence of "God" as we humans know that term. That explanation accounts for a living being, or beings, on some other distant planet, making purposeful decisions, and being directly involved in our lives. Those creatures, who may or may not be like human beings, would be "gods" to us. They would be our "creators."

It's not too "sexy," and it doesn't begin to answer anywhere near all the questions we continue to have regarding how anything came into existence, but it is, in my mind, a logical explanation. Please keep in mind that this is an imperfect world. Bad things happen all the time, like earthquakes, floods, hurricanes, shifting tectonic plates, climate change, exploding volcanoes, droughts and other natural disasters are commonplace. Okay, tectonic plates don't happen every day, but they move ever so slightly every day, we are told. Those things happen with science experiments.

The idea that a civilization from a different planet is experimenting with us does explain, to some extent, how ancient civilizations, such as the Sumerians from Mesopotamia, the Indus Valley civilization from India, the Mayans and the Incas from Central and South America, the Egyptians, the ancient Greeks and Romans, to name a few, were so far advanced from the rest of the human race during their days on earth.

Also, it would explain how some "special" people came to earth with "super-powers," and extraordinary talents, like Ramanujan, the uneducated peasant from India who was a mathematician with inexplicable ability. There are many such examples of people who seem to have been "placed" here on earth. They were way "ahead" of their time. Personally, I think Elon Musk is just such a person. To me, his talents are far beyond extraordinary.

Hinduism recognizes the concept of "avatars," which is said to be an incarnation of the deity Vishnu on earth in the form of a human, or one who "descends" to restore balance to the earth. Some say that Siddartha Gautama, the original Buddha, and Jesus, were avatars. There are a few humans who exerted an extraordinary influence over the world, such as Sri Krishna, Abraham, Moses, the Buddha, Confucious, Jesus, Mohammad and a few others.

That is not to say that religion, regardless of its theology, is not absolutely necessary for humans to function in a decent manner while on earth. To the contrary, what would humans do without a world order premised upon the most basic principles that we all hold dear, which is that if you lead a good, decent life, you will go to heaven! That there is a reward, an after-life, awaiting those who behave well on earth is THE most basic incentive to cause human beings to live a good, decent life.

If that were not the case, if religions, and all of them, did not provide a good moral code for humans to live by, only the laws of men would govern the actions of men. If a person disobeys the laws of a country, that person could be incarcerated or killed. Jails are made for those who disobey the laws of men. Hell is made for those who disobey the laws of religions.

To a large extent, the laws of the religions of the world coincide with the laws of the countries of the world, with some notable exceptions. Sometimes, the laws of the religion were the laws of the country. The United States of America was formed, to a large extent, on the basis of freedom of religion, so that people from Europe, primarily, could escape religious intolerance and discrimination. Religions had become brutal and totally unyielding in their insistence that their rules be followed with absolute and unconditional obedience.

Most human beings need religion to provide them with answers to the questions which they otherwise have no answers for. There are atheists and agnostics, but they are a very small number, and they just totally ignore such philosophical discussions. They want to be left alone.

Some communistic countries, like China and Russia, when Stalin was its ruler, totally banned religion. Both have relaxed their positions of late, but religion has no place in government in either country. The laws of the land, not of any religious leader, were to be followed with no resistance tolerated.

Again, my "theory" regarding the existence of "god," with a small "g," is that "god" is a civilization which is a higher form of life than we humans are. It has preceded us by millions, if not billions, of years. I have no answer, not even a guess, as to how life began, so my "answer" is incomplete and inadequate, and I readily acknowledge that, but it's the best I can come up with.

However, and this is extremely important – Jesus, Siddhartha, Confucius, Mohammad and the others could come from that civilization. They are "avatars." They could have been sent here to advance the human race, which is a flawed species. That would make Jesus, Siddartha and the others, like "gods" to us. I am comfortable with that notion.

Some say "life" happened spontaneously, but I ask who and what created the gases, or the dense, fireball that exploded. We don't know and probably never will know – not in our lifetimes, that's for sure. How did something come from nothing? I cannot get past that most basic question. Period. End of story. I'm not going to go there.

And that theory does provide an answer the next question which all human beings ask, and that is: Is there an afterlife? If there is a "higher civilization," on a different planet, within a different galaxy, our "souls" could go there after our human bodies have disintegrated. What that life consists of is an entirely different question and it can be whatever we want it to be.

Personally, I think that the "higher civilization" is looking for "good" souls to join them. They might be a part of an experiment themselves, or maybe they're just trying to improve the genetic pool on their planet. I have no idea, but I like the idea.

Every religion on earth, to my knowledge, is in agreement that there is an after-life. Of course, not all agree on what that after-life consists of. Many think that we return to earth in a different body, called "reincarnation." I'm okay with that, too.

The "higher forms of life" may be trying to create a better form of human being. That would be the "purpose" of all of us being here. Whether or not we are divided up into males or females, different races, different ethnicities and all the rest is another matter, but that does make life more interesting, doesn't it? What would it be like if we were all the same? But maybe that's what they want. Who knows?

I heard Ted Turner say on television one night that if he thought that going to heaven meant that he could fish all day, every day, then he was all for it, but he didn't want to float around on some cloud for the rest of eternity. That made me laugh.

What is heaven? Is it eternal? What would that be like? Put in that context, as Ted Turner did, it doesn't sound all that desirable, does it? I don't think that's what "heaven" would be like, even for all of those people who believe that if they've been good on earth they're going to heaven.

Knowing human beings as I do, and as we all do, I'm sure, we'd be bored to death after a very short period of time, right? Would we eat? Drink? Party? Have sex? Play sports? What would we do in heavenly bliss? Retirement isn't all that easy. What will eternity be like? I just don't see that happening.

Buddhists, Hindus, Sikhs, Taoists and others believe that we "return" to this earth after death to lead more lives until we reach a point where we don't need to return to earth again, that we have advanced to the point where reincarnation is no longer necessary.

Christians seem to think it's a "one and done" kind of deal. Either you make it to heaven or you don't. The idea of a "purgatory," or a mid-point, went out with the changes enacted by the Catholic Church in 1966. So there is no "limbo." Either you're "IN" or you're "OUT." That's a bit harsh, don't you think? So if there is "reincarnation," what is reincarnated? The obvious answer is your "soul."

Most people believe that humans have a "soul," something that is not a physical thing, not matter, that survives death. Our physical bodies age, decay and otherwise give out, but we think that our "soul" survives.

As I have already acknowledged, I have communicated with people, who I call "conduits," who are intermediaries between what exists on earth and what exists beyond what we humans can see, hear, touch, feel or smell. I have no idea what's out there, but I believe that there is something out there and that there is a purpose for which we humans exist on this earth.

In my view, we reincarnate until we have improved to the point where we no longer need to come back again. We are to lead good lives and advance our selves, or our "souls," to a higher level of consciousness so that when we reincarnate we will have returned in a higher form of life, whatever that might be.

Maybe that means becoming a more gifted human being, or advancing to a higher "class" of human. Hindus are famous for their caste system, though not as much nowadays as in prior generations. In fact, in India there are now laws to prevent a rigid enforcement of a caste system, though one continues to exist, whether in a formalized manner or not.

To Buddhists, Hindus, Sikhs and others it means getting closer to "nirvana," which is a transcendent state of awareness which does not require any further incarnations. Most adherents of those religions are from South Asian countries. They all practice meditation and daily mindful prayer practices, as most religions do, but not to the extent that Buddhists, Hindus, Sikhs and others do. Chanting is common, as well.

Buddhists have an "eightfold" path to nirvana, which involves right view; right resolve, right speech, right action, right livelihood, right effort, right mindfulness and right concentration. Needless to say, just what is the "right" attitude for any of the eight steps along the path is somewhat subjective.

However, I would say this about what Buddhists and Hindus view as living a "good life" is concerned, as I understand it, and that is this: I don't think sitting, chanting, and meditating for hours on end is the best way to live life. I think life is meant to be lived, and by that I mean enjoyed, to the fullest. That's what the Dalai Lama says – "Be happy!"

For other religions, like Christianity, there isn't much of a standard, except for be good, do good and hope for the best. For Catholics, it is said that you can't "earn" your way to heaven, you must be chosen. Jews think that they are the "chosen ones." That makes even more difficult. I don't ascribe to that one.

Everyone has to find their own path in life, and do the best they can with whatever they have chosen to do or be. It's that simple. Some don't have the same opportunities, due to lack of talent, money, drive, determination or whatever else it takes to succeed in life. Everyone does the best they can, or they fail for some reason or another.

Nobody is perfect. Everyone has good qualities and qualities that aren't so good. Everyone has failed at one thing or another. I don't know too many people who I would say have transcended the trials and tribulations of life and are ready to move on to heaven or nirvana – Mother Teresa, maybe? The Dalai Lama? Mahatma Gandhi? Who else, in our lifetime? Who am I missing?

It seems to me that everyone is flawed in one way or another, right? Who does it perfectly on the first time around? Not me, that's for sure, although I have no idea how many times I've been around, and that's another thing - since we can't remember prior incarnations, how are we supposed to know how we're doing? It's a catch-22.

Therefore, and in conclusion, I say that we all have a soul, that it is transmutable, a distinct and separate entity unto itself, and that it represents who we are, as individuals, once we strip away all of the trappings of family, society, culture, ethnicity, race, sex and everything else that makes up our ego and our wants, needs and desires – in a word, our "essence."

Our souls are an energy source, not matter, and they survive the death of our bodies. Our souls reincarnate. Our purpose is to become better souls. We want our souls to reach "heaven," which is to become a member of that higher civilization. That makes sense to me. I can live with that, until I come to some different level of understanding or awareness.

Maybe it's not so important that we become better human beings – maybe human beings aren't the higher life forms that are our "gods." Who knows what other life forms are out there? Planet earth is a testing grounds for us human beings. The way things are going, planet earth might not survive human beings.

Regardless, and in any event, we all want to be the best "souls" we can be. We all want to move on to the best place we can go. No one knows where that is or how to get there, so all we can do is just be the best we can be. It's that simple, but we make things so much harder than we have to, don't we? I do.

Everyone knows right from wrong. I think our souls are somewhere beyond our hearts. Our hearts make mistakes. Our souls are like the ancient sphinx of Egypt. They look with clear eyes and minds and they endure all the mistakes and mis-steps that our frail human bodies make, but what are they?

My soul is the goodness in me. My soul never does the wrong thing. My heart will … my mind will … my body will… but not my soul. My soul is eternal. My soul is all that is good about me. That is my "inner" self. My "outer" self still needs a lot of work, but it's about to reincarnate!

In the process of writing this book, I have "found" answers to the questions I asked at the beginning of the book. It might be hard for some of you to believe, but I really didn't find some of those answers until the very last day. The idea that Jesus, Siddhartha and the others are from that "higher civilization" that is conducting experiments with planet earth didn't occur to me until that very day. Jesus IS God. Siddhartha IS God, and so are the other avatars. Like Mehkaeil in my five-book series on religion, I found an answer I could take home. I am comfortable with that answer.

However, I am ever mindful of things Socrates said, and I, like him, candidly acknowledge that I "know nothing." I have examined my life, just as Socrates told us we should all do, and what is contained herein are my answers to the questions I ask myself. I wish you all good luck in finding the answers to all of the questions you ask yourselves.

I hope that you enjoyed reading what I have written.

THE END

About the Author

Pierce Kelley is a retired lawyer and educator who received his undergraduate degree from Tulane University, New Orleans, Louisiana in 1969. He received his Doctorate of Jurisprudence (JD) from the George Washington University, Washington, D.C. in 1973. He now lives in Vero Beach, Florida.

Printed in the United States
by Baker & Taylor Publisher Services